DATE DUE

OC 27 '99		
NO 18 '99		
11/8/00		
APR 12 2011		
APR 13 2011		

CHARLOTTE PERKINS GILMAN

A Study of the Short Fiction

Twayne's Studies in Short Fiction

General Editors
Gary Scharnhorst, *University of New Mexico*
Eric Haralson, *State University of New York at Stony Brook*

CHARLOTTE PERKINS GILMAN
Courtesy of Walter Stetson Chamberlin

CHARLOTTE PERKINS GILMAN

A Study of the Short Fiction

Denise D. Knight

State University of New York College at Cortland

TWAYNE PUBLISHERS
An Imprint of Simon & Schuster Macmillan
New York

PRENTICE HALL INTERNATIONAL
London Mexico City New Delhi Singapore Sydney Toronto

Twayne's Studies in Short Fiction, No. 68

Copyright © 1997 by Twayne Publishers

Twayne Publishers
An Imprint of Simon & Schuster Macmillan
1633 Broadway
New York, NY 10019

Library of Congress Cataloging-in-Publication Data

Knight, Denise D., 1954–
    Charlotte Perkins Gilman: A Study of the Short Fiction / Denise
D. Knight
        p.   cm.—(Twayne's Studies in Short Fiction ; no. 68)
    Includes bibliographical references and index.
    ISBN 0-8057-0866-9 (hardcover: alk. paper)
    1. Gilman, Charlotte Perkins, 1860–1935—Criticism and
interpretation.   2. Women and literature—United States—
History—20th century.   3. Women and literature—United States—
History—19th century.   4. Short story.   I. Gilman, Charlotte
Perkins, 1860–1935.   II. Title.   III. Series.
PS1744.G57Z734 1997
813'.4—dc21   96–44447
                                                                              CIP

10 9 8 7 6 5 4 3 2 1

Printed in the United States of America

Contents

Contents

PART 3. THE CRITICS

Preface

Although the social and literary contributions of author and lecturer Charlotte Perkins Gilman were virtually forgotten by the time of her death in 1935,[1] the resurgent interest in her life and literature dating back to the mid-1960s has been nothing short of extraordinary.[2] Recent books on Gilman have included two biographies, a nonfiction reader, an examination of her utopian fiction, collections of critical essays, a reprint of her autobiography, a monograph exploring her oeuvre, publication of her personal diaries, and anthologies containing dozens of her short stories. Yet, Gilman's literary reputation rests largely on a single work, the frequently anthologized and much-analyzed story "The Yellow Wall-Paper," first published in 1892.[3] Depicting the nervous breakdown of a young wife and mother, the story is a potent example of psychological realism.

Gilman (1860–1935) was able to write with authority about the terrifying consequences of chronic depression. From early adulthood, she struggled with episodes of severe melancholia. After her engagement and subsequent marriage to her first husband, Charles Walter Stetson, her depression deepened. Following the birth of her daughter, Katharine, in 1885, Charlotte Stetson became dangerously despondent and at the age of 26 undertook the rest cure for neurasthenia from the renowned nerve specialist Dr. Silas Weir Mitchell of Philadelphia.[4] Deprived of intellectual stimulation as part of the treatment, she subsequently suffered a nervous breakdown. She gradually recovered her health after separating from Walter Stetson in 1888 and divorcing him six years later. "The Yellow Wall-Paper," drawn in part from her own experiences with acute depression, was both an indictment of the rest cure and an attack on nonegalitarian marriages. Having herself come "so near the border line of utter mental ruin that [she] could see over,"[5] Gilman was able to realistically capture the psychological torment of her fictional narrator.

Despite her insistence that "The Yellow Wall-Paper" "was no more 'literature' " than her other works (*Living*, 121), Gilman clearly recognized both its artistry and its appeal. She enjoyed discussing the story with houseguests, and impromptu readings were a frequent form of entertainment when she traveled on lecture tours. In 1933, more than 40 years after its initial publication, Gilman briefly pondered the possibility of staging "The Yellow Wall-Paper" as a dramatic monologue. To her cousin and literary executor Lyman Beecher Stowe she wrote, "Look here, I've had an idea! Why, wouldn't ["The Yellow Wall-Paper"] make a *gorgeous monologue*! Stage setting of the room *and the paper,* the four windows, the moonlight on the paper—changing lights and *movement*—and the woman staring! ... Perhaps Kate Hepburn would consider it—though she's pretty young."[6] Gilman never lived to see "The Yellow Wall-Paper" dramatized onstage; in recent years, however, it has been adapted in film versions, including a television production, and performed by at least two touring actresses.[7]

By the time Gilman ended her long career, she had amassed an extraordinary list of publications, including nearly 200 short stories, the majority of which appeared in *Forerunner,* the monthly magazine that Gilman single-handedly wrote and published between 1909 and 1916. Her plans to publish "volumes of short stories" in later life never materialized,[8] and it was not until Ann J. Lane reprinted 11 stories in *The Charlotte Perkins Gilman Reader* (1980) that any of her short fiction appeared together.

With the notable exception of "The Yellow Wall-Paper," critics have not been wildly enthusiastic about Gilman's fiction for a host of reasons: it is heavily didactic, uneven in quality, and defies easy classification within the arbitrary categories by which American literature is currently defined. Moreover, Gilman was primarily a lecturer rather than a writer of fiction, and she fully acknowledged her artistic deficiencies by "disclaim[ing] any pretension to literature."[9] Her singular purpose in writing was to advance her ideas about social reform. As she recalled in her autobiography, "What I saw in the world was not its foolish, unnecessary troubles, but its splendid possibilities; as a competent promoter sees in some tottering business the success he can make of it." Her business, she said, "was to find out what ailed society, and how most easily and naturally to improve it" (*Living,* 182–83).

Indeed, after recovering from her breakdown and divorcing Walter Stetson, Gilman pursued in earnest her desire to reform society. In the early 1890s, she became a convert to Nationalism, a movement promoting an end to capitalism and advancing the peaceful, progressive, ethical, and democratic improvement of the human race. Her support for reform Darwinism—a philosophy advocating conscious intervention in the evolutionary process for the purpose of controlling human destiny— also shaped her ideological views. The publication of *Women and Economics* in 1898 launched Gilman into the international spotlight, and by the early part of the twentieth century, she had emerged as one of the intellectual leaders of first-wave feminism. She enjoyed a celebrated public career until 1925, when she virtually disappeared from the public eye. In 1935, after battling inoperable breast cancer for three years, Charlotte Perkins Gilman ended her life. Her choice of death by suicide was intended, in part, "to be of social service in promoting wiser views" on the question of euthanasia (*Living*, 333–34). Her death, like her fiction, was meant to be instructive.

Part 1 of this volume opens with a discussion of Gilman's didacticism, which includes an examination of various influences on her fiction—her feminism, her ideological views, her advocacy of reform Darwinism. An extended discussion of "The Yellow Wall-Paper" follows. The next section addresses Gilman's other early fiction, including a series of stories written in imitation of various well-known authors—Hawthorne, Poe, Freeman, Garland, and Twain among them—for inclusion in the *Impress*, a literary weekly edited by Gilman in California from 1894 to 1895. An overview of several autobiographically inspired stories follows. Part 1 concludes with an analysis of selected stories that originally appeared in the *Forerunner*.

Part 2, "The Writer," provides Gilman's reflections on writing "The Yellow Wall-Paper," including excerpts from her autobiography, in which she recounts both its publication history and its reception. Also included in part 2 is an excerpt from "Thoughts and Figgerings," an unpublished collection of miscellaneous notes, in which Gilman ponders the value of writing short fiction. Her views on masculinist literature and literary trends also appear in this section, along with an excerpt on Gilman's writing by her friend and fellow author Amy Wellington.

Part 3, "The Critics," is a collection of contemporary criticism of several of Gilman's short stories, including, of course, "The Yellow Wall-Paper." Because scholarly essays on that particular story are both plentiful and accessible, however, I have chosen to reprint only two, in order to include essays on some of her other works so that readers might expand their appreciation of Gilman's range as a writer of short fiction.

Notes

1. Although Gilman also published short fiction under the name Charlotte Perkins Stetson, I have for the sake of consistency referred to her throughout this edition as Charlotte Perkins Gilman when discussing her literary works.

2. Carl N. Degler reintroduced Gilman's *Women and Economics: A Study of the Economic Relation Between Men and Women as a Factor in Social Evolution* in 1966 (New York: Harper and Row). Hereafter, *WE*.

3. The word "wallpaper" appears variously in the story's title as one word (Wallpaper), two words (Wall Paper), and as a hyphenated word, with both a lowercase and uppercase *p* (Wall-paper; Wall-Paper). In quoting titles of critical articles, I have retained the spelling as it appears. In general discussion of the story, I have used "Wall-Paper," taken from the manuscript version of the story.

4. The rest cure, introduced as a treatment for nervous disorders in the nineteenth century and popularized by Dr. Silas Weir Mitchell of Philadelphia, required the patient to undergo prolonged periods of bed rest, to be secluded from friends and family, and to eat a special, often high-fat diet.

5. Charlotte Perkins Gilman, "Why I Wrote The Yellow Wallpaper?" *Forerunner* 4 (October 1913): 271.

6. Beecher-Stowe Collection of Family Papers, Schlesinger Library, Radcliffe College, folder 416. Quoted by permission.

7. In addition to film versions intended for classroom use, Masterpiece Theatre aired a film version of *The Yellow Wall-Paper* on PBS in 1989, and in 1992, actress Ann Timmons began a touring production of "Off the Wall: The Life and Works of Charlotte Perkins Gilman," which originally opened off-Broadway. A theater-in-the-round adaptation of "The Yellow Wall-Paper" has been staged by Brochu/Dumais Productions.

8. Gilman, "To My Real Readers." *Forerunner* 7 (December 1916): 326.

9. Gilman, *The Living of Charlotte Perkins Gilman* (Madison: University of Wisconsin Press, 1990), 285. Hereafter, *Living*.

Acknowledgments

I am grateful for permission to use the following material:

Excerpts from *The Living of Charlotte Perkins Gilman*, by Charlotte Perkins Gilman. Copyright 1990 by Radcliffe College. Reprint of the 1935 edition published by the University of Wisconsin Press. Published by permission of Radcliffe College, Cambridge, MA.

Excerpts from the Charlotte Perkins Gilman Papers at the Schlesinger Library, Radcliffe College. Published by permission.

" 'Out at Last?' 'The Yellow Wallpaper' after Two Decades of Feminist Criticism," by Elaine R. Hedges, from *The Captive Imagination: A Casebook on 'The Yellow Wallpaper,'* Catherine Golden, ed. Copyright 1992 by the Feminist Press. Reprinted by permission.

"The Writing of 'The Yellow Wallpaper': A Double Palimpsest," by Catherine Golden, from *The Captive Imagination: A Casebook on 'The Yellow Wallpaper,'* Catherine Golden, ed. Copyright 1989 by *Studies in American Fiction* and Northeastern University Press. Reprinted by permission.

"Charlotte Perkins Gilman's 'The Giant Wistaria': A Hieroglyph of the Female Frontier Gothic," by Gary Scharnhorst, from *Frontier Gothic: Terror and Wonder at the Frontier in American Literature*, David Mogen et al., eds. Copyright 1993 by Fairleigh Dickinson University Press. Reprinted by permission.

Excerpts from "Consider Her Ways: The Cultural Work of Charlotte Perkins Gilman's Pragmatopian Stories, 1908–1913," by Carol Farley Kessler, from *Utopian and Science Fiction by Women*, Jane A. Donawerth and Carol A. Kolmerten, eds. Copyright 1994 by Syracuse University Press. Reprinted by permission.

The State University of New York College at Cortland English Department, and the Cortland chapter of the United University Professionals, deserve my sincere thanks for supporting my application for a Nuala McGann Drescher Award, which provided release time for my work on this project. Gretchen M. Gogan of the interlibrary loan department at the State University of New York College at Cortland also deserves my thanks for processing numerous requests for material in a cheerful and timely manner.

I am indebted to Gary Scharnhorst, coeditor of Twayne's Studies in Short Fiction, who was most generous in providing guidance throughout this project and in sharing material on Gilman from his personal files. I also appreciate the support from series coeditor Eric Haralson and Twayne assistant editors Pauline J. Sultana and Anne Davidson.

I am grateful for the friendship and kindness of Walter Stetson Chamberlin, who generously provided the photograph of his grandmother used in the frontispiece.

Finally, I wish to thank my husband, Michael K. Barylski, for his continued support of my work on Gilman.

Part 1

THE SHORT FICTION:
A CRITICAL ANALYSIS

Writing with a Purpose

When William Dean Howells asked Charlotte Perkins Gilman for permission to reprint "The Yellow Wall-Paper" in his forthcoming anthology, *The Great Modern American Stories*,[1] she readily agreed but "assured him that it was no more 'literature' " than any of her other works, "being definitely written 'with a purpose.' In my judgment," she insisted, "it is a pretty poor thing to write, to talk, without a purpose."[2]

A descendant of the prominent Beecher family of New England, Charlotte Perkins Gilman inherited both the Beecher talent for preaching and the family's "urge to social service" (*Living*, 6). From an early age, she "looked ahead to a steady lifetime of social study and service," promoting "the evolution of the human race" through preaching, lecturing, and writing (pp. 74, 42). Regardless of the forum, Gilman's purpose in communicating was always the same: to advance her belief that a reformed society—one that advocated the positive development of the human race—was not only desirable but attainable. Virtually all of her writing, including her fiction, was written "with a purpose"—to educate her audience about "the gradual steps by which we might advance to an assured health, a growing happiness" (p. 183).

As a result of Gilman's heavy reliance on didacticism to advance social reform, the quality of her fiction often suffered. Even her first husband, Walter Stetson, complained about her penchant for didacticism: "I confess I wish she'd strive more for beauty . . . than for didactics, for when she does let herself forget to preach she writes very very tender & lovely things," he wrote.[3] But Gilman candidly acknowledged her literary deficiencies and viewed didacticism as a means to an end. "I am not a poet," she insisted. "I'm only a preacher, whether on the platform or in print."[4] In 1916, having written fiction for seven years in her self-published magazine, the *Forerunner*, Gilman reiterated her views about literature in a short essay titled "A Summary of Purpose."[5] "The subject matter, for the most part, is not to be regarded as 'literature,' but as an attempt to set forth certain views of life which seemed to the author of real importance to human welfare," she wrote ("Summary," 286).

Indeed, the subjects depicted in Gilman's fiction were the same as those addressed in her essays and lectures—the move toward economic independence for women, the benefits of professional housekeeping, the need for expert child care, the advantages of dress reform, the practical necessity of the kitchenless home, the pervasiveness of yellow journalism, the problem of nonegalitarian marriages. Fiction became just another vehicle through which Gilman might convey her message. "I have nothing to offer the world but what I *think*," she wrote her future second husband, Houghton Gilman, in 1897.[6] "I think that the thing I am here to do is a big thing—the truth. I see deep basic truths; and that I have been given unusual powers of expression."[7]

Although Gilman had "unusual powers of expression" and claimed that "to write was always as easy to me as to talk" (*Living*, 98), she found writing "the stories, which called for composition," to be "more difficult" than writing other forms of literature (p. 100). Moreover, her literary methods were not well defined. "As far as I had any method in mind, it was to express the idea with clearness and vivacity, so that it might be apprehended with ease and pleasure," she remarked in her memoirs (pp. 284–85).

Owing to continual haste, Gilman rarely revised her writing, and artistry was always subordinated to message. In fact, much of her fiction was formulaic, particularly since Gilman wrote most of it to fit an allotted space: typically $4^1/_2$ to 5 pages for stories appearing in the *Forerunner* and even less for those published in the *Impress*. These self-imposed space limitations impeded Gilman's ability to develop her story lines; hence, her characters are frequently flat, her dialogue forced, her settings often inconsequential. But if Gilman wasn't an eloquent fiction writer—Mary Austin once complained that "everything she wrote was in the same key"[8]—she was at least aware of the power of the printed word to show her readers the possibilities of a world reformed. In short, her stories re-create the world according to her vision of the ideal. "There is nothing to prevent humanity developing a type as beautiful, as strong, as intellectually able as any in the past; and with a far wider vision, a vast increase of knowledge, a measureless gain in power; and the spirit of love which belongs to a conscious world," she wrote in "A Summary of Purpose" (p. 290).

Various influences gave shape to Gilman's agenda for social reform. Her own unhappy experiences in her first marriage, for example, gave rise to her tireless campaign for gender equality. "Women ought to feel a glorious new pride in their sex," she wrote. "They ought to feel an unbounded hope and power in their ability to remake the race and to help manage it on better terms than ever before. And they ought also to burn with shame, deep scorching shame, at the pitiful limitations with which so many of them are still contented."[9] Gilman used her fiction in part to demonstrate viable alternatives to the long-ingrained social traditions that kept women oppressed. By depicting strong women who led useful and productive lives outside of the home, Gilman hoped to simultaneously educate her reader and correct the predominantly male literary tradition that cast women characters (and women writers) into peripheral roles.

One of Gilman's complaints about existing literature was that the story of the "conscientious woman"—the strong and self-reliant female who would leave an abusive husband and risk poverty, loneliness, and disgrace rather than endure a destructive marriage—had not been adequately told. "When our women writers emerge from the smothering pressure of [the male] literary tradition, and recognize their distinctive place and power," she wrote, "we shall have a new portent—the woman, as an artist" to express a fuller and more realistic view of woman's world and all its multifaceted layers.[10]

Perhaps the single greatest influence in shaping Gilman's philosophy was her support for reform Darwinism, a modified version of traditional Darwinism that gained popularity in the late nineteenth century. Her friendship with Lester Ward, the country's leading reform Darwinist, whom she described in her autobiography as "quite the greatest man I have ever known" (*Living*, 187), was instrumental in refining her social philosophy. Reform Darwinists believed that conscious intellectual intervention in the evolutionary process (as opposed to allowing for the strictly biological process of natural selection) was both necessary and desirable. Intervention could help to remediate human suffering, poverty, and inequality. Simply stated, people could help to control their own destiny; Gilman's fictional world would show them how.

Her support of Nationalism, a movement that relied on some of the basic tenets of reform Darwinism, also significantly shaped Gilman's evolving ideology. Heavily influenced by Edward Bellamy's socialist-utopian novel *Looking Backward, 2000–1887*, the Nationalist movement rejected capitalism, class distinctions, and other forms of inequality. Gilman not only embraced the tenets of Nationalism but began to promote Nationalist reform through lectures and writings in the early 1890s. It was, in fact, her activities on behalf of the Nationalist movement that first thrust her into the public spotlight.

In "A Summary of Purpose," Gilman conceded that "Our dawning social consciousness finds us bound, suffering, thwarted, starved, crippled in many ways. The more we see the possible joy of human living, the more painful become present conditions—if unchangeable. But they are changeable," she insisted (p. 290). Infusing her fiction with socialist and feminist ideology was a way for Gilman to demonstrate how progress and democracy in society could be advanced if only people would act on the need for change.

Gilman once characterized her collection of verse, *In This Our World*, as "a tool box . . . written to drive nails with."[11] That same characterization applies equally to her short fiction: driving home her point was almost always her primary objective.

"The Yellow Wall-Paper"

Just six months prior to her May 2, 1884, wedding to Rhode Island artist Charles Walter Stetson, Charlotte Anna Perkins remarked in her diary that one of the things she had done that day was to "Paint [a] lugubrious picture of 'The Woman Against The Wall.' "[12] When she showed the painting to Stetson a few days later, he recognized the work as a troubling self-portrait of his bride-to-be. *His* diary entry described the painted figure as "a wan creature," a "worn-out" woman facing "an insurmountable wall which extended around the earth." Stetson characterized the artwork as "powerful" and "a literal transcript of her mind" (*Endure*, 244). More than 40 years later, near the end of a highly visible career, Gilman searched for that painting, hoping to reproduce it in her forthcoming autobiography.[13] She never found it. But worn-out women and wall imagery would be forever associated with Gilman as a result of her most famous short story, "The Yellow Wall-Paper," a chillingly realistic depiction of a nervous breakdown.

"The Yellow Wall-Paper" was written in the summer of 1890, during Gilman's "first year of freedom" (*Living*, 111), shortly after her permanent separation from Walter Stetson. It was composed over a two-day period in Pasadena, California, during a heat wave that sent the thermometer soaring to 103 degrees.[14] In August, Gilman sent the story to William Dean Howells, who had written earlier that year to praise her poem "Similar Cases," which appeared in the April 1890 edition of the *Nationalist*. Howells passed the story on to Horace Scudder, editor of *Atlantic Monthly*, who returned it to Gilman with a curt reply: "I am returning herewith the manuscript of 'The Yellow Wallpaper.' I should never forgive myself if I made other people as miserable as reading your story has made me"("History").[15] Gilman persisted in her efforts to publish the story, placing it with a literary agent in the fall of 1890. Finally, in January 1892, "The Yellow Wall-Paper" appeared in *New England Magazine*. A chapbook edition was published in 1899 by Small, Maynard, and Co., and in 1973 the Feminist Press issued a reprint edition. Since 1973, "The Yellow Wall-Paper" has been widely anthologized.

Based loosely on her experiences in undergoing the rest cure for neurasthenia but with "embellishments and additions,"[16] "The Yellow Wall-Paper" was Gilman's attempt to document what might have been the "inevitable result, progressive insanity" (*Living*, 119), had she not cast her doctor's "advice to the winds" (*FR*, October 1913). That doctor, the noted nerve specialist Silas Weir Mitchell of Philadelphia, treated the 26-year-old Gilman during the spring of 1887, after she had struggled with severe postpartum depression for more than two years following the birth of her daughter, Katharine. Mitchell greeted his patient with open contempt, citing the self-recorded "history of the case" that she prepared for his review as evidence of "self-conceit" (*Living*, 95). He also confessed his "prejudice against the Beechers," having previously treated two of her female relatives (p. 95).

After she had undergone several weeks of bed rest, Mitchell concluded that "there was nothing the matter" with his young patient and sent her back to Providence, Rhode Island, with the following prescription: " 'Live as domestic a life as possible,' " which included having the baby with her at all times; " 'have but two hours' intellectual life a day. And never touch pen, brush or pencil as long as you live.' " (*Living*, 96). For three months following her return home, Charlotte Stetson tried to follow Mitchell's advice. In doing so, she came perilously close to the "utter mental ruin" that claimed her fictional narrator (*FR*, October 1913). Clearly, her temperament—and particularly her desire to work—was ill-suited for such radical restrictions as Mitchell prescribed.

The "real purpose" of "The Yellow Wall-Paper," Gilman insisted, "was to reach Dr. S. Weir Mitchell, and convince him of the error of his ways" in treating nervous prostration (*Living*, 121). The story "is a description of a case of nervous breakdown beginning something as mine did," Gilman wrote (pp. 118–19). But she never experienced "hallucinations or [had] objections to [her] mural decorations" (*FR*, October 1913), and the end of the story is strikingly different from her own ordeal. Although Gilman suffered prolonged "mental agony" and "profound distress" (*Living*, 96), she ultimately garnered enough emotional strength to reclaim her independence, leave an unhappy marriage, and carve out a successful career. Her fictional narrator, on the other hand, goes insane.

Despite its implicit didacticism—the common element in nearly all of Gilman's fiction—the story stands apart from the others in her vast oeuvre. In artistry and execution, it is superior to any of her other literary works. As Elaine Hedges documents in her historical overview

" 'Out at Last'? 'The Yellow Wall-Paper' after Two Decades of Feminist Criticism," the collective criticism of the story offers "a dazzling and significantly disparate array of interpretations."[17] Indeed, critics have disagreed vehemently over the meaning of the story, variously arguing the significance of everything from linguistic cues and psychoanalytic interpretations to historiographical readings.

While some critics have hailed the narrator as a feminist heroine, others have seen in her a maternal failure coupled with a morbid fear of female sexuality. Some have viewed the story as an exemplar of the silencing of women writers in nineteenth-century America; others have focused on the gothic elements, comparing the story to some of "the weird masterpieces of Hawthorne and Poe," which critic Amy Wellington dismissed as "only a lazy classification for a story which stands alone in American fiction."[18] Undoubtedly, because the story is so unusual and provocative, it will continue to engender debate and controversy with the passage of time.

The opening of "The Yellow Wall-Paper" quickly establishes the narrator's circumstances.[19] She is spending the summer in "a colonial mansion" with her husband, John, a "physician of high standing" who "is practical in the extreme" (*YW,* 10, 9). She is suffering from an illness, which John dismisses as "temporary nervous depression—a slight hysterical tendency" (p. 10). As part of her treatment, she is "absolutely forbidden 'to work,' " a remedy with which she strenuously disagrees. "Personally, I believe that congenial work, with excitement and change, would do me good. But what is one to do?" the narrator muses (p. 10). Along with his sister/housekeeper Jennie, John appropriates all of his wife's power, providing her with "a schedule prescription for each hour of the day" and taking "all care" from her (p. 12). Writing of any kind is prohibited, since John has cautioned her "not to give way to fancy in the least" (p. 15). But the narrator, Jane, is convinced that writing might prove therapeutic. "I think sometimes that if I were only well enough to write a little it would relieve the press of ideas and rest me. . . . It is so discouraging not to have any advice and companionship about my work" (p. 16). Despite John's admonitions, however, the narrator does write, recording her impressions in a secret diary.

Through these diary entries, which comprise the text of the story, the reader learns much about the narrator's state of mind. As the story unfolds, it becomes apparent that she is suffering an acute form of postpartum depression, a condition acknowledged neither by John nor by the late-nineteenth-century medical community of which he is a part.

Part One

"John does not know how much I really suffer," the narrator confides. "He knows that there is no *reason* to suffer, and that satisfies him" (p. 14). Since pragmatism and reason are fundamental aspects of John's personality, he instructs the narrator to simply use "will and self-control" to make herself well (p. 22). If she doesn't show rapid improvement, John warns, "he shall send [her] to Weir Mitchell in the fall" (p. 18), a scenario she clearly wants to avoid.

So extreme is the narrator's depression that the care of the new baby has been assumed by a nursemaid, Mary. "Such a dear baby! And yet I *cannot* be with him, it makes me so nervous," the narrator confesses (p. 14). Deprived of the freedom to write openly and relinquishing care of the infant to a nanny, the narrator gradually shifts her attention to the wallpaper in the attic nursery where she spends most of her time. The paper is the worst she has ever seen, depicting "one of those sprawling flamboyant patterns committing every artistic sin," and "the color is repellant, almost revolting; a smouldering unclean yellow," she writes (p. 13). Soon she begins to detect a subpattern in the wallpaper, "a strange, provoking, formless sort of figure" that "gets clearer every day" (pp. 18, 22). Eventually, the dim shape crystallizes into the image of a woman attempting to escape from behind the wallpaper, on which the narrator gradually begins to discern prisonlike bars. The entrapped woman tries to break free and "takes hold of the bars and shakes them hard" (p. 30). As the woman behind the wallpaper becomes increasingly desperate to effect an escape, the narrator comes to her aid. "I got up and ran to help her. I pulled and she shook, I shook and she pulled, and before morning, we had peeled yards off that paper," she writes (p. 32). Eventually, the narrator's own identity becomes merged with that of the entrapped woman, and she begins to collaborate in her own escape. Having tolerated enforced rest for weeks, the narrator reclaims her right to "work" by joining her symbolic sister in bondage in vigorously stripping the walls of its paper with the "strangled heads and bulbous eyes and waddling fungus growth just shriek[ing] with derision!" (p. 34). At the end of the story, John breaks into the locked room, discovers his wife crawling on the floor, and faints "right across my path by the wall, so that I had to creep over him every time!" (p. 36).

Although Gilman fared better than her fictional protagonist, the biographical dimension, particularly as regards her oppressive first marriage to Walter Stetson, is nevertheless instrumental in understanding the power of the story. Obscuring the biographical link, however, is Gilman's own disclaimer: her insistence that the "real purpose" of "The Yellow

Wall-Paper" was to convince Dr. S. Weir Mitchell that his rest cure treatment, albeit well intended, was not only misguided but dangerous. By examining the three primary metaphors embedded in the text, however—the color yellow, the insurmountable walls that entrap, and the various functions of the paper itself—and by exploring the applications of these images in Gilman's own life, the reader can clearly see that Walter Stetson is implicated along with Mitchell in the intricate patterns encoded in the text.

While the various theoretical approaches to the text—psychoanalytical, linguistic, new historicist, deconstructionist, reader response, and the like—open endless debates about infantile regression, referentiality, and triumph or defeat, the process of creating it was, for Gilman, a major act of empowerment, an act both defiant and personally triumphant. Whether Jane is victorious or defeated at the story's end is perhaps not as significant as the fact that Gilman succeeded in providing an exposé about the devastating effects of work deprivation on intelligent women. It is unlikely that Gilman would have written the story merely to condemn the treatment of her illness, or even the practitioner who prescribed it, without also intentionally exposing one of the primary sources of that illness. While Mitchell's involvement in Gilman's life lasted only a few weeks—he is mentioned only briefly in the story—her marriage to Walter Stetson lasted 10 years, and the imbalance of power in their marriage is as much at issue in the cause of the illness as are the dangers of the "cure."

Walter Stetson understood Charlotte Perkins's reluctance to marry; she constantly articulated her fear that wedlock would require a total subordination of her life's work. "Were I to marry, my thoughts, my acts, my whole life would be centered in husband and children. To do the work that I planned I must be free," she told Stetson early in their relationship (*Endure*, 32). A few weeks later, she was even more adamant: "As much as I love you I love *WORK* better, & I cannot make the two compatible" (p. 63). Stetson persuaded her, however, that should she consent to be his wife, he would not object to her earning an income through writing (p. 69). As if to reinforce his commitment, Stetson occasionally presented his future wife with small gifts—including tablets of paper and stylograph pens—to encourage her writing. But his promises, however well intended, were short-lived, and his gifts of blank paper became an ominous reminder of Gilman's forfeiture of self—a symbol recalling her failure to produce meaningful work and to serve humanity. As various critics of "The Yellow Wall-Paper" have observed, deprived of the freedom to write, the narrator symbolically inscribes her "text" onto the wallpaper in that large attic nursery.[20] Through her fictional alter ego, Gilman projects the trauma of her own first marriage onto the substitute text in a bizarre configuration that "slaps you in the face, knocks you down, and tramples upon you. It is like a bad dream," the narrator writes (*YW,* 25). Moreover, we are told that the paper is "hideous," "unreliable," "infuriating," and "the pattern is torturing" (p. 25), descriptors that can all be applied to Gilman's marriage to Stetson. The protagonist also asserts that "there are things in that paper that nobody knows but me, or ever will" (p. 22). Indeed, the barred paper is at once both a nagging reminder of her silencing in marriage and a frightening tableau depicting the narrator's torment under the care of her physician/husband. Her statement that "there are things . . . that nobody knows" is ultimately untrue, since Gilman makes certain through the discourse of the text that the community of readers will know the details of her marital entrapment. The remark is also strikingly similar to an entry that Gilman recorded in her diary the day before she left Providence to seek the rest cure from Dr. Mitchell: "No one can ever know what I have suffered in these last five years. Pain pain pain, till my mind has given way." Then follows a revealing passage in which Walter Stetson is directly addressed: "I leave you—O remember what, and learn to doubt your judgement before it seeks to mould another life as it has mine" (*Diaries,* 18 April 1887). Just as John attempted to exert control over the narrator's life, Walter Stetson apparently sought to "mould" his young wife.

On the day that Charlotte Stetson left for Mitchell's sanitarium, she first took her young daughter to her friend Mary Phelon, who occasionally served as Katharine's caretaker (significantly, the nursemaid in the story is also named Mary), and returned home to find herself locked out of the house. "Doors locked. No key to be found. Struggle in at bay window with much effort. . . . Begin to write an account of myself for the doctor" (*Diaries,* 19 April 1887). In an ironic reversal in "The Yellow Wall-Paper," the oppressive physician/husband is locked out at the end of the story and has difficulty finding the key that will allow him entrance to the attic room. Gilman's fictional narrator appropriates power, in part, by rendering her physician/husband more marginal than even she is at the story's end; he is on the outside trying in vain to get in while she creeps around the perimeter of the room. If, as critics such as Jeffrey Berman, Mary Jacobus, William Veeder, and Linda Wagner-Martin argue, the narrator's fear of sexuality contributes to her breakdown, then the final scene, in which John urgently attempts to gain entrance, has added significance. When he does finally enter the room, Gilman has him faint, effectively reducing him to a prone and impotent lump on the floor. Significantly, however, he is still blocking his wife, literally and symbolically obstructing her path so that she has to "creep over him every time" (*YW,* 36).

While the diary, of course, was a private document in which Stetson is directly implicated, "The Yellow Wall-Paper" was created for a public audience and thus invites the reader to interact with the text. The narrator's assertion, then, that "there are things in that paper that nobody knows but me" actually entices the reader into exploring further that particularly enigmatic statement and into reading the patterns in the wallpaper. It is at this point in the story that color imagery, walls, and paper—and the significance of the three in Gilman's own life—begin to coalesce.

The color yellow—lurid and revolting—has been variously interpreted as the narrator's sexual repression, her sexual fear, her disgust of sexuality. Indeed, the yellow in the story exemplifies the negative. It is "not beautiful . . . like buttercups"; rather, it reminds the narrator of "old foul, bad yellow things" (p. 28), and it is "smouldering," "unclean," "repellant" (p. 13). Moreover, in the original manuscript of "The Yellow Wall-Paper," Gilman includes a sentence that describes the color as "a sickly penetrating suggestive yellow," a descriptor that doesn't appear in published versions of the story until 1994 and that reinforces the narrator's fear of sexuality as posited by various critics.[21] The color also has extratextual relevance. Less than two months prior to her wedding, Charlotte Perkins cheerfully attempted to play the role of attentive wife-to-be at an opening-night reception honoring her fiancé's latest art exhibition. In dressing for the evening, she virtually swathed herself in yellow, adorning herself with "yellow ribbons, yellow beads, [a] gold comb, [an] amber bracelet, [a] yellow bonnet, [and] yellow flowers"(*Diaries,* 4 March 1884). Unlike Kate Chopin's protagonist in *The Awakening,* Edna Pontellier, who casts aside society's expectations in an effort to formulate an independent identity, Charlotte Perkins was attempting to appropriate "that fictitious self which we assume like a garment with which to appear before the world."[22] She was exceedingly ill at ease in the role, however: rather than feeling exhilarated at the success of Stetson's exhibition, she complained of feeling "strangely tired," and within days was "lachrymose," praying that her "forebodings of future pain . . . be untrue" (*Diaries,* 9 March 1884). Unfortunately, her worst fears about marriage and motherhood were confirmed.

In his essay "Who Is Jane? The Intricate Feminism of Charlotte Perkins Gilman," William Veeder traces "the intricate dramatization of conjugality" between Gilman's biography and "The Yellow Wall-Paper."[23] Using a psychological model exploring ego boundary and object-relations theories, Veeder offers an extended analysis of the color yellow, arguing that "the peculiar yellow odor suggests urine and that the permeated wallpaper represents—among other things—the saturated diaper of childhood" (p. 48). Likewise, Ann J. Lane posits that the foul odor is "a smell, perhaps, of a child's feces."[24]

There is evidence in Gilman's diaries to corroborate the theories of Veeder, Lane, and others who have suggested that the yellow color and smell of the wallpaper might variously be associated with urine, with the narrator's fear of motherhood, and with her regression to an infantile state that finds her creeping around on the attic floor. Gilman's own early experiences with maternity left her nervous, exhausted, and despondent, particularly after Katharine became chronically ill with "bad diaper," Gilman's euphemism for diarrhea (*Diaries*, 6 May 1885). Not only did Katharine's frequent illnesses cause Gilman to question her maternal competence, but her own mother's ease and pleasure in caring for Katharine reinforced Gilman's insecurities. "Mother . . . takes all the care of the baby . . . with infinite delight. I fear I shall forget how to take care of the baby," she confided to her diary (10 May 1885). She was also still desperately anxious to engage in meaningful work. When Katharine was just five months old, Gilman expressed resentment that she had been "forced to be idle and let things drift. Perhaps now I can pick up the broken threads again and make out some kind of a career after all" (*Diaries*, 5 August 1885).

Gilman became increasingly angry at her husband, who not only failed to honor his prenuptial pledge to allow his wife the freedom to write but also imposed a two-week moratorium against her reading anything "about the woman question."[25] In his own diaries, he reviled the drudgeries of housework and engaged in a double standard that mimics the source of much of the tension found in "The Yellow Wall-Paper":

> There is housework to do and though [Charlotte] does what she can, I find enough to tire me and make me feel sometimes that I am wasting my energy, power that should be applied to my art. For love's sake, one must bear all things. . . . But I feel certain that other work is not so well done because of it. I cannot let my mind roam in sweet fancy's field

now. It is utterly impossible. . . . I cannot afford, nor would it be right for me, to give up all my time and strength to such things [as housework]. (*Endure*, 276)

Not surprisingly, Gilman's own sentiments toward the need to indulge *her* fancies—toward her need to accomplish "meaningful" work—mirrored those recorded in her husband's diary. The theme of work, and the earnest desire to indulge the "need" to work, is foregrounded in "The Yellow Wall-Paper." The narrator laments that she is "absolutely forbidden to 'work' until well" and vehemently "disagree[s] with [her husband's] ideas" (*YW,* 10). Near the end of the story, the narrator temporarily assumes control by asserting, "I must get to work" (p. 34), effectively subverting what John had "prescribed" for her. The narrator echoes Gilman's sentiments about the importance of work, that "first duty of a human being" (*Living*, 42). Like the fictional John, Walter Stetson seemed not to recognize the importance of work to his future wife's well-being. Stetson's diary entry for March 13, 1884, is telling: "My love is . . . depressed. *I* think she is unwell." And, like John, he offers his own prescription: "I think a cure will come with marriage and *home*" (*Endure*, 256). Home, for Charlotte Stetson, was analogous to prison. By tearing down the paper, her narrator symbolically destroys the walls that have kept her bound and entrapped—walls Gilman alluded to in her landmark feminist treatise *Women and Economics*, which advocates economic independence and employment for women, "the very walls of [the subordinate woman's] prison" (p. 133).

Although Walter Stetson tried to accommodate his fiancée's desire "to make a name for herself in the world by doing good work," (*Endure*, 144) he paradoxically viewed it is as sinful: "It is sin—surely sin: anything that takes woman away from the beautifying and sanctifying of home and bearing children must be sin," he rationalized (pp. 144, 148). Stetson was exceedingly conventional in his advocacy of a gender-based division of labor, a practice Gilman emphatically rejected on both philosophical and ideological grounds. (It is likely that Gilman's outrage at Stetson's conventional notions helped to inspire *Women and Economics*, published just four years after their divorce became final.) "The Yellow Wall-Paper," then, actually became a vehicle through which Gilman could encode her rage toward Stetson over a host of matters: his broken promises, the loss of her personal freedom following Katharine's birth, her enforced economic dependence, her obsequious status and entrapment in the marriage, and even the pressure Stetson exerted on her to marry while she was still obviously mourning the loss of her longtime friend Martha Luther Lane.[26]

Gilman's resentment at being coerced into assuming the role of wife and mother not only emerges in diary entries and in the painting depicting a defeated woman literally up against a wall—a potent symbol of her unattainable quest to serve humanity should she marry—but is embedded deep within the framework of "The Yellow Wall-Paper." The arbitrary restrictions that John imposes on his wife—particularly forbidding her to write—symbolize artificial walls between the narrator and the work she aspires to perform.

One of the basic requirements of the rest cure was that the patient be denied liberties of all kinds, including the freedom to write. Again, an intriguing bit of extratextual evidence sheds light on Gilman's distress at being forbidden to write. In the diary entry made the day before she left for S. Weir Mitchell's sanitarium, she writes, "I have kept a journal since I was fifteen, the only blanks being in these last years of sickness and pain. I have done it because it was useful. Now I am to go away for my health, and shall not try to take any responsibilites [*sic*] with me, even this old friend" (*Diaries*, 18 April 1887). Charlotte Stetson obviously resented the forced abandonment of her "old friend"; hence, she creates a fictional narrator who outwits her husband by hiding a secret diary in which she documents the cause of her gradual descent into madness.

Perhaps one of the most crucial links between Gilman's biography and "The Yellow Wall-Paper" lies in the narrator's enigmatic assertion at the end of the story: " 'I've got out at last,' said I. . . . 'And I've pulled off most of the paper, so you can't put me back!' " (*YW*, 36). In looking for a parallel to this declaration of independence in Gilman's own life, we are reminded of the pivotal moment when, after "crawl[ing] into remote closets and under beds—to hide from the grinding pressure of that profound distress" (*Living*, 96), she "recovered some measure of power" by reclaiming an identity independent of that thrust on her by Walter Stetson (*FR*, October 1913). "Coming out of the closet," which evokes images of suffocation, constraint, and secrecy, involves a public disclosure of one's formerly concealed identity and breaking the silence—exposing to the world the truths about one's life.

Although Gilman deflected direct blame from Stetson by instead implicating Mitchell and "the error of his ways," there is little doubt that Stetson recognized in John of "The Yellow Wall-Paper" a thinly disguised portrait of himself. But even though (or perhaps because) he was disconcerted by what he read, Gilman seemed smugly satisfied by his reaction. In a letter to Martha Luther Lane, she urged: "When my awful story 'The Yellow Wallpaper' comes out, you must try & read it. Walter says he has read it *four* times, and thinks it is the most ghastly tale he ever read. . . . But that's only a husband's opinion."[27] As an unintended but ironic commentary on their relationship, Gilman described the story to Lane as one that was "highly unpleasant." But to openly state that the purpose of the story was to paint Walter Stetson as a villain would have been needlessly cruel, as Gilman undoubtedly recognized. She was, after all, still married to Stetson when the "The Yellow Wall-Paper" was first published, and an open indictment would have proved personally embarrassing to him. In her essay "Why I Wrote The Yellow Wallpaper?" Gilman states that casting aside Mitchell's advice and returning to work enabled her to recover "some measure of power" (p. 271). And loss of power was precisely the issue around which much of her apprehension toward marriage was originally focused. The act of writing an exposé of her breakdown—the price exacted for succumbing to the pressure to marry—helped to restore her sense of control.

Gilman's indictment of S. Weir Mitchell is, in part, a psychological maneuver: by deflecting criticism from Walter Stetson, she also avoided confronting the vulnerable part of herself that had reluctantly submitted, against her better judgment, to a marriage of servility.[28] It also served a therapeutic purpose. She could simultaneously retaliate against her oppressor, restore a sense of power, and ultimately practice the very craft she had been for so long denied. Regrettably, although she remained remarkably prolific, she would never again write a story that rivaled the power and poignancy of "The Yellow Wall-Paper."

Early Fiction and "Studies in Style"

One very early review of her fiction reported that "as a writer of short stories Charlotte Perkins Stetson possesses a constructive skill, and a dramatic power peculiarly her own. Most of her stories are somewhat lurid, particularly those of a ghostly nature."[29] While the nature and character of her stories would change dramatically in future years, Gilman wrote several early stories in the gothic tradition. In addition to "The Yellow Wall-Paper," which was often characterized as a ghost or horror story in the years following its initial publication,[30] Gilman's gothic stories include "The Giant Wistaria" (1891), "The Rocking-Chair" (1893), and "The Unwatched Door," written in imitation of Poe's narrative style.[31]

"The Giant Wistaria," written in March 1890 just a few months before Gilman completed "The Yellow Wall-Paper,"[32] is a remarkable work comprised of two related stories set one hundred years apart. The first episode, set in late-eighteenth-century New England, opens with a young unwed mother, recently arrived from England with her parents, nervously breaking shoots off of her mother's newly planted wistaria vine. Reproached by her mother for damaging the plant, the unnamed young woman begs to see her new baby, who is being cared for by a "hard-faced servant woman" (*GW*, 480). The young mother, wearing "a small carnelian cross that hung from her neck," appeals to her own mother's sense of maternity in pleading for her child: "Art thou a mother and hast no pity on me, a mother? Give me my child!" she cries (p. 480). Her solicitations are abruptly interrupted by her embittered and abusive father, Samuel Dwining, who violently strikes his daughter across the mouth and orders her to her chamber. After her departure, Dwining states his wish that his daughter had drowned during the ocean voyage to spare his "house from open shame" and announces to his wife that he has arranged for his daughter "a new life to cover the old" (p. 480). The new life will require her to abandon the baby and set sail for England the following day to marry her cousin. The first section of the story concludes with Samuel Dwining striding "heavily across the porch, till the loose planks creaked . . . with his arms folded and his brows fiercely knit above his iron mouth" (p. 480). Meanwhile, his wan daughter watches silently from the window of the chamber to which she has been sent.

In the second part of the story, Gilman moves the narrative forward one hundred years, and the somber tone in the first section is quickly eclipsed by the exuberant chatter of Jenny, a young bride who is elated over the prospect of spending the summer in a remote old mansion she is sure must be haunted. Once a lease is secured, she and her husband, George, invite two other couples for an extended stay. Together they explore the old house "from top to bottom, from the great room in the garret, with nothing in it but a rickety cradle, to the well in the cellar . . . with a rusty chain going down to unknown blackness" (p. 482). Outside the mansion, their attention is drawn to the gnarled wistaria vine, which gains new prominence in the second part of the story. The vine has grown so huge that its roots have buckled the planks on the floor of the porch. "The trunk [of the vine] rose at the corner of the porch by the high steps, and had once climbed its pillars; but now the pillars were wrenched from their places and held rigid and helpless by the tightly wound and knotted arms" (p. 482). The young vine with tender shoots in the first part of the story has, over the course of a hundred years, become a sinister force, "a knitted wall of stem and leaf" (p. 482).

Young Jenny is intrigued by the decaying old house and the desolate setting. "I'm convinced there is a story, if we could only find it," she remarks. "You need not tell me that a house like this, with a garden like this, and cellar like this, isn't haunted!" (p. 482). George, a young and rather pragmatic physician, gently mocks her interest in ghosts, while Jack Waterbury, a reporter on a New York daily, assures her with considerable amusement that "if we don't find a real ghost . . . I shall make one [up]" (p. 482). The men belittle the women, who insist that the mansion "is a *real* ghostly place." Soon the women imagine that they "see bloodstains and crouching figures" in the landscape. One of them also remarks that the great wistaria trunk "looks for all the world like a writhing body—cringing—beseeching!" (p. 482).

Over breakfast the next morning, Jenny announces that she awakened during the night with a "dreadful feeling" and heard "that old chain down [in the cellar] rattle and creak over the stones" (p. 483). Jack Waterbury, still in a festive mood, reports having had a dream in which he saw a female ghost "all wrapped up in a shawl" and wearing "a little red cross that hung from her neck" rifling through the drawers of a bureau. He humorously concludes that what he saw "was the genuine,

19

legitimate ghost of an eloping chambermaid with kleptomania!" (p. 484). While the women are disappointed by Jack's levity, George rather solemnly confesses that during the night he too encountered the figure of a woman in the cellar wearing a little red cross. Although he speculates that his vision may have been the result of indigestion, he is clearly unnerved by what he has seen.

Together the three couples decide to search the cellar well. "The fresh cambrics and pretty boots were gallantly escorted below by gentlemen whose jokes were so frequent that many of them were a little forced," the narrator states (p. 484). In the bucket of the well, they make the horrifying discovery of a month-old infant's tiny skeleton preserved in the lime, which George estimates to be about "a century" old (p. 485). As the couples quietly contemplate their discovery, the silence is broken by a cry from some workmen who have been repairing the loose planks on the front porch. "They had removed the floor and the side walls of the old porch, so that the sunshine poured down to the dark stones of the cellar bottom. And there, in the strangling grasp of the roots of the great wistaria, lay the bones of a woman, from whose neck still hung a tiny scarlet cross on a thin chain of gold" (p. 485).

Gilman has created in this intriguing work both a ghost story and a tale about the suffering of women under patriarchal rule. The giant wistaria is at once both a symbol of maternal sacrifice and a grotesque reminder of the silencing of the woman whose skeletal remains are literally and metaphorically rooted in a "strangling grasp" (p. 485).

In his critical analysis of the story, Gary Scharnhorst persuasively argues that the story can be read as "an experiment in the female frontier gothic" wherein Gilman has created a character who becomes "a natural hieroglyph in the hallucinatory wilderness or liminal frontier."[33] Gloria A. Biamonte writes that in addition to being read as a ghost story, the text "suggests the different conceptual and perceptual worlds that women live in" compared to men.[34] Both critics raise questions, which Gilman refuses to answer, about the circumstances leading to the deaths of the young mother and her infant. Was the young woman murdered by her father for her refusal to submit to his demands? Did she take her own life? Was she a victim of incest? Who drowned the baby? While Scharnhorst rightly concludes that "Gilman's tale resolves no mysteries of historical causation" (p. 161), subtle textual signifiers in both sections of the story, although speculative at best, suggest a murder-suicide committed by the desperate young mother.

The inconsolable young mother in the first episode of the story is provided no first name, which underscores her loss of identity as both a new mother (her infant has been taken from her) and as a daughter (she is persecuted by her tyrannical father). She is, however, given the surname Dwining. Derived from the Middle English word *dwinen*, the term means to languish, pine away, wither, or fade. Indeed, in her appeal to Samuel Dwining, Mistress Dwining expresses the fear that their daughter will either die of grief or take her own life: "Art thou not afeard for her life?" she asks. "She grieveth sore for the child, aye, and for the green fields to walk in," a veiled reference, perhaps, to the relative freedom of death when compared to her confinement in the upstairs chamber. "Nay," Samuel Dwining responds to his wife. "She hath lost already what is more than life" (p. 480).

The young mother is, in effect, an archetypal death-in-life character. While Gilman provides little physical description, she allows that the young woman has "weary eyes that yet had a flickering, uncertain blaze in their shaded depths" (p. 480). Similarly, in the last scene in the first episode, "the shadows flickered mockingly across a white face . . . with eyes of wasted fire" (pp. 480–81). The pale young woman is presumably weak as a result of her recent travail, and the flickering suggests that the flame of life will soon be extinguished. Moreover, having "lost already what is more than life," and effectively silenced by her father's hand, the young woman has little motivation for living. Not only will she be "bound" as a punishment for disobedience, but her baby will be left in the new world in the care of strangers, and she will be forced to marry her cousin, "a coarse fellow" whose attentions she has "ever shunned" (p. 480).

Also suggestive of a murder-suicide is that the young woman overhears her father's remark that he would have preferred that his "child drowned, than live to this end" (p. 480). The young woman apparently enacts the same fate for her infant child, choosing the method of death identical to the one her father expressly wished for. In an act both defiant and rebellious, the woman drowns her infant in the basement well. The sacrifice of the innocent, and her own subsequent death, constitute a morbid repudiation of her father's declaration that his daughter "hath small choice" but to leave the baby and marry her cousin.

No less significant is the image of the tender vine in the first episode. In what might be seen as a subconscious gesture foreshadowing the murder of the infant, the young woman "[breaks] the tender shoot," which leads her mother to chide her for meddling with the plant that was a gift from her husband (p. 480). In the second part of the story, the plant's "knitted wall of stem and leaf" forms an ironic parallel to Samuel Dwining's "fiercely knit" brows after he announces his plans to dispatch his daughter to distant shores. Both the exposed part of the great vine and that which is rooted deep beneath the surface suggest the power struggle between father and daughter. Samuel Dwining's persecuting spirit is entwined in the giant wistaria, looming above his daughter's "cringing, beseeching" one. Moreover, Dwining's inventing "a new life to cover the old" obviously suggests concealment (p. 480). Likewise, the girl's presumably unbridled passion, which resulted in her pregnancy, is mimicked one hundred years later in the wild, primeval garden that was once carefully groomed. Nature's uncontrolled proliferation is emblematic of the girl's untamed carnal desires that led to her illegitimate pregnancy.

Perhaps the strongest evidence pointing to a murder-suicide is in the apparent reenactment by the woman's ghost that now haunts the house where she once dwelled. According to Jack, the apparition he saw carried under her arm "a big bundle" and moved "in frantic haste and terror." She also appeared to be removing items from the bureau drawers before creeping "noiselessly from the room" (p. 483). The bundle suggests the child she is about to sacrifice, and she might conceivably be searching for some device to assist her in taking her own life—a rope, a weapon, some lethal substance, perhaps? We can only speculate, since Gilman leaves unclear the reason for the search of the bureau drawers. We do know, however, that while Jenny only hears the bucket moving in the well, George actually sees the woman take "hold of the chain" to which the bucket is attached (p. 484). Both the chain that holds the cross and the chain that holds the bucket link the woman to her child and to death. The cross establishes her as a martyrlike figure, willing to take her own life and that of her child rather than endure a forced separation, and the chain on the bucket might signify her determination to be unshackled from her father's suffocating authority. Significantly, she lowers the bucket deep into the well—ceremoniously burying not only her illegitimate child but also her father's scheme to "maketh an honest woman of her" (p. 480). The persecuted woman in the first episode is, however, still subject in death to the penetrating force and "strangling grasp" of patriarchal authority, as symbolized by the roots belonging to the vine that her father presented to her mother a century before.

Despite the dark nature of this tale, Gilman has some fun at the expense of one of her male characters, the roguish newspaper reporter Jack Waterbury. A jovial man who insists that he is "not horrid by nature" but only by profession (p. 484), Jack has learned to be skeptical as a result of his job. He unrelentingly teases the other guests, makes puns and wisecracks, and wildly embellishes his account of seeing the ghost to make a better story. Fittingly, Gilman gives him the first name Jack, perhaps to reflect his often-asinine antics, and the surname Waterbury, to not only foreshadow the grisly discovery in the well but to underscore both his shallowness and his self-absorption. Just as Samuel Dwining invented "a new life to cover the old," Jack Waterbury will concoct a story about a ghost if necessary. His name also suggests how easily the truth may be submerged, concealed, or denied when it presents a scenario too sinister for the rational mind to assimilate.

Although "The Rocking-Chair" was not published until 1893, Gilman began working on it in August 1890, just two days after she completed work on "The Yellow Wall-Paper."[35] Replete with gothic elements that include the specter of a beautiful young woman, a rocking chair that mysteriously "walks" across the room, and the disclosure of a coffinlike chamber, this story, like "The Giant Wistaria," culminates with the discovery of a brutal murder.

The story opens with two "young newspaper men, 'penny-a-liners,' " searching for lodging in "the dreary dimness of a narrow city street" (*RC,* 453). Their attention is drawn to "the golden head of a girl in an open window" rocking in a high-backed chair (p. 453). After spotting a sign in a first-floor window that lodging is available in this "ordinary" house (p. 453), the unnamed narrator and his lifelong friend Hal approach the landlady, "an old woman with a dull, expressionless face and faded eyes," and promptly lease two rooms. Hal takes the room with the rocker, a "high-backed chair . . . with heavy square corners . . . mounted in brass" (p. 454). The narrator meanwhile moves into a smaller room adjoining Hal's. The men admit to one another that they are drawn to the house in part by the golden-haired young woman, but they also sense the lure of another "compulsion" that neither man can immediately identify (p. 454).

Both men hope to see the young woman face-to-face, but several days pass without a sighting. They hear "her light movements," however, and occasionally detect her "soft girlish laugh" (pp. 454, 453). From the street below, each man believes that he sees the other in the room with the young woman, and there soon develops between them "a dreadful sense of concealment" (p. 455). The tensions quickly escalate, and the narrator is seized with feelings of "jealousy and hate" toward Hal (p. 458). Each man angrily accuses the other of lying, and when Hal flings open a previously locked door expecting to find the woman in hiding, both men are astonished to discover only "a closet, two by four, as bare and shallow as an empty coffin" (p. 458). Hal turns "white with rage," while the narrator admits that "So wild a wave of hate rose in my heart that I could have trampled upon him where he lay—killed him like a dog—but with a mighty effort I turned from him and left the room" (p. 458). Early the next morning, he returns to an empty house with "no sign of human occupancy" (p. 458). Not only has the landlady mysteriously disappeared, but when the narrator enters Hal's room, he finds him "[d]ead, and most horribly dead. Three heavy marks—blows—three deep, three-cornered gashes—I started to my feet—even the chair was gone!" (p. 459). In utter terror, the narrator flees the house to the sound of the "whispered laugh" (p. 459). When he reaches the safety of the street, he "cast one shuddering glance at the fateful window" (p. 459). There in the rocking chair sat the young woman with "the sweet face, down-dropped eyes, and swaying golden head" (p. 459).

Juliann E. Fleenor points out that both men view the elusive young woman as "a feminine enigma" since she is described as possessing "a strange beauty, infinitely attractive, yet infinitely perplexing" (*RC*, 455).[36] Fleenor also suggests that "Gilman appears to be satirizing the male proclivity to worship . . . a non-existent woman" (p. 231). Indeed, the beautiful, younger woman in the story appears only as a vision, and she is silent, except for the "faint, soft, silver laugh" that both men hear (*RC*, 458). She is symbolically static, confined to the house and primarily to the chair at that. Similarly, the older landlady, whom the men presume to be the girl's mother, "murmurs monotonously" and refuses to provide room service or meals to her tenants, although she takes apparent pride in her old Spanish rocking chair, whose brass corners she mechanically polishes with the edge of her apron. Meanwhile, the men go out into the world to collect their news stories, and see themselves as "part of that struggling crowd of aspirants who are to literature what squires and pages were to knighthood in olden days" (p. 453). Their perception of themselves as "winning [their] spurs" (p. 453), however, is shattered both by the reality of their "slow work, unpleasant, and ill-paid," and, significantly, by the chair itself, which although apparently cherished by both women, inflicts "manifold bruises" on the men "with an ease and violence equally astonishing" (p. 456). Despite their painful "encounters" with the rocker, so compelling is their romantic association of it with the golden-haired beauty who graces it "evening after evening" that neither man wants it removed (p. 457).

As Fleenor suggests, Gilman seems in part to be satirizing the male addiction to feminine beauty at any cost. Their bumps and bruises are greeted by the quiet laughter of the feminine specter, who eludes the men at every turn. The older landlady, too, whose presence in the house seems innocuous enough, is apparently a cold-blooded murderer who brutally crushes the skull of the younger woman's would-be suitor.

As she does in "The Giant Wistaria," Gilman leaves several questions in "The Rocking-Chair" unanswered. Why the young woman haunts the dwelling, for example, we do not know. And whether the ghost and the landlady are one and the same we cannot say, although they never appear together. It is perhaps possible that the ghost has the ability to assume the guise of the older woman, who appears harmless, while in reality she carefully polishes the "dark glittering" corners of the rocking-chair-turned-murder-weapon (p. 456).

Interestingly, both "The Giant Wistaria" and "The Rocking-Chair" anticipate Gilman's contempt for newspaper reporters, which began to develop in 1892. Her frequent disputes with reporters over their sordid interest in her divorce from Walter Stetson led her to conclude that journalists, in general, were unethical and untrustworthy.[37] Her distrust seemed evident even as she wrote these early stories, shortly after her formal separation. The two aspiring journalists in "The Rocking-Chair" "had small honor for those above [them] in their profession, with but too good reason" even though they, "of course, should do far nobler things when [their] spurs were won!" (*RC,* 453). And as we saw in "The Giant Wistaria," Jack Waterbury will invent news, if necessary.

Gilman's experiments with the gothic mode early in her career were preceded by a handful of other fictional works, including her first story, "A Transparency," a parable on brotherhood that appeared in the 1 December 1886 issue of *The Alpha*. Nearly 3 $^1/_2$ years passed before her next story, "That Rare Jewel," a short piece examining courtship and marriage, appeared in the May 1890 issue of *Woman's Journal*.[38] "Circumstances Alter Cases," which also appeared in 1890, is discussed in the section "Autobiographical Fiction."

Another early story, "The Unexpected," deserves mention for its well-rendered narrative style.[39] Gilman's male narrator, Edouard Charpentier, is a struggling Europeanized American "artiste," who is fickle, pretentious, and humorously melodramatic in his love for a distant cousin, Marie, whom he meets when he travels to the States. He surrenders himself to the "[f]ate [that] rules all men" (*Yellow,* 118) and, like Walter Stetson, quickly proposes marriage. But the more he persists in his proposals of marriage, the more Marie resists. "I think that girl refused me nine times," he states (p. 118). Unperturbed by her rejection, however, Edouard is determined to win her, and finally Marie, with her "face of fire and roses," agrees to marry him (p. 118). A fortnight later, Edouard suspects his new bride of infidelity, although he knew her only a week before wooing her and wooed her only a month before marrying her. His greatest dilemma is whether to kill only the man he presumes to be his wife's young and handsome lover or both of them. The denouement is predictable: Marie is herself an artist, and the attractive young man is merely her model. Despite the contrived ending, in which Edouard and Marie contentedly share a double studio in Paris, the narration is entertaining and Edouard delightfully whimsical.

"My Poor Aunt," originally published in *Kate Field's Washington* in 1891 and later reprinted in the *Forerunner*,[40] contains all of the didactic elements that would become standard fare in Gilman's later reform fiction. The story centers around the future of Kate Bennett, a young woman who rejects marriage, much to the dismay of her meddlesome mother. Constantly compared by her mother and other relatives to her estranged "poor aunt Kate," the younger Kate is both intrigued by and wary of her namesake's legacy. (Coincidentally, one of Gilman's lifelong friends was the "kind and helpful" Kate Bucklin, after whom she named her daughter, Katharine. Like the fictional "Aunt Kate," Bucklin was "somewhat older" than Gilman and enjoyed her independence [*Living*, 49].) "I had grown up with a dim, unpleasant sense of naughtiness about Aunt Kate, and regarded her, in spite of my inward sympathy, as an epitome of all iconoclasm and unwomanly rebellion," the narrator states (*FR*, 310–11). After rejecting the proposals of three suitors and being subjected to an extended argument about why she should marry by her "uncommonly homely" and priggish male boarder (p. 310), young Kate realizes that she is a reasonable person of legal age and is empowered to make her own choices about marriage. As she finishes her impassioned rejoinder to the boarder's uninvited counsel, her long-lost Aunt Kate melodramatically bursts into the room, offers Kate a job, and gives her "hope and strength and courage with every breath" (p. 313). The paradigm of the older and wiser woman paired with the younger, less experienced woman recurs in several of Gilman's later stories.

Three of Gilman's other early stories, "Society and the Philosopher," "Society and the Baby," and "An Extinct Angel," all published in 1891 in *Kate Field's Washington*,[41] combine Gilman's interest in Nationalism and reform Darwinism with her predilection for didacticism. Each advances her theories about human nature and the responsibility incumbent on the individual to effect positive change. Written primarily in dialogue form, "Society and the Philosopher" effectively illustrates Gilman's belief that society's ills can be cured "in a reasonable time" if society has the fortitude to make "certain radical changes" (p. 94). "Society and the Baby" is more political, and, perhaps unwittingly, reflects what might be seen to epitomize the contemporary and contrary philosophies of the two major American political parties. To Society's insistence that the Baby "can't stay on the face of the earth without paying for it" (p. 165), the perplexed Baby responds, "I'll pay with all my heart when I'm bigger. Just feed me well now, and when I'm grown I'll be a credit to you. The more you do for me now, the more I'll do for you then—see? And I can pay back compound interest, for the work of a smart person is worth vastly more than his keep" (p. 165). But Society doesn't buy it. "It is immaterial to me whether you live or die," Society answers. "You have got to pay for everything you get" (p. 165). When the Baby points out that Society is made up of people and is invariably healthier when those people are well cared for, Society balks. But the Baby rails against its indifference: " 'There you sit and plaster your wounds, and nurse your diseases, and fight your vices, and pretend you own the earth! You are a hollow, crack-brained, discrepant old rudiment.' . . . But Society, though on its last legs, was bigger than the Baby," and the Baby inevitably dies (p. 166). "But there are more Babies," the narrator notes as she ends the tale with a glimmer of optimism reflecting her continued belief in people's ability to shape their future (p. 166).

"An Extinct Angel" is a brilliant satire telling the story of the "angel in the house," a metaphor for a perfect wife and doting mother, and how she eventually becomes extinct. Presented as a fairy tale but with an unmistakable subtext rooted in historical fact, the story notes that in the old days, "almost every family had one" of these angels (p. 199). "It was the business of the angel to assuage, to soothe, to comfort, to delight." Even though the impassioned "owners" of the angel sometimes became unruly "even to the extent of legally beating [his] angel with 'a stick no thicker than his thumb,' the angel was to have no passion whatever" (p. 199). The "human creature" who went out to work every day "was apt to come home tired and cross," but the angel in the house was trained to greet him with "a soft, perennial, heavenly smile" (p. 199). In a second reference to domestic violence, Gilman writes that "when an angel fell the human creature" would punish her "with unrelenting fury" (p. 200). The angels "waited on the human creatures in every form of menial service, doing things ... which the human creature loathed and scorned" (p. 200). Unfortunately, Gilman's narrator confides, "The angels—I say it under breath—were not very bright!" (p. 200). Because "the human creatures did not like intelligent angels" since "it was harder to reconcile things when the angels had any sense[,] ... every possible care was taken to prevent the angels from learning anything" of value. Nevertheless, "little by little, owing to the unthought-of consequences of repeated intermarriage between the angel and the human being, the angel longed for, found and ate the fruit of the forbidden tree of knowledge. And in that day she surely died" (p. 200). Although rumors persist that the species survives in remote areas "where no access is to be had to the deadly fruit," the "race as a race" is finally extinct. A call for the elimination of domestic servility in women is beautifully illustrated in "An Extinct Angel."

Published in *Pacific Monthly* in 1891, "A Walk for Two" examines the contest of wills between Ella Graves, "a damsel of twenty-one" (p. 194), and "young Sanders," a "spare and feeble youth" (p. 195), whose "tireless attentions" toward Ella "hardened her heart as she remembered his immovable conceit and persistence" (p. 198).[42] To the disappointment of her mother and aunt, who "considered her a predestined old maid" (p. 194), Ella, who has no desire to marry, declines numerous invitations from Sanders, the son of a wealthy mill owner. Finally, however, Ella, a "tomboy" in peak physical condition, accepts his proposal to go for a walk on a "very hot summer Sunday afternoon ... an invitation that left her free to act, and on her own ground" (p. 196). Ella gleefully leads the perspiring youth through miles of country meadows and valleys, while he feebly struggles to keep up. When they have finally come full circle, hours later, the exasperated and exhausted Sanders attempts to extort a kiss from Ella, declaring, "You owe me something for such a trick as that!" (p. 198). When he seizes her hand and tries to draw her near him, Ella uses "the arm that was used to racket and rein" and "threw off his hand so that he almost fell" (p. 198).

Gilman makes several points in this story. The protagonist, who rejects marriage in favor of a career despite the fact "that she's *had* offers—and good ones" (p. 194), is the epitome of health and happiness. Although her mother and aunt "grieved over Ella," (p. 194), she has an enormously positive self-image. Moreover, the cultivation of her physical strength has given her both the confidence and the ability to defend herself against her would-be accoster. (Gilman herself was exceedingly proud of her physical fitness in her early twenties and was instrumental in garnering support for the Providence Ladies Gymnasium, which opened in the fall of 1881.)

Dress reform and fiscal management are the subjects of another early story, "Their Dressmaker," in which the first-person narrator is, interestingly, a patient undergoing the rest cure in a sanitarium.[43] She is, however, in decidedly better spirits than her counterpart in "The Yellow Wall-Paper." "One of the amusing things in a rest-cure is the way the nurses congregate in the invalids' bedchambers and chatter like merry magpies," she remarks. "Your own friends you may not see—nor books nor papers; the doctor's calls are short and quiet; no outside influence is allowed to break the charmed silence of the sick room; but these merry nurses, full of health and spirits, flit in and out as freely and converse as fluently as though the rest-cure was an afternoon tea" (p. 202).

The subject of conversation among the nurses is their "recalcitrant dressmakers," who routinely fail to deliver promised garments on time. Although the narrator considers all the nurses her "good friends," her "short stock of patience gave out" and she "assailed them" from her bed, which they took "meekly enough," particularly since "invalids are allowed to be irritable" (p. 202). Gilman's narrator uses her sharp analytical mind to reason calmly and logically. As she listens to their complaints, she concludes that anyone overhearing them would think "that they were bond slaves of some awful potentate; helpless sufferers at the hands of this august being who made . . . their dresses" (p. 202). With a pencil and paper that "the doctor would never have allowed" (p. 202), the invalid narrator draws up a plan under which the nurses could collectively hire their own dressmaker, with whom they would have an exclusive annual contract. Gilman's point is twofold: not only are seemingly insurmountable problems ultimately solvable, but pooling resources for a common good can have widespread social and economic benefits.

The direction of Gilman's fiction took a twist during the summer of 1894, when she assumed management of the *Impress*, a California literary weekly and the official publication of the Pacific Coast Woman's Press Association. In addition to "articles, verses, editorials, ethical problems . . . and reviews" (*Living*, 173), Gilman "instituted a series of 'Studies in Style,' " designed to provide readers with "a wide knowledge and more delicate appreciation of distinctive literary methods."[44] To this end, Gilman produced 16 short stories and one play over 18 weeks "in avowed imitation" of such well-known authors as Louisa May Alcott, George Eliot, Hamlin Garland, Nathaniel Hawthorne, Henry James,

Edgar Allan Poe, Olive Schreiner, Mark Twain, and Mary E. Wilkins [Freeman] (*Living*, 173). The quality of these studies, like all of her fiction, is uneven. Several of the stories, however, are deftly sketched and demonstrate an ear for dialect and a talent for descriptive imagery that undoubtedly could have been developed had Gilman had time to "give her mind to it," as author Mary Austin once suggested (p. 285).

Despite the "delicate appreciation of distinctive literary methods" that Gilman offered as the purpose for writing the "Studies in Style," the series was little more than an advertising gimmick to promote the *Impress*. "I could not write a good story every week, much less buy one," Gilman confessed in her autobiography (p. 173). To relieve both the pressure of time and the need for original creative expression, her "Studies in Style" was born. The first reader to correctly identify the author being imitated would "receive a copy of one of that author's books" (p. 173).

One of the stories featured in the "Studies in Style" series was "Clifford's Tower," written in imitation of Nathaniel Hawthorne.[45] Gilman hailed Hawthorne a "great and deep" writer whose work was "honored as one of the distinctive glories of American literature."[46] She had, in fact, become familiar with his work at an early age. When she was just 16, she was present for the opening-night performance of the stage version of *The Scarlet Letter*, produced at the Boston Theatre; also present were William Dean Howells, James Russell Lowell, and Henry Wadsworth Longfellow.[47] Gilman's exposure to Hawthorne's work continued over the years; in 1882 she read *Mosses from an Old Manse*, and in 1883 she counted among her Christmas presents a new "silk umbrella & a book of Hawthorne."[48] Although Gilman praised the "greatness" of Hawthorne's writing, "Clifford's Tower" stands alone as the only one of her stories that can be properly attributed to "the School of Hawthorne," to borrow Richard Brodhead's phrase.[49]

Of the 17 sketches that Gilman produced for the "Studies in Style" series, she found "Clifford's Tower" among the most difficult to write. "Not the greatest and deepest characteristics of so great and deep a writer [as Hawthorne] could be rendered in this brief story," she lamented.[50] "Its brevity was one of the essential difficulties in this case, the style of Hawthorne being comparitively [*sic*] diffuse." Although Gilman was satisfied with her rendering of Hawthorne's "elegant diction" and "the old New England background," she was less pleased with the story's "most Hawthornesque features . . . the tone of sadness and hint of supernaturalism, the family strain of pride and unforgiven injury

long past, and the sudden dark catastrophe which brings it to an end."
Space constraints had left these elements inadequately developed, she
conceded in the 3 November 1894 *Impress* (p. 4).

Indeed, the plot of "Clifford's Tower" is predictable, the characters
underdeveloped, and the dialogue weak. Set in the charming and color-
ful New England countryside, "Clifford's Tower" recounts the story of
Herndon Clifford, one of the country's original settlers, who sets out to
build a castle "which should rival in this new world the ancestral glory
of his family in the old" (p. 5). Clifford's intention is to build the castle
as a tribute to his bride-to-be, Mabel Hurd. When Mabel undergoes a
change of heart and returns to her first love, Clifford abruptly halts construction of the castle and spends the remainder of his life in exile.
Generations later, one of Clifford's descendants, the "fair pale Agnes
whose short life was passed in the very shadow of the [castle] tower"
(p. 5), falls in love with Robert Hurd, grandson of the woman who left
Clifford to return to her first love. Agnes's mother, Catharine Clifford, a
chronically ill but exceedingly strong-willed woman, forbids the union
between the two young lovers. "While I live, and while this tower shall
stand, you shall not marry this man!" she commands Agnes (p. 6). An
obedient daughter, Agnes reaffirms her duty to her sickly mother. Late
one evening, however, while her mother is asleep, Agnes slips outside in
the midst of a violent thunderstorm to say good-bye to Robert one last
time. In an utterly contrived and melodramatic climax, a stroke of light-
ning destroys the castle, killing Catharine Clifford and freeing Agnes to
marry Robert. "Clifford's Tower" offers a baldly superficial imitation in
its attempt to represent Hawthorne's New England landscape and character types.

Although Gilman admired Hawthorne's eloquence, applauded his
artistry, and even attempted to imitate his work, her rendition of his
style lacked the power and passion that characterized his fiction. This is
not to say, however, that Gilman, like so many other writers at the turn
of the century, did not appropriate some of Hawthorne's most prominent themes in some of her other works. Indeed, the Hawthornesque
themes of sin, morality, guilt, redemption, and obsession figure prominently in Gilman's fiction; however, she reshaped the conflicts, the
characters, and particularly the resolutions in the majority of her stories
to argue more explicitly her central thesis: that a reformed society is not
only desirable but also within reach.[51] Whereas Hawthorne's Hester
Prynne could only look forward, vaguely, to "some brighter period, when
. . . a new truth would be revealed, in order to establish the whole rela-

tion between man and woman on a surer ground of mutual happiness,"[52] Gilman's characters are able to effect a "new truth" and to enact a positive change. Again and again, the bulk of Gilman's fiction offers solutions to seemingly untenable social and domestic problems.

In another story, "The Unwatched Door," Gilman invokes such devices as the gothic mansion, the demented narrator, and the secret tomb in an attempt to capture Poe's distinctive literary style.[53] But rather than a successful imitation, "The Unwatched Door" is, at best, a parody, combining elements from several of Poe's best-known stories in a tale that fails to achieve his trademark "unity of effect." The story opens with a female narrator describing the "marble house" in which she lives and around which "flowers grew, rich brilliant flowers, in eddying sweeps of color that pulsed and flowed up to the white walls, over the wide steps, and out into the vivid velvet of the lawn" (p. 4). The mausoleumlike marble structure, expanse of velvet lawn, and bright flowers all suggest a cemetery, and indeed, by the second paragraph, the description becomes more macabre. "The trees were not very tall yet, not tall enough to give the place the air I wanted, and some which I had eagerly transplanted died after a little while and stood withered and stiff among the flowers. But even those the vines soon covered, riotous climbing things that shot creeping fingers of pale delicate green, which turned to clutching hands, and then to embracing arms that only death would loosen" (p. 4). In paragraph three, the narrator reports that her house is "full of . . . curious things; memorials of past ages and other lands, and specimens or strange unusual growths and freaks. . . . But the strangest thing of all . . . was a singular low sound I heard sometimes among my curiosities. A low, faint, irregular, throbbing sound" (p. 4). Gilman draws on descriptions reminiscent of Roderick Usher's portentous studio combined with the emphasis on sound in "The Tell-Tale Heart" to create a mood of suspense. Less effective is her introduction of a Prince, who routinely visits the narrator and one day inquires about the source of her sadness. Although she denies being sad, he insists that something is wrong. "Show me your heart!" he suddenly demands. "I have none," she responds. "My heart is dead. . . . It died many years ago. I myself drove deeper every stroke that slew it. I sealed it in linen and folded it in lead. I laid it in a stone coffin, a monolith, bound with iron. I buried it under seven vaults and built this fair house over it," she confesses.

Suddenly seized by "a horrible thought," the narrator runs madly toward the door of the tomb. "At first I thought I caught again the low sound I knew above, but it had stopped wholly now, and as I turned to face him at the last door, my face white with terror, there was no breath of sound, no pulse of motion anywhere," she says (p. 5). When she opens the door of the tomb, a "little crouching thing ... suddenly sprang up and ran upon us with unearthly eyes—on us—over us like an escaping beast, up the echoing stairs and out into the hot, sweet night with frantic leaps and wavering senseless cries. My heart was mad" (p. 5). Where Gilman fails in this attempted imitation is in placing the nightmarish terror outside of the narrator's psyche. By transforming it into an external object—into a cartoonlike being with "unearthly eyes" that sprouts legs, springs free, and escapes into the sweet night air—she completely loses the primordial fear of death, discovery, and insanity so characteristic of Poe's work. As Gilman acknowledged in her "Story Studies" the week following the publication of "The Unwatched Door," "When the element of horror [in Poe's works] is allowed to verge on loathing, it no longer horrifies—it merely disgusts and repels."[54] Unfortunately, the ending of "The Unwatched Door" neither disgusts nor repels; rather, its fantastical departure from Poe merely amuses the reader.

"An Unpatented Process," a story in imitation of Mark Twain's anecdotal humor, appeared in the 12 January 1895 *Impress*. The use of colloquial language, the irony and exaggeration, and the frequent inclusion of unusually long sentences renders this sketch an effective imitation of Twain's style. More to the point, Gilman captures a theme common in Twain's domestic tales: the clash between the clearheaded woman and the absentminded man.

Gilman recounts the story of a couple on the eve of their wedding, noting that "there was an alarming discrepancy between their characters. . . . They were about as well calculated to get along together as an eight-day clock and a California rainy season" (p. 4). Despite emphatic warnings from Nettie Hines's well-meaning friends that to marry her fiancé, Hank Richardson, a doctor, would be "rank suicide," she "was not going to be deterred from marrying the man of her choice by any such paltry objections as these" (p. 4). They had "tried to get married two or three times, but Hank slipped up on it, and it was awfully mortifying to Nettie. . . . The first time was more excusable, because of not having had any experience, and perhaps not rightly appreciating the importance a young girl attaches to a little matter of ceremony like that" (p. 4). On the evening they planned to have their first wedding, for example, there "was an outrageous storm that night, there's no denying it; and living as they did, in the country, it was difficult and really somewhat dangerous to get around." But "the minister got there all right," and so do great numbers of guests, because "country people don't mind a little weather when its [*sic*] a question of sociability—but Hank never showed up at all. So after awhile Nettie's brothers set out to look for his body" (p. 4). When they arrive at his house, "Hank came down and opened the door, half dressed" in preparation for bed (p. 4). To the brothers' demands about whether Hank realizes it is his wedding night, he responds, "[W]hy yes, I know that, but it rained so I thought they wouldn't have it." The forgetful male is a stock character in many of Twain's autobiographical anecdotes, as are women characters who frequently attempt to clean up the messes that men leave behind.[55]

Eventually, Hank and Nettie do get married, but not before Nettie "had insisted on one thing . . . that they should go off somewhere for a year before they settled down" (p. 4). In a clever imitation of Twain's colloquial style, Gilman writes: "When they really did start; when the gang plank was off and all those dear friends one has on those occasions had stood around to the last moment and made you feel every emotion you had in your bosom several times over, and were now standing all along the edge of the pier to make you feel them over again—or maybe a new one—I thought I saw a peculiar expression of—well, of scientific enthusiasm, in Nettie's eye" (pp. 4–5). When they return home after a year, Hank has changed dramatically, much to everyone's surprise. "We all thought it was a miracle, or that maybe he had been changed at nurse, or something of that sort; but my sister found out the whole process after a while and told me" (p. 5). Nettie has devised a kind of Pavlovian technique to train Hank "to focus and carry on at the same time" (p. 5). Nettie functions in this tale as both civilizer and savior of the inept male. Proud of her success in training Hank, Nettie "beamed and glowed like a young mother" (p. 5), the narrator reports. "She was a young mother, in course of time; and, if you'll believe me, Hank Richardson could tell you that baby's age as well as he could the increase in the local death rate. But if I tell you any more, perhaps you'll discredit the whole story," the narrator concludes (p. 5).

Gilman candidly acknowledged that some of her imitations were failures. In her attempt to capture Henry James's work, for example, she admitted that her sketch " 'One Way Out' falls a little short of the standard of excellence desired to be maintained in these studies; perhaps because the author represented is so finished in his mastery of the art

of wordsmanship as to render imitation an inefficacious flattery. . . .
The execution is unequal and lacking in the deliberate finish of this
master."[56]

Other stories appearing in the "Studies in Style" series included "A
Day's Berryin' " in imitation of Mary E. Wilkins [Freeman], and "Ad'-
line" in imitation of Hamlin Garland.[57] Gilman admired Freeman's writing, with its "country dialect, . . . strain of pathos, clear local color, and
bits of vivid personal description."[58] She also recognized that "under
the dialect and color, under the pathos and the description, in the very
least and briefest of these stories, lies a whole human life . . . revealed
not by direct narration, but by subtle . . . touches; by what seems almost
a chance phrase, yet which reveals years of tragedy in its casual mention" (*Impress*, 5).

"A Day's Berryin' " centers on the lives of two middle-aged sisters
who are spending part of the afternoon picking berries. Gilman captures
both the New England setting and the dialect that are so characteristic
of Freeman's short stories.

> The sun was very hot on the round humpy little hills above "the
> smut." It was hot enough down there, on the black cracked surface of
> the peat bog; or where the still blacker pools reflected the cloudless
> sky in filmy lustre.
>
> But up here it was hotter, and the lovely white moss crumbled
> under foot as you walked on it.
>
> "That moss makes first-rate kindlin' if you keep it dry," said Dothea
> Hopkins, crushing through the brittle masses. "That is, I've always
> heard say it did—I ain't never tried it." (p. 195)

Almira, the more assiduous of the two berry-picking sisters, "had
married a 'city dweller' " in her youth, and although she "mourned him
decorously in whole, half and quarter mourning when he died; still it
was observed that she did not marry again" (p. 196). Despite "plenty of
chances," Almira has embraced the independence that being widowed
has brought, "serenely declin[ing]" further offers of marriage and preferring to live "up stairs in her small city home" and renting out rooms
on the first floor (p. 196). During a break in the berry picking, Almira
tells Dothea the story of Car'line Hines, one of her boarders. Car'line
lives with her mother, "works like a horse," and "pays reg'lar board"
(pp. 196–97). When a young suitor begins paying Car'line attention,
Mrs. Hines instructs her daughter not to see him. Car'line, however,

stands up to her mother by announcing that if she cannot receive her friends, she will move out. "So he's comin' yet, but her mother don't speak to him, and I think he feels kinder stiff there now," Almira concludes (p. 198).

The story "seemed to stir some faint memory" in Dothea, who had been similarly oppressed by her own mother "until that good woman, after five years in her house and two in her bed, had died" (p. 197). We learn little more about Dothea, except that she was a "nurse by profession, not by choice" and was "unimaginative and unromantic," presumably because she spent some of her best years under her mother's thumb. At the conclusion of Almira's story, the two sisters notice Bijah Stearns, a potato farmer, riding toward them on a horse-pulled wagon. " 'Is he waitin' on you agin?' Almira eagerly inquired" of Dothea. " 'He has called once or twice,' slowly assented Dothea, looking far over the sun-burned meadows to where the white, dusty road lay like a piece of faded tape between its yellow-green border" (p. 198). The good-natured Bijah invites the sisters into his wagon and offers to drive them home, since it's about to rain. Almira, who "was rather nearsighted," exclaims, " 'How lucky 't you should come along! . . . Its [*sic*] a special providence, *I* think' " (p. 198).

Gilman ends the story on an ambiguous note, failing to confirm whether Bijah's sudden appearance was by design or by chance. But she effectively captures "the piteous starved lives of the New England villages and outlying farms" so familiar in Freeman's fiction (*Impress*, 20 October 1894: 5). "The sum of [Freeman's] work is a patient melancholy, broken by occasional light gleams of hope. Two notes of grief are sounded oftenest—failure to marry, and failure to pay the mortgage. Also there is the frequent spectre of family intolerance and oppression," Gilman wrote (p. 5). Indeed, Almira's story of an independent woman who refuses to tolerate her mother's meddling strikes a chord in Dothea, who undoubtedly regrets the lost opportunities caused by caring for her mother. Gilman gave only the merest suggestion of pathos in Dothea's situation, averring that in Freeman's work, "it is only hinted at and shown by inference. . . . The suggestion of buried lives—of the patient martyrdom that makes no sign and bears the pang without the palm" is authentically rendered (p. 5).

"Ad'line," representing Hamlin Garland's style, is also a fairly skillful imitation. "No writer of the new school of American realists has made a stronger impression than Hamlin Garland," Gilman wrote.[59] "His governing spirit is a passionate realization of the wrong and suffering of the

American farming class, especially in the middle west. There is suppressed fury in his presentation, not unlike the smouldering rage of the French peasant before the revolution; a futile rebellion that falls back helpless from the limiting walls of circumstance, yet seems to swell with gathered force in presage of some outbreak that shall change the face of events materially" (p. 4).

The story opens with a description of George Crandall returning East to marry Ad'line after spending 10 years in the Midwest eking out a living as a farmer. The train on which he is riding passes the "thick, soily water" of the Missouri River creeping "along the mudbanks at its sides" (*Yellow*, 199). George feels a sense of restlessness and isolation on the train, and his fellow travelers with their "perfectly appointed traveling array . . . stirred in him a smouldering rage" because they "made him painfully conscious of how unfit his own appearance was" (pp. 199–200). He begins to reminisce about Ad'line's refusal to marry him earlier. "I can't go," Ad'line told him. "And what's good of askin'? Here's father, old now, and needs me more every year, 'n mother ain't strong—she ain't been able to do the housework since last summer" (p. 200). In the meantime, George has moved three times to find "a place that should be a home in due season," but "at last he had something he could call a home and bring Ad'line to" (p. 200). Still, "it stirred him to the depths of bitter resentment that he should be driven so many miles away, and she held so fast by the same inexorable pressure" (pp. 200–201). Although George has managed to build a home, he still has "nothing to show for his ten year's [*sic*] struggle, but the tickets in his pocket" (p. 201).

Because George "never was much of a writer, and grew less so as his hands stiffened with long toil" (p. 201), his homecoming is a surprise to Ad'line, who has told him previously "that she could never leave her mother, and that he had better take a wife among his Western neighbors" (p. 201). George, however, has refused to surrender hope that "poor little Ad'line" is still waiting for him. When he arrives at her home, he finds her sitting quietly on the narrow porch "in the light of a low golden sun" (p. 201). Ad'line fails to recognize him at first, and he is surprised at how thin and frail she has become. When he announces to Ad'line, "I've come for you," she explains that she cannot go with him; her father has died, her mother is bedridden, and it is incumbent on her to care for her mother and 14-year-old sister. "Then he saw how very thin she was, and the glow on her cheeks that was not all the sunset light. . . . 'It looks as if you were in the right of it,' he said slowly. 'But I'm sorry, Ad'line' " (p. 202).

37

Gilman's depiction of "the courage and unfailing resolution of the young farmer ... and the same qualities more negatively expressed in the girl" (*Impress*, 10 November 1894: 5) is a close rendering of Garland's impressionism. The constant struggle to survive, the effect of grueling labor on the body, and the brutal natural forces over which we have no control make "Ad'line" a compelling imitation of Garland's powerful style.

Gilman's 17th and final foray into "Studies in Style," "My Cousin Mary," was published in the 9 February 1895 issue of the *Impress*. (For reasons unknown, Gilman failed to identify the author being imitated in either this story or the one preceding it.) One week later, with the February 16 issue, the paper abruptly folded. Although Gilman had hoped to make the *Impress* into a "good family weekly" that would be "varied and interesting" (*Living*, 171, 173), the publication lasted for only 20 weeks. A "clean and handsome paper," judged by "a competent critic as the best ever published on the [west] coast" (p. 173), the *Impress* became a casualty of the public outcry against Gilman's unconventional lifestyle. According to her account in *The Living of Charlotte Perkins Gilman*, the paper's demise was a direct result of the sentiment expressed by "the San Francisco mind" that judged her to be immoral (p. 173). Not only was she a divorcée, but her decision to relinquish custody of her nine-year-old daughter to her ex-husband was greeted by many with open contempt. Adding to the public condemnation was Gilman's decision to publish in the *Impress* "a beautiful poem, of a nobly religious tendency" by her longtime friend Grace Channing Stetson— Walter Stetson's new bride (p. 173). Gilman's "continued friendship" with both Walter Stetson and Grace was something that the public "could not endure. . . . That we three should have remained in friendly correspondence, with mutual understanding, affection and respect . . . was to them incomprehensible" (p. 167).

Embittered by the open hostility that followed her divorce from Walter Stetson, Gilman left California in 1895 and spent much of the next five years on the lecture circuit. Although she continued to write stories occasionally, it was not until 1909, when she launched the *Forerunner*, that she produced them with any regularity.

Autobiographical Fiction

In addition to the autobiographically inspired classic "The Yellow Wall-Paper," a handful of other stories can be linked to episodes in Gilman's life. Three stories—"Mary Button's Principles" (1912), "The Hypnotizer" (1914), and "Spoken To" (1915)—have their roots in actual incidents described in *The Living of Charlotte Perkins Gilman*. Three other stories based on actual events but written with considerable embellishments are "Circumstances Alter Cases" (1890), "An Unnatural Mother" (1895), and "The Lake of Mrs. Johnsmith" (1898). Each of these works is heavily steeped in irony and allows Gilman to comment on the negative aspects of social conservatism. "Through This" (1893) can be read as a companion piece to "The Yellow Wall-Paper," while another story, "Dr. Clair's Place" (1915), reveals Gilman's vision of an effective alternative to the conventional treatment for neurasthenia.

Two of the autobiographical stories, "Circumstances Alter Cases" and "Through This," were written during particularly difficult periods in Gilman's life.[60] The first, "Circumstances Alter Cases," composed shortly after her separation from Charles Walter Stetson, is revealing in its presentation of the circumstances leading to their marriage in 1884, which are well documented in Gilman's autobiography, in her diaries and letters, and in biographical studies of the author. The story opens with a discussion between a man and a woman about the status of their relationship. The woman, Hilda Warde, like Charlotte Anna Perkins, is reluctant to marry because, as she explains to her fiancé, "I am, unfortunately, one of those much-berated New England women who have learned to think as well as feel; and to me, at least, marriage means more than a union of hearts and bodies—it must mean minds, too. It would be a never-ending grief to me, starvation and bitter pain, to have you indifferent or contemptuous to my most earnest thoughts and beliefs" (p. 85). The man, George Saunders, who is clearly modeled after Stetson, "turned over several things in his mind before replying. It was really difficult. Masculine habits of thought, dominant for centuries, were strong within him" (p. 85).

After this brief opening scene, Gilman shifts the action ahead to a discussion between two old "college chums and partners at law," George Saunders and Howard Clarke, who are standing outside the ocean-view cottage belonging to the now "travelled, cultured, experienced, and 'peculiar' " Hilda Warde (p. 86). Although Clarke "had loved her, vainly," he had "gotten safely over it" (p. 86). Saunders, however, is still in love with her, but he is prepared to go abroad to get on with his life if she continues to refuse his proposals. Hilda soon joins the two men on the beach along with a friend of hers, a young Russian count, and announces that she wants to tell a story. It is "a true story; and I want your honest opinions on the merit of the case," she remarks. She recounts the circumstances of a young man, who "had great notions [about] the work he was going to do" although no one "believed in his reformatory ideas" (p. 87). A young woman, "handsome and clever" and a highly gifted musician, fell in love with him and wanted to get married. He, however, "was resolved never to marry" so that he might pursue his work as a "rabid reformer" (p. 87). The woman relentlessly played "upon his masculine nature," and eventually, reluctantly, he married her (p. 87). Predictably, the marriage "upset his work," and when the couple had a child, "the extra care and unusual demands, and the miserable state of mind he was in . . . quite ruined him. He felt that he had been false to his mission," and he "went insane and killed himself" (p. 87). At the conclusion of her story, Hilda asks the three men to offer "an opinion on the relative guilt of the two parties" (p. 87). All three men quickly pin the responsibility on the woman. "She was most cruelly to blame," says one. "She was a criminal!" opines another (p. 88). Hilda then admits that she has made an error in presenting the facts of the story: she has accidentally reversed the genders. "The facts are all the same, but the sexes are reversed. It is the story of my friend May Henderson and her husband" (p. 88). Saunders vehemently objects to the new information and tries to retract his condemnation of the woman. "Why, Hilda, it's not the same case at all," he protests. Not only was John Henderson "a genius," but his "wife [was] a nervous hypochondriac" whose departure was "the kindest thing she ever did" (p. 88). Hilda reminds him that May "used to be a paragon of health, and of most brilliant promise." And, she adds, "she told him she did not wish to marry—was not able or willing" (p. 88). To Clarke's observation that "It's a wholly different matter when you change the sex," Hilda's simple response, "So I see," affirms the existence of the double standard that reduces women to mere role-playing. Only the count, an exile from his country who now makes his living by writing, is willing to point blame at the man for coercing the woman into marriage. The story is, in effect, a portrait in miniature of Gilman's courtship with and marriage to Stetson. She continually refused his marriage proposals (the first of which was made only $2^1/_2$ weeks after they met) and cited her devotion to social reform work as the reason. Moreover, despite episodes of chronic depression that began in early adulthood, Gilman didn't become "a nervous hypochondriac" until she experienced motherhood, which forced her to confront the reality of her domestic bondage. "How irrevocably bound I am, for life, for life," she wrote in her diary a few months after giving birth. "Unless [Walter] die and the baby die . . . there is no way out" (*Diaries*, 30 August 1885). And while the fictional John Henderson (actually his wife, May, when the genders are reversed) felt "that he had been false to his mission," Gilman likewise declared herself "a traitor to my cause" (*Diaries*, 31 December 1886) for entering a marriage against her better judgment. Still, the story points blame at Stetson, who, like George Saunders, "took advantage of the freedom of their friendship" (p. 87).

"Through This" was written when Gilman was simultaneously managing a boardinghouse with nine tenants, caring for her terminally ill mother, approaching the end of a volatile relationship with newspaper reporter Adeline "Delle" Knapp,[61] and attempting to earn a living through lecturing and writing. Gilman consulted her physician, Dr. Kellogg Lane, on how to cope with the enormous strain.[62] Among her concerns was that her domestic responsibilities consumed too much of her time and energy and interfered with her ability to work. Just a week prior to writing "Through This," in fact, Gilman recorded her frustration in her diary: "Get no work done today—only houseservice," she complained (*Diaries*, 17 January 1893). The theme of "houseservice" versus "real" work figures prominently in "Through This."[63]

"Through This" first appeared in 1893, a year after "The Yellow Wall-Paper" was published in *New England Magazine*.[64] Like "The Yellow Wall-Paper," "Through This" requires a figurative reading, since Gilman avoids the heavy didacticism that characterizes much of her later work. Also connecting "Through This" to "The Yellow Wall-Paper" is its attack on the patriarchal institution of marriage, which typically entrapped women in "feminine" roles. Throughout her professional career, in her lectures and essays, Gilman encouraged women to cultivate their nondomestic skills, lest they become victims of "sexuo-economic" relationships with men. In *Women and Economics*, for example, Gilman argues that "Although marriage is a means of livelihood, it is not honest employment where one can offer one's labor without shame, but a relation where the support is given outright, and enforced by law in return for the functional service of the woman, the 'duties of wife and mother.' Therefore, no honorable woman can ask for it. . . . It is economic beggary as well as a false attitude from a sex point of view."[65]

As was the case in Gilman's first marriage, "Through This" depicts a woman entrapped in a relationship where she is bound to perform the "duties of wife and mother," a condition she expounded on at some length in her polemical work *The Home*.[66] Unlike the narrator of "The Yellow Wall-Paper," the narrator of "Through This" expresses no conscious desire to engage in "forbidden" work; rather, she seems content in her role as a doting wife and mother. Yet, there are intriguing similarities between the two stories. For example, the cast of characters in "Through This" is strikingly similar to that of "The Yellow Wall-Paper." Husband John, Jennie, Mary, Jane's brother, and a male first-born child all either appear or are alluded to in "Through This." But Gilman has effected a dramatic role reversal by casting the narrator of "Through This" in the role of enthusiastic housekeeper played by Jennie in "The Yellow Wall-Paper." Further, the Jennie in "Through This" appears to have the freedom and independence longed for by Jane in "The Yellow Wall-Paper." But although the narrator of "Through This" appears to exude cheerful enthusiasm for her traditionally "feminine" roles, she shows subconscious signs of resentment of her roles as wife and mother. Beneath the gracious veneer lies a seriously conflicted woman who embodies what Gilman feared she would herself become should she consent to marry Walter Stetson: "Were I to marry . . . I fear I should give all up and become of no more use than other women" (*Endure*, 33). Gilman's first marriage confirmed her worst fears; her subsequent writing became both a forum for political expression and a kind of self-therapy. Significantly, "Through This" was published just one year before her divorce from Walter Stetson became final.

Written in part as an exposé of "the obedient house-servant" and in part as a psychological profile, "Through This" chronicles a typical day in the life of a young married wife and mother. Repeatedly, the protagonist attempts to convince herself and the reader of her profound happiness. Still, the effects of subjugation are apparent in every phase of her existence, and despite her declarations to the contrary, her stream-of-consciousness narrative is riddled with tension, contradictions, and enormous ambivalence.

In this restructured protagonist, Gilman has created Jane's alter ego, a woman who can carry out the mission Jane intended but abandoned in "The Yellow Wall-Paper": to be "such a help to John, such a real rest and comfort" (*YW,* 14). The new Jane fulfills the role that Stetson wished his wife to play in their marriage when he wrote, "[Charlotte has become] more like what is best in other women—more thoughtful, bland, gracious, humble, dependent" (*Endure,* 140). "Through This" is an obvious vehicle through which Charlotte Stetson could express just how demeaning and repugnant she found that role to be. Ironically, Stetson, too, found housework to be laborious and time-consuming, and complained about the way it eclipsed his "other" (i.e., "real") work: "I have striven to make a home for her that should be pleasant. . . . I have done more than I ought. . . . So far it has counted for little in her favor—too little it seems to me. On account of all this I have lost the power I used to have so strongly, to conceive of colors & forms and pictures clearly" (*Endure,* 282).

Charlotte Stetson's sentiments about work mirrored those recorded in her husband's journal. To vent her frustration about her own lost power, she crafted her unnamed protagonist in "Through This," whose identity is defined exclusively by her subservient roles, to show what happens to obedient women who give up all their time and strength to "such things" as even Walter Stetson objected to for himself. The protagonist neglects her own needs in order to perform "the sweet home duties through which my life shall touch the others!" (*Yellow,* 54). As her family "grows happier and stronger by [her] living," the narrator's strength and energy is proportionately depleted. Indeed, in the course of one day, we witness her living through actions that constitute a veritable litany of self-annihilation: buying baked goods, making breakfast, washing dishes, ordering groceries, soaking tapioca, cooking beets, baking potatoes, bathing the baby, cutting and basting nightgowns, watching the children, dealing with solicitors and salesmen, making the noon meal, discussing her husband's job with him, worrying about house repairs and fuel consumption, running downtown, worrying about her mother's health, buying sewing notions, rushing home again, preparing dinner, apologizing to her husband for the milkman's tardiness, putting the children to bed, reciting nursery rhymes to them, and finally, justifying to herself her failure to write a letter because of fatigue.

The story also offers an intriguing stylistic parallel to "The Yellow Wall-Paper." Set forth in short, halting sentences, the narrative is confused and fragmented. The narrator's language is as chaotic as is her day. The limited vocabulary Gilman allows the weary woman parallels the limitations in her life: her restricted choices, her troubled state of mind, her repressed anger. Like Jane, the protagonist in this story has a fixed schedule for each hour in the day, which necessitates a rigid adherence, which in turn robs the woman of the freedom to escape domestic drudgery, even through fantasy.

Significantly, the wall imagery that was so prominent in "The Yellow Wall-Paper" recurs in "Through This." The narrative begins with the protagonist noticing the dawn colors reflecting off her bedroom wall at daybreak. But the beauty of the new day is limited by the verb used in her description: "The dawn colors *creep* up my bedroom wall, softly, slowly" (p. 54; emphasis added). Readers familiar with "The Yellow Wall-Paper" are immediately reminded of the throng of creeping women behind the wallpaper and in the garden outside the nursery window. The verb "creep" suggests furtive, sly movement, and indeed, the woman seems to be unconsciously captivated by the colors, the only variegation in an unbearably bland and predictable routine. Only in the few quiet moments before she slips out of the soothing embrace of sleep to begin her day can she allow her mind to wander, to create, to envision. Like "Wall-Paper's" Jane, this protagonist possesses a fanciful imagination that is frustrated, not because she is explicitly forbidden to cultivate it, but because the demands of her roles preclude any opportunity for intellectual stimulation. After the first four sentences, the softness and slowness of the narrative is consumed by the frenzied pace of the housewife's activities.

We are told that "with the great sunrise great thoughts come" (p. 54). But the woman's "great thoughts" never reach fruition. Four times during her busy day she drifts into reveries that are aborted either consciously, because of deep-seated guilt, or inadvertently, because of external intrusions. The first two early-morning daydreams of a domestic utopia are interrupted by the realistic demands of the woman's socially prescribed roles. It is significant that the other two reveries, which take place later in the morning, just before the noontime meal, are no longer idealistic visions of a well-ordered home but rather escape fantasies that are abruptly interrupted by the call of domestic duty. As the day wanes, so too does the narrator's conscious idealism. The aborted escape fantasies were to be contemplations of life after the children were grown, of a life in which the woman would finally be free.

The third interruption, significantly, is by someone who apparently invites the narrator to join a "progressive" organization. The woman initially expresses an interest in joining: "Ah, well—yes—I'd like to have joined. I believe in it, but I can't now." (Can't believe in it?) "Home duties forbid" (p. 55). The juxtaposition of "I can't now" with "home duties forbid" reveals much about the narrator's unstated ambivalence. That she is forbidden by "home duties" transfers blame away from herself (and from John) but paradoxically empowers an inanimate object (the home) to require her to perform tasks that forbid engaging in interests or activities outside the domestic realm. She follows this statement with an almost defensive-sounding "This is my work" (p. 55), elevating to a loftier level the monotony of cooking, sweeping, sewing, and washing dishes. Immediately after she makes this statement, she attempts for the fourth time to escape into a reverie about the future, but is interrupted again by the doorbell, which not only brings an abrupt end to her daydream but awakens the baby as well, marking an end to her escape attempts and a return to her housework.

The narrator explicitly defends housework when she declares, "I like to cook. I think housework is noble if you do it in a right spirit" (p. 55). The clause beginning with "if" suggests that housework is *not* noble unless it is performed in the right spirit. Again, the ambivalence underlying the narrator's statement is apparent. She is trying to live her whole life according to the *right* spirit, which implies that any deviation from the rigidly prescribed role is the *wrong* spirit. Like Jane, the woman is imprisoned in her own home, but as long as she is incarcerated she will do her best to be a model inmate, conforming to the rules of the institution (marriage).

In the meantime, the husband and children parasitically draw nourishment and sustenance from the woman's existence: "Through this man made happier and stronger by my living" (p. 54). Clearly, the woman is drained by her family's dependence. But her only happiness, her only purpose, she would have us believe, lies in relation to what she can give to others—a literal giving of her self. The entire story, in fact, centers around a very pronounced forfeiture of self. Gilman breathes more viability into the inanimate props in the setting than into her protagonist. The morning light *grows*, the fire's swift kindling and gathering roar *speak* of accomplishment, the rich odor of coffee *steals* through her house. While her time is occupied, her mind remains stagnant, as she automatically surrenders herself to meeting the needs of others. The protagonist's own mother, too, is imbued with a sacrificial spirit: "Mother looks real tired. I wish she would go out more and have some outside interest. Mary and the children are too much for her, I think. Harry ought not to have brought them home. Mother needs rest. She's brought up one family" (p. 56).

Ironically, the protagonist's own actions contribute to her mother's fatigue: "So glad you could come, mother dear! Can you stay awhile and let me go down town on a few errands?" (p. 56). Although employing her mother as a temporary caretaker allows the protagonist brief escape from the confinement of her home, she unintentionally subjects her mother to the servitude that she herself has just condemned. Even when her mother leaves her own home, her role as "mother" remains intact. Furthermore, the demands placed on the two women do not allow them even an opportunity to visit with one another. We never see either woman relaxing for a moment, stopping to sip a cup of tea or glance at a newspaper. The protagonist's "escape" downtown is merely an extension of her home duties, as she hurriedly searches for sewing notions and contemplates winter clothing for her oldest child. The narrator's grandmother, too, although an absent figure in the story, unwittingly perpetuates the protagonist's domestic bondage by sending her knit edging to be used in sewing nightgowns for her great-grandchildren (p. 55). The edging becomes a subtle metaphor characterizing the implicit borders that define the protagonist's domain. The only "free" maternal figure in the story is Amaranth, the cat, who leisurely "lies on the grass under the rosebush, stretching her paws among the warm, green blades" (p. 54). She stands in contrast to the other mothers in the story; she is the picture of bliss, as her kittens playfully tumble over her.

Like John in "The Yellow Wall-Paper," John in "Through This" is a powerful patriarchal force. Although Gilman has changed his occupation from physician to politician, his influence and control over his wife is visible throughout the narrative. That he is a politician, in fact, pegs him as an opportunist who has symbolic license to legitimate the "sexuo-economic" laws by which his wife must abide.

John's likes and dislikes, needs and whims, shape the narrator's day. John likes flowers on the breakfast table; John likes the way his wife cooks his steak; he has to go out early to campaign for election; he is annoyed that his wife didn't prepare a dish he likes; he hates to have her wait up for him. It is obvious that John's wife complies with his every whim. Her economic dependence on him further disempowers her, and disempowerment limits her self-confidence. She engages in self-deprecation when asked for suggestions concerning a civil matter: "Why no—not *personally*—but I should think *you* might [have one]. What are men for if they can't keep the city in order" (p. 55). Her deliberate and emphatic reticence in speaking out on public issues reinforces the intellectual boundaries created by her limited sphere within the home. At the same time, her remark "I should think *you* might [have a suggestion]" underscores the extrinsic value of his life outside of the house (p. 55). While she soaks tapioca and recites nursery rhymes, her husband shapes government policy. The contrast between their two spheres, hers contained within the house and his "out there," is enormous. Further, Gilman's frequent reference to John by name underscores his prominence and, at the same time, diminishes the nameless narrator's status. She has become John's helpmate, but in doing so she has had to forfeit an independent identity.

Like the "Wall-Paper" Jane, this narrator, too, is consumed by guilt: "I must get the dishes done and not dream" (p. 54). "I meant to have swept the bed-room this morning. . . . It does look dreadfully" (p. 55). "I ought to take the baby out in the carriage . . ." (p. 55). But a more significant feature both stories share recalls Gilman's old grievance: the frustration of not being able to write. In "The Yellow Wall-Paper," the protagonist, like Gilman, was forbidden to write as part of the rest cure for nervous prostration. In "Through This," the narrator, also like Gilman, is plagued by a fatigue so debilitating that she cannot muster enough energy even to compose a letter.

The segment of the story concerning Jennie's letter is the most crucial revelation of the narrator's ambivalence about her own roles. "It's no use, I can't write a letter tonight, *especially* to Jennie" (p. 56; emphasis added). Earlier in the day, the narrator reminded herself that she really "ought to answer Jennie's letter. She writes such splendid things, but I don't go with her in half she says. A woman can't do that way and keep a family going. I will write to her this evening" (p. 55). By delaying the task until later, the narrator is postponing a confrontation between both her conscious self-denial and her subconscious desire to be free and Jennie's alluring life, about which Jennie writes "such splendid things." After consciously deferring the matter until later, the narrator immediately lapses back into thoughts of the excitement and enthusiasm that characterize Jennie's life. "Of course if one *could*, I'd like as well as anyone to be in those great live currents of thought and action" (p. 55). But clearly she cannot be. Her role as wife and mother, her "home duties," have condemned her to a life of banal predictability. The "great *live* currents" to which she alludes underscore her own unarticulated mourning for her past, since she immediately follows that statement with a nostalgic memory: "Jennie and I were full of it in school. How long ago that seems" (p. 55). Her life used to be "full"; now it is simply busy. And her rather wistful remark "How long ago that seems" suggests how swiftly the protagonist's identity has been subsumed by the demands of her marriage. And then comes a retraction. "But I never thought then of being so happy. Jennie isn't happy, I know—she can't be, poor thing, till she's a wife and mother" (pp. 55–56). The narrator moves from an expressed wish ("if one *could*") to a denial ("but . . .") to an unconvincing expression of sympathy for Jennie, whose failure to fulfill her feminine "duties" is bound to leave her unhappy, despite her immersion in "the great *live* currents of thought and action." Again, the action and freedom that characterize Jennie's life make the narrator's domestic obligations resemble a primitive form of obsequious bondage.

When the narrator returns to thoughts of Jennie later that evening after the children are finally asleep, she still cannot confront her ambivalence: she is too tired, even though it is still "early." Because such a confrontation with herself is too threatening, it is dismissed. The fatigue the narrator cites is a classic symptom of depression, suggesting that she is simply too conflicted to write to her friend. In truth, Jennie's letter paradoxically represents an affirmation of the narrator's subconscious desire to be free and a repudiation of her conscious choice to be enslaved. Jennie, who was the "perfect and enthusiastic housekeeper" in "The Yellow Wall-Paper," has been dramatically transformed in "Through This" into a dynamic activist at the center of current thought, much like Jane could have been had she been permitted to indulge her intellectual inclinations. Gilman has created a dramatic reversal, with the protagonist of "Through This" assuming the docility of "The Wall-Paper"'s Jennie while at the same time repressing the tendency to acknowledge her anger, unlike "The Wall-Paper"'s Jane. While Jane occasionally vents her anger ("I get unreasonably angry with John sometimes"; "I get positively angry with the impertinence of [the wallpaper]"; "I am getting angry enough to do something desperate" [*YW*, 11, 16, 34]), the narrator of "Through This" represses any expression of frustration or resentment.

The perhaps most enigmatic line of "Through This" appears near the end, when the narrator states, "I'll go to bed early. John hates to have me wait up for him late. I'll go now, if it is before dark" (*Yellow*, 56). The "if" raises the obvious question as to why the protagonist will go to bed only *if* it is not yet dark. Her decision may suggest a fear of the dark or perhaps some kind of unacceptable subconscious association. Or perhaps the dark is a literal and figurative allusion to the woman's subconscious despair and resentment. Either way, by going to bed, the narrator is able to escape the threatening darkness that increasingly surrounds her life. Even Gilman's title suggests that the narrator's survival, and perhaps even her sanity, depends on her ability to get "through this." The reader is left wondering how long it will be before the narrator transforms the wall's creeping colors into objects of her imagination, into concrete projections that will be emblematic of her repressed psyche. The "Wall-Paper" narrator, after all, hated both the moonlight and the sunlight that crept through the window. "I hate to see it sometimes, it creeps so slowly, and always comes in by one window or another" (*YW*, 23).

In his 1985 essay on "The Yellow Wall-Paper," Conrad Shumaker posed the question, "What happens to the imagination when it is defined as feminine (and thus weak) and has to face a society that values the useful and the practical and rejects all else as nonsense?"[67] The answer Gilman seems to offer in both stories is that it figuratively runs up against a wall, walls being powerful symbols of both separation and entrapment. Like the "Wall-Paper" narrator, who as a child used "to get more entertainment out of blank walls . . . than most children could find in a toy store" (*YW*, 16–17), the narrator in "Through This" indicates that her creative imagination has been arrested and replaced by socially sanctioned behavior. Thus, the dawn colors that arrive with the narrator's morning may be emblematic of hope, promise, and optimism, but they are replaced by evening shadows, which suggest weariness, disappointment, and despair.

By publishing these two suggestive stories a year apart, and in contrasting the two female protagonists—one who tries to cope, and one who cannot—Gilman ironically shows two sides of the same coin. Both stories demonstrate what inevitably happens to women who subordinate their own needs to those of others. While the loss of identity is poignantly obvious in "The Yellow Wall-Paper," it is shrouded somewhat in "Through This" by the narrator's pretense of normalcy. Still, there is no mistaking it. "Through This" begins and ends in metaphorical darkness.

Another story that addresses women's roles is "An Unnatural Mother," first published in 1895.[68] Gilman used the story to expose the hypocrisy and narrow-mindedness of people who vilified her for relinquishing custody of her daughter, Katharine, to ex-husband Walter Stetson and his new wife, Grace Ellery Channing, in 1894. Gilman defended her choice in her autobiography, arguing that Katharine benefited immeasurably from Walter's companionship. Gilman also maintained that "no one suffered from [the arrangement]" but herself, and that she was subjected to "furious condemnation" stemming from charges that she had "given up" her child (*Living*, 163). Her unqualified response to "those pious condemners" came in the form of "An Unnatural Mother," which, significantly, was published three times during her lifetime (p. 164).

Gilman's protagonist, Esther Greenwood, is a healthy, free-spirited woman who is ostracized by her community because of her unconventional behavior. As a child, Esther "wan't like other girls—she never seemed to care for dress and company and things girls naturally do," according to one of the townspeople, Miss Jacobs. Indeed, she grew up in a liberal environment, her father teaching her the facts of life and allowing her to go barefoot, as Gilman did in her childhood, much to the dismay of the nosy neighbors (p. 21). Eventually Esther marries; her husband, like Walter Stetson, is an artist. The two are apparently "very happy together" (*CPG*, 62), and she bears a child—a girl. She allows her daughter to "roll round in the grass like a puppy with hardly nothin' on" (p. 63). Despite the fact that her daughter grows into "a great strappin' girl," the townspeople insist that Esther's child-rearing skills are inappropriate and that she lacks "maternal feelin' " (p. 63).

These criticisms are rooted in Gilman's own maternal experiences, as she candidly acknowledges in her autobiography. "The good mamas of Pasadena were extremely critical of my methods. . . . They thought it scandalous that I should so frankly teach [Katharine] the simple facts of sex" and allow her to play "barefooted in the . . . California sunshine. . . . For all this I was harshly blamed, accused of 'neglecting my child,' " she stated (*Living*, 161).

Gilman uses "The Unnatural Mother" to respond to her detractors by depicting Esther Greenwood as a martyred heroine. Greenwood is misunderstood by nearly everyone in the village, with the exception of a 36-year-old single woman, Maria Amelia Briggs, who remembers Esther fondly as "a real nice girl" who was "kind and pleasant" (*CPG*, 60). It is Maria Amelia, herself an unconventional woman, who defends Esther's actions.

When Esther discovers that a dam is about to break and threatens to destroy three neighboring towns, she runs to the nearest village to warn its inhabitants of the imminent danger rather than return home to save her daughter. Esther drowns while saving the 15 hundred townspeople, yet they fail to acknowledge that her sacrifice was ultimately responsible for their collective survival. Her daughter is saved, as are all of the villages' inhabitants. At the end of the story, the townspeople continue to pass judgment on Esther's actions. "A mother's duty is to her own child!" one of them remarks. "Yes," adds another, "and here's her child, a burden on the town! She was an unnatural mother!" (p. 65).

This story was born out of Gilman's personal anguish. On numerous occasions, she found herself defending her choices. On Christmas Day, 1899, for example, she was "violently slapped in the face" by an old friend who accused her of being an "unnatural mother." The accusation both saddened and upset her. "It was painfully surprising," she confessed in a letter to Houghton Gilman.[69] "I haven't felt so uncomfortable inside for ever so long."

Apparently, Gilman's daughter, Katharine, never fully understood her mother's action either. According to Gilman biographer Ann J. Lane, during an interview with the 93-year-old Katharine in 1978, Katharine still harbored "feelings of resentment and rejection" and claimed that her mother "abandoned" her when she "was nine years old."[70] But Gilman remained adamant that her choice was "the right thing to do" (*Living*, 163), and at least some of her friends shared her views. Her longtime friend and confidante Harriet ("Hattie") Howe wrote supportively of Gilman's decision in her essay "Charlotte Perkins Gilman—As I Knew Her." "By all the facts of reason, wisdom, and common sense it was undisputably best that the child should go, for the period of her school years, where she would have the greatest possible advantages, besides being tenderly and devotedly loved by two people whom the child herself devotedly loved.... Which is the greater love, the demanding, possessive, clutching love of the average mother, or the self-denying love of this mother which gave and gave and gave, that her child might have the best, better than even her own love could bestow? Yet for this supreme love was she criticized by those who could not fathom its depth."[71] Likewise, in her autobiography, *Earth Horizon*, Mary Austin defended Gilman against the affront of "public opinion" that arose from the incident.[72]

"The Lake of Mrs. Johnsmith," originally titled "The Haughty Mrs. Johnsmith," was based on Gilman's encounters with her landlady, Mrs. Jones, during her stay at Cold Spring Harbor, Long Island, during the summer of 1898.[73] Although references to their interactions are brief in Gilman's diaries, the scattered allusions suggest that there was considerable tension between the two women. One rather telling entry indicates that Gilman and Katharine, who was spending part of the summer with her mother, had decided to "Go rowing on [the] lily pond—in spite of Mrs. Jones!" (*Diaries*, 23 June 1898). Apparently, Mrs. Jones, like her fictional counterpart, Mrs. Johnsmith, tried to ban Gilman and Katharine from using the pond. The day after they went rowing "in spite of Mrs. Jones!," Gilman produced a scathing portrait of her in "The Lake of Mrs. Johnsmith," which was accepted three weeks later by *The Criterion* (*Diaries*, 18 July 1898).

Mrs. Johnsmith, an intolerant and supercilious woman, addresses her "pleasant-faced" boarder with impatience and condescension. To the boarder's request that she be permitted to row in the pond with her young son, Kenneth, Mrs. Johnsmith responds that she does not "know of any way" that it might be arranged (p. 3). As the pleasant-faced boarder retreats, Mrs. Johnsmith remarks to another boarder, Miss Lark, that she finds "such ordinary people" to have "no sense of propriety" (p. 3). With "contempt" she launches into an indictment of the pleasant-faced boarder. "Such vulgar people as they are!" she complains. "I see this woman go by here every day, with that longlegged boy of hers. Look at her dress! That is cloth they make jumpers and overalls of—for common laborers!" (pp. 3–4). In an effort to change the topic, she asks Miss Lark to read to her from a book by Helen Ellacomb, "a great woman" writer whose work "is not yet publicly known." But "suddenly a distressing sight appeared on the water of the Lake. . . . Mrs. Johnsmith gasped. 'There is that woman!. . . They're after the lilies!' " So "positively disgusting" was the boarder's behavior that "Mrs. Johnsmith led her guest into the dark parlor, where their eyes might no longer be offended by the audacious intruders upon the sacred waters of her private lake" (p. 4).

In the next scene, at the end of the long summer, the action shifts to the New York residence of Mrs. Johnsmith, where she is entertaining several of her "munificent friends" with talk about emerging literary giants. A short time later, she is invited to a literary salon to meet Helen Ellacomb, the woman whose work she has so admired. In a rather predictable denouement, Ellacomb is none other than the "pleasant-faced boarder" herself. Mrs. Johnsmith turns "a painful purple color" when she hears herself characterized by Ellacomb, who is describing her summer boarding experiences to another woman. "One local dignitary I called on once to ask about a boat for Kenneth—and you would have been amused to see the lordy air with which she answered me that it was 'private water!' " (p. 4). Ellacomb is gracious to Mrs. Johnsmith, however, underscoring Gilman's point that "sometimes very great people are in straightened circumstances" (p. 4). Indeed, chronic poverty was a condition that she knew only too well, particularly before her second marriage, to her cousin Houghton Gilman in 1900. As a result, Gilman often devised inexpensive ways to entertain Katharine during her visits.

While it is not clear what exactly transpired between Gilman and her landlady that summer, Gilman undoubtedly resented being chided for rowing on the lily pond with Kate. Her landmark book *Women and Economics* had just been released a month before, and she was on the brink of achieving international celebrity. Clearly, Gilman saw herself as infinitely more gracious than Mrs. Jones, who is depicted as arrogant and superficial. "The Lake of Mrs. Johnsmith" is in part a fantasy of retaliation, revealing how Gilman might have liked the encounter to eventually play out. Significantly, Gilman's "pleasant-faced" fictional counterpart has the last word.

Another story with a basis in fact blends two separate incidents that Gilman mentions in her memoirs. One occurred in 1890 when she was living in Pasadena, California. She was approached one evening by an elderly migrant worker who asked for overnight lodging in her little cottage to spare himself a long return trip the next morning (*Living*, 117–18). The other incident occurred during her youth, when a friend demanded the truth about whether Gilman had accused her of lying (pp. 59–60). Both incidents tested Gilman's ethical values, and she combined them in a story titled "Mary Button's Principles."[74]

Gilman's fictional version of the incidents appears to have been embellished very little. In the actual account of the overnight-lodging story, for example, when the elderly man asked for lodging, Gilman acquiesced, believing that it was the right thing to do; so does Mary Button. After spending an uneventful night on the little lean-to porch, the man inquired as to the whereabouts of Gilman's husband. When the man learns in "Mary Button" that the husband is back East, "an expression of overwhelming reproach came over" his face. " 'Well!' said he, with decision, still gazing on her as one misled, 'if I'd 'a' known *that*, nothing in the world would have indooced me to stay here' " (*Yellow*, 61). "So that's what I got by facing scandal to do a kindness," Gilman concluded, "and it paid richly in amusement" (*Living*, 118).

To understand the subtle subtext in the story, one must examine Gilman's personal conduct following her separation from Walter Stetson. She not only took "extreme precautions" to conduct herself in a manner that would discourage public criticism of her lifestyle, but apparently, her interactions with men were beyond reproach. So "absurdly careful" was Gilman that she even refused to "take a soda in a drug-store" with the budding poet Edwin Markham (p. 171), who had not yet attained fame.[75]

Gilman, along with providing entertainment value in the story, also used the narrator as a mouthpiece for her own moral values. The narrator recalls the overnight-lodging incident with her girlhood friend, and the friend admits both having called her a liar and that "[the narrator's] principles had made her brave in the very face of terror" (*Yellow*, 58–59). Gilman also exposes the pettiness of neighbors who utter "creeping slanders" when she separates from her husband (*Living*, 171). While she found the thought of a strange man spending the night on her porch alarming, "far worse than terror was the thought of what the neighbors would say" (*Yellow*, 58).

Another story, "The Hypnotizer," was based on an actual incident that occurred on 22 March 1897 during Gilman's boardinghouse days in New York.[76] Houdini and magic shows were immensely popular at the time, and Gilman was so amused by witnessing a "private exhibition of hypnotism" that she included a rather detailed account of the experience in her autobiography (*Living*, 220–22). In the fictionalized version, Gilman's first-person male narrator is objective enough to acknowledge the pros and cons of hypnosis until his girlfriend, Sophie, volunteers to take part in a demonstration. The narrator becomes incensed by her eagerness to subject herself to the spell of the male hypnotist and admonishes her against taking part. Sophie will not be bullied, however, and insists on participating. When the hypnotist commands her, in whispers, to meet him for a clandestine tryst the following evening, the narrator overhears him and becomes quietly enraged. Later that evening, he engages her in his own hypnotic spell and directs her to "never think of that man again, nor see him, without contempt and loathing" (*Yellow*, 87). While Gilman wanted to entertain the reader with a story "which was as funny as could be desired" (*Living*, 220), she also used it to demonstrate the sexual politics at work. Sophie is presented as a strong-minded woman who, despite her suitor's protests, voluntarily agrees to undergo hypnosis. But her self-empowerment is undermined, not only by the hypnotist, who instructs her to meet him (*Yellow*, 85), but also by the narrator himself, who purports to love her while failing to recognize the irony and hypocrisy inherent in his own use of mind control.

"Spoken To" (1915) examines the issue of women going out alone, a topic Gilman addresses in the "Power and Glory" chapter of her autobiography (*Living*, 72–73).[77] In recalling the joy of acquiring youthful independence, Gilman writes in her memoirs that "one new indulgence was to go out evenings alone," which she perceived as "not only a right but a duty" (p. 72). When "a stalwart man" once insisted that "any true man" should be "ready to go with a woman at night" because "he is her natural protector," Gilman pointed out that "the thing a woman is most afraid to meet on a dark street is her natural protector" (p. 72). Although her mother objected to her lone excursions, Gilman argued that "there did not seem to be any real danger" and "so out I went" (p. 72).

The fictionalized version of her assertion of independence bears some striking similarities to her own circumstances. The cast of characters in "Spoken To" parallels that of her own family: an overly protective mother, a brother who teases, an aunt who resides in their home, and an absent father.[78] When the story's 21-year-old protagonist, Lucille Wright, announces that she intends to start "going about alone at night," her mother expresses grave reservations about the wisdom of doing so. "Why you might—you might be *spoken to*," she argues (*FR*, 29). Like the youthful Gilman, Lucille is depicted as a strong woman who has "just secured a position as teacher in a girls' gymnasium" and is not easily dissuaded (p. 30).[79] When her brother assumes the persona of the "stalwart man" and announces that "Man is woman's natural protector," Lucille's response is identical to what Gilman's would have been: "Against what?" she asks (p. 30). While her mother seems unable to offer a compelling argument and "felt only a maternal terror and that deep-seated dread of the unconventional which . . . is stronger than the fear of hell," Lucille's aunt Marie, who hails from France, is more direct. "In my country, you foolish child, no young girl of any birth and breeding is allowed to go out alone, even in daylight" (p. 30). Brother Hervey eventually moves to Paris, and the remainder of the story, with the exception of the denouement, is somewhat reminiscent of the plot of James's *Daisy Miller*, which Gilman read in 1879 at age 18.[80] When Lucille and Aunt Marie travel to Paris to visit Hervey, Marie again attempts to instill in Lucille the importance of being chaperoned in public. "You must *not* go alone in the streets of Paris," she cautions. "It is not—respectable . . . you must have company," she tells Lucille (p. 32). She also confides that years earlier, she had been "spoken to" by what appears to be the very image of James's Mr. Giovanelli: a man with "a reputation most terrible" who was "handsome as the devil . . . beautifully dressed, with a cloak-overcoat, with an ebony and gold stick; with a waxed moustache" and "eyes of an infinite audacity!" (p. 32).[81] Although Lucille attempts to honor the custom of European chaperonage by going out only with an escort, one day she succumbs to the temptation to "stroll and look about, all by herself" (p. 33). During her walk, she is approached by the same audacious man who spoke to her aunt years before. Lucille, however, is prepared; she has learned to steel herself against would-be accosters. When she hears "the unmeasured insult of his whispered words," she responds by unabashedly depositing "two cents" in his glossy hat, which he has swept off his head "with a magnificent air" (p. 33). The "gentleman" is duly embarrassed by Lucille's gesture, and Lucille "passed on quite undisturbed, as one who has performed a good action" (p. 33).

"Dr. Clair's Place" is linked to Gilman's autobiography to the extent that it presents an alternative to the conventional rest cure treatment for neurasthenia that she underwent in 1887.[82] In this story, Octavia Welch is an archetypal death-in-life character who is contemplating suicide after battling neurasthenia for many years. Her personal history is strikingly similar to Gilman's: her health has been "utterly broken" since age 24, her happiness "buried in shame and bitterness," and her experience with motherhood "had and lost." "I am too weak even to support myself," she confesses. "I have no money. I have no friends. I have no home. I have no work. I have no hope in life" (*Yellow*, 177).

A passenger on the train in which Welch is traveling gently persuades her to see Dr. Willy Clair, a woman who has opened a sanitarium where she specializes in neurasthenia and other "psychopathic work" (p. 178). Most significant is that Dr. Clair has "developed methods of her own" for the treatment of chronic melancholia (p. 178). She particularly resists traditional approaches in which the patients "have nothing to do but sit about and think of themselves and their 'cases' " (p. 179).

After her own near-tragic experience with the rest cure, Gilman sought unconventional methods for treating the chronic depression that would plague her throughout her life. In late 1901 and early 1902, for example, she underwent mild electric shock therapy at the hands of Dr. Mary Putnam Jacobi, who also prescribed "phospho-glycerates in wine" with good effect (*Diaries*, 17 December 1901) and encouraged Gilman to undertake relatively simple intellectual tasks to "set that inert brain to work" (*Living*, 291). The activities gradually became more challenging, and Gilman found herself "improving under Dr. Jacobi's treatment" (*Diaries*, 2 January 1902).

Similarly, the fictional Dr. Clair resists the treatment prescribed for Jane in "The Yellow Wall-Paper" by instead encouraging reading and other activities that will engage the patient intellectually. Attention is also paid to the patient's physical environment. When Octavia Welch arrives at the sanitarium, for example, she is placed in a "quiet fragrant rosy room" with a "rose-draped balcony" (*Yellow*, 182–83), much like the one Jane longed for in "The Yellow Wall-Paper," with "roses all over the window" but that "John would not hear of" (*YW*, 12). Most important, she is free to control her treatment, and at the end of a month, she is so much improved that she begins physical conditioning by swimming and climbing mountains. Her "misery and pain and shame seemed to fade into a remote past" (*Yellow*, 184), and at the end of the story, she has taken a position as an associate at the sanitarium, where she helps other people get well. The themes in "Dr. Clair's Place" are similar to those in many of her stories: the issues of control, empowerment, and work are of paramount importance, as they were in Gilman's own life.

The *Forerunner* Fiction

Just 10 years after winning international acclaim with the publication of *Women and Economics* (1898), Charlotte Perkins Gilman was having difficulty placing her writing. Part of the problem stemmed from her self-imposed boycott of journals owned by publishing mogul William Randolph Hearst, whom Gilman had held in contempt since 1892, when he began publishing sensational accounts of her separation and subsequent divorce from Walter Stetson.[83] Hearst had acquired a sizable number of newspapers and magazines, in which Gilman refused to publish. But an equally significant problem was that her "principal topics were in direct contravention of established views, beliefs, and emotions" (*Living*, 304). "My work grew in importance but lost in market value," she concedes in her memoirs. "I wrote more and sold less" (pp. 303–4). By 1909, "more and more" of her manuscripts were being rejected; indeed, as she recalls in her autobiography, they "accumulated far faster than I could sell them" (p. 304). When she attempted to place her writing with Theodore Dreiser, then editor of the *Delineator*, he "gloomily" suggested that she "should consider more what the editors want" (p. 304). Although Gilman realized that "the market is necessarily limited" when "one writes to express important truths" (p. 304), she decided to spurn Dreiser's advice. Rather than compromise both her integrity as a writer and her agenda for social change, Gilman instead formulated a bold new plan—to single-handedly write, edit, and publish her own monthly magazine, the *Forerunner*, in circulation from 1909 to 1916. The *Forerunner* would become the most ambitious project of Gilman's long career.

In addition to essays on current social issues, the *Forerunner*, which sold for 10 cents a copy or a dollar a year,[84] boasted annually one complete novel, one nonfiction book, several short articles, a dozen or more poems, 12 short sermons, commentary on various news items, numerous book reviews, and 12 short stories. It was, in fact, the forum in which the majority of Gilman's fiction appeared.

The purpose of the *Forerunner* was identical to the purpose of the majority of the stories it featured: "to stimulate thought; to arouse hope, courage and impatience; to offer practical suggestions and solutions, to voice the strong assurance of better living."[85] As with nearly all of her writing, Gilman's objective in producing *Forerunner* fiction was primarily didactic. So determined was Gilman "to express important truths" that she risked financial ruin to undertake the new venture (*Living*, 304).

Despite the existence of a number of magazines that addressed themselves to issues of concern to women, such as Alice Stone Blackwell's suffrage publication, *The Woman's Journal*, or such narrowly conceived and gender-specific monthlies as *Ladies Home Journal* and Hearst's *Good Housekeeping*, the *Forerunner* broke new ground. Although the majority of the 15 hundred subscribers were women, Gilman insisted that the magazine was about people. "It . . . treat[s] all three phases of our existence, male, female, and human," she wrote (*FR*, November 1909: 32). Not only did the *Forerunner* advocate human rights, but it also became a vehicle through which Gilman could call for social reform. On the pages of the *Forerunner*, Gilman used her fiction to proselytize on topics ranging from venereal disease and prostitution to the need for child labor laws and academic freedom.

Gilman insisted that the *Forerunner* was intended to be non-gender-specific, yet she constantly sought to change the traditional depiction of women in her literary works. The problem with existing "women's" magazines was that they were "not truly for women at all, but only for dressmakers, cooks, nurses, houseservants, and those who need books on etiquette. . . . These housekeepers' manuals are not the literature for the new woman," she complained (*FR*, September 1915: 235). Rather, Gilman sought to create fictional characters who would more accurately reflect the courage and convictions of the new woman.

While most of the stories had a similar purpose—to educate the reader—the origins of the stories varied markedly. At times Gilman invented her fictional scenarios from scratch; in other cases, as we saw, she would draw on incidents from her own life to form the basis of a story. If we examine the entire collection of *Forerunner* fiction, however, several distinctive themes emerge. The most common include women struggling to circumvent limitations imposed by an androcentric society, the need for economic independence, violations of human rights, and the advantages of utopian communities. Gilman also frequently used social satire to make her point.

Economic Independence

Economic independence for women was one of Gilman's priorities, both on the lecture circuit and in her groundbreaking work *Women and Economics*,[86] in which she took umbrage with the subservient roles played by women in life and in fiction:

> In old romances the woman was nothing save beautiful, high-born, virtuous, and perhaps 'accomplished.' She did nothing but love and hate, obey and disobey, and be handed here and there among villain, hero, and outraged parent, screaming, fainting, or bursting into floods of tears as seemed called for by the occasion. In the fiction of to-day women are continually taking larger place in the action of the story. They are given personal characteristics beyond those of physical beauty. And they are no longer content simply to *be:* they *do.* They are showing qualities of bravery, endurance, strength, foresight, and power for the swift execution of well-conceived plans. They have ideas and purposes of their own; and even when, as in so many cases described by the more reactionary novelists, the efforts of the heroine are shown to be entirely futile, and she comes back with a rush to the self-effacement of marriage with economic dependence, still the efforts were there. Disapprove as he may . . . no feature is more distinctive of this time than the increasing individualization of women. (*WE*, 150–51)

Of the 134 stories published in the *Forerunner*, no less than 19 address economic self-sufficiency; several also depict women helping other women to attain economic independence, a demonstration of Gilman's philosophy that the "splendid sisterhood" that had "battled and suffered for half a century" had done so, "not for themselves alone, but for one another" (*WE*, 167).

A story that combines the issue of economic self-sufficiency with the theme of sisterhood is "Mrs. Beazley's Deeds" (1911).[87] Gilman relied in this story on a pairing common in her fiction—the wiser, somewhat older, and invariably more experienced woman counseling the distraught and disillusioned younger woman.

The protagonist, Maria Beazley, lives under the thumb of her abusive and manipulative husband, William, who espouses the philosophy "Wives submit yourselves to your husbands" (*Yellow*, 165). Although she is only 32, Maria Beazley is described as a "faded little woman" with a "dragged out appearance," whose husband has forced her to sign over property deeds that she inherited from her father (*Yellow*, 170, 163).

When only one deed remains—the title to her old family homestead—
Maria's vehement protest that she wants "to keep it for the children"
falls on deaf ears (p. 165). Reminiscent of Adoniram Penn in Mary E.
Wilkins Freeman's "The Revolt of 'Mother,'" who wished his wife
would "'tend to [her] own affairs" rather than question his authority,[88]
William Beazley "minded her outcry no more than he minded the
squawking of a to-be beheaded hen" (*Yellow*, 164). In a further assertion
of his patriarchal rule, William arranges to keep a boarder but provides
Maria with virtually no advance notice and no say in the matter.

Although Maria dreads her arrival, the boarder, Miss Lawrence
(whose profession is suggested by her name), is a bright, dynamic, and
sympathetic 37-year-old attorney. Mrs. Beazley confides to Miss
Lawrence her sense of helplessness in having to "submit" to her husband's demands: "O, Miss Lawrence, you don't understand—here am I
and here's the children, and none of us can get away, and if I don't do as
he says I must, he takes it out of us—that's all. You can't do nothing
with a man like that—and him with the Bible on his side!" (pp.
169–70). But Miss Lawrence decides to "commit the unpardonable sin
of interfering between man and wife—in the interest of the children"
(p. 170). She explains to Mrs. Beazley that she not only has legal rights
that will protect her but that she has a moral obligation to "make a stand
for the children's sake" (p. 171). Miss Lawrence finally alters Mrs. Beazley's perception of her condition, and Mrs. Beazley begins to see herself as a victim of both domestic imprisonment and emotional bondage.
With Miss Lawrence's counsel, she wisely invests her remaining property, becomes economically self-sufficient, and garners the strength to
leave her unhappy marriage. Gilman ends the story with a twist of irony:
in the final scene, it is William Beazley who is himself forced to sign a
deed—of separation.

Another story in which economic self-sufficiency is a prerequisite to
happiness is "Mrs. Elder's Idea" (1912).[89] Grace Elder is a middle-aged
woman with two grown children who realizes, after her children leave
home, how little in common she has with her husband. "Mr. Elder's
concerns in life had never been similar to his wife's," says the narrator
(p. 139). While Mrs. Elder thrives in the city, her husband is at peace in
the country. She enjoys shopping; he does not. He finds smoking pleasant; to her it is a useless vice.

When Mr. Elder announces one day that he has sold his business and
purchased a farm, his wife is incensed. "I know you won't like it at first,
Grace, but it will do you good," he tells her (pp. 141–42). Grace, how-

ever, perceives life on a farm as analogous to "penal servitude," and there arises in her "a slow, boiling flood of long-suppressed rebellion" (p. 142). She begins to formulate a plan, and within a few weeks she makes an announcement of her own: "I am going to board in Boston. I have rented a furnished floor" (p. 144). Standing firm against his protests, Grace launches a career as a professional shopper. She assures her husband, however, that he will always be welcome in her new home. In the end, "the Elder family maintained a city flat and a country home; and spent their happy years between them" (p. 145). Gilman demonstrates how well a commuter marriage can work, particularly when "two half homes and a half happy wife, were really more satisfying than one whole home, and a whole unhappy wife, withering in discontent" (p. 145).

Several of Gilman's stories perform double duty. "Mrs. Mann's Clothes," for example, both demonstrates the importance of economic security and makes a statement about dress reform, a topic Gilman addressed in lectures, fiction, poetry, and, most extensively, in her 12-part essay "The Dress of Women," serialized in the *Forerunner* in 1915.[90] Dress reform was an issue about which Gilman felt strongly; she "despised" fashion and was criticized for once appearing "corsetless" and "petticoatless" in public (*Living*, 66).[91]

Women's clothing, Gilman argued, was "unhealthful, unbeautiful, immoral. . . . [yet] physical suffering has been so long considered an integral part of woman's nature . . . that a little more or less is no great matter."[92] Moreover, women who were "slaves of fashion . . . lifting their skirts, baring their backs, exhibiting their legs, powdering their noses," were guilty of "behaving just as foolishly as ever" (*Living*, 318).

The protagonist of "Mrs. Mann's Clothes" is another empty nester who is near despair after "tramping the long blocks, and the long aisles of a score of stores, without being able to find a dress to suit her" (*FR*, 114). The fashions designed by "Parisian geniuses" gracing the New York stores where Mrs. Mann shops are ill-suited to her full figure, and frustration give way to a "consuming rage" (p. 114). But, as the narrator points out, "A consuming rage is a great stimulus" (p. 114). Mrs. Mann begins to realize that there is a market for the thousands of women who "wanted to look 'stylish,' but would be thankful indeed if they could preserve that appearance, to a reasonable degree, and yet have clothes that would wear—and be comfortable" (p. 114). Mrs. Mann decides to open a shop that sells "sensible" women's clothing, and predictably, the business is successful, and Mr. Mann is proud of his entrepreneur wife.

The concept of social motherhood was another area of reform Gilman promoted. She advocated a system in which the child would be removed from the home and placed, for several hours of the day, into a "baby-garden" (her term for a day-care center). This arrangement would subsequently free the mother to contribute to the economic security of her children by engaging in employment with remunerative benefits. Rather than being a detriment to the emotional health of the child, Gilman believed, children entrusted to trained education specialists would be happier, safer, and better attended than those raised exclusively at home. "What is there in the make-up of any ordinary house designed to please, instruct, educate and generally benefit a child?" she asked in *The Home* (p. 118). "To what sort of a place is the [infant] introduced? To a place built and furnished for several mixed and conflicting industries; not to a place planned for babies—aired, lighted, heated, coloured, and kept quiet . . . but a building meant for a number of grown people to cook in, sweep and dust in, wash and iron in, cut and sew in, eat and wash dishes in, see their friends in, dress, undress, and sleep in; and incidentally, in the cracks and crevices of all these varied goings on, to 'bring up' children in" (p. 234).

Moreover, Gilman's theory of "the new motherhood" would allow "the fullest development of the woman, in all her powers, that she may be better qualified for her [maternal] duties,"[93] particularly since "a mother economically free, a world-servant instead of a house-servant; a mother knowing the world and living in it,—can be to her children far more than has ever been possible before" (*WE*, 269). Because not every woman has the talent, training, or experience to make her an effective mother, children who are raised by professional caretakers are healthier, brighter, and better adjusted, Gilman believed.

Certainly Gilman's lingering doubts about her own maternal competence shaped her views, and she crafted several stories that illustrate the benefits of social motherhood. The concept of social motherhood, depicted in "A Garden of Babies," published in 1909, and several of Gilman's short sermons on motherhood and child-rearing, is also demonstrated in the story "Making A Change."[94]

In "Making a Change," Gilman once again depicts the older woman counseling the younger woman and combines her advocacy of day-care centers and social motherhood with her call for economic independence. The story's protagonist, Julia Gordins, is a young wife and mother who discovers that abandoning her career as a musician to become a full-time, housebound caretaker for her infant son involves such a forfeiture of her self that suicide seems the only means of escape. The narrator tells us that Julia "spent her days in unremitting devotion to [the baby's] needs and to the care of her flat" a combination that has left her exhausted and dangerously depressed (*CPG*, 67). After an early-morning quarrel with her husband, Frank, over her inability to quiet the crying infant, Julia mechanically goes through the motions of bathing the baby, feeding him, and cleaning up the tub. Then, in an uncharacteristic gesture, Julia relinquishes the infant to the care of her mother-in-law, who resides with the Gordins, and quietly slips into her room to end her life. Julia's mother-in-law discovers her intentions in time to prevent the suicide, and the two women together effect a solution to the crisis. Without telling Frank, they conspire to have Julia return to work outside of the home by giving music lessons, and the mother-in-law happily indulges her own desires by opening a "baby-garden" on the roof of their apartment building. Gilman's point is that the removal of child care from the home engenders positive changes on a number of levels. Not only is Frank's mother providing a valuable community service by doing something useful, something she enjoys immensely, but more important, the restructuring of the environment frees Julia to return to the music world that was her livelihood prior to marriage. This same paradigm, involving architectural innovations or revisions of domestic space, appears in dozens of Gilman's *Forerunner* stories.

Gilman recognized that the home served vastly dichotomous functions for each gender. For men, it was a haven to retreat to after a long day's work. For women, it was a place of entrapment—a veritable prison that transformed intelligent women into mere "house-slaves" who were relegated to an obsequious role by virtue of the nonegalitarian function of their domestic responsibilities. But Gilman envisioned an architecturally liberated environment that would benefit all the inhabitants of the home. In her two major feminist polemics, *Women and Economics* and *The Home*, in hundreds of public lectures, in numerous essays, in her poetry, and in her fictional works, Gilman proposed architectural innovations that, she believed, would dramatically change the quality of family life.

In Polly Wynn Allen's seminal work on Gilman's architectural theory, Allen affirms that Gilman "recognized that the layout of physical spaces [in the home] is both arbitrary and political, thus alerting [the inhabitants] to the environmental dimension of their efforts to harmonize family and job."[95] Specifically, Gilman argued that such routine daily tasks as cooking, laundry, and child care should be removed from the home altogether, not only because of the traditional gender bias in the assignment of those tasks but, more significant, because of the "mental myopia" that housebound women were doomed to suffer in performing those tasks. "Human creatures, to keep healthy," Gilman asserted, "*must* mingle with one another. The house-bound woman cannot; therefore, she does not maintain a vigorous and growing mind" (*Home*, 12).

As a remedy for mental stagnation, not only must the home be modified, Gilman argued, but the women must become productive members of the civilian work force. Here, Gilman's social theories of both the home and of human labor tend to overlap. She believed that the home, and domestic servility in particular, was the main source of political, social, and economic disparity in male and female relationships. Gilman reasoned that as long as women were confined to the domestic sphere, they would remain economically disempowered; furthermore, unless they lived useful and productive lives that required work *outside* of the home, women could not fulfill their lives as human beings. She believed that a rearrangement of the space within the home was a crucial first step toward attaining economic democracy (Allen, 77).

Gilman proposed a radical modification of the home into what she fondly referred to as "a kitchenless house," one that would provide private living quarters for the family (bedrooms and bathrooms in particular) while featuring a communally shared kitchen, laundry, and child-care center. She described her vision in *Women and Economics* as follows: "The apartments would be without kitchens; but there would be a kitchen belonging to the house from which meals could be served to the families in their rooms or in a common dining room, as preferred. It would be a home where the cleaning was done by efficient workers, not hired separately by the families, . . . and a roof-garden, day nursery and kindergarten, under well-trained professional nurses and teachers, would insure proper care of the children" (*WE*, 242).

The immediate effect would be to free the woman from the drudgery of time-consuming domestic industry; the larger effect would be, in Gilman's words, to "have homes that are places to live in and love in, to rest in and play in, to be alone in and to be together in; and they will not be confused and declassed by admixture with any industry whatever" (pp. 267–68). One of the most compelling benefits of the architectural modification that Gilman proposed would be to simultaneously reduce tension in the household and promote harmony in the family. "Take the kitchens out of houses," she wrote, "and you leave rooms which are open to any form of arrangement and extension; [furthermore], when

parents are less occupied in getting food and cooking it, in getting fur-
niture and dusting it, they may find time to give new thought and new
effort to the care of their children" (p. 301). In addition to releasing
women from domestic bondage, Gilman argued, the kitchenless home
would result in meals being safer, more economical, more nutritious,
and invariably more appetizing. Since so few women were skillful cooks,
she reasoned, meals would be better prepared by professional chefs who
could provide healthy and tasty meals. Moreover, Gilman argued that
having a kitchen in every individual home was wasteful, costly, and inef-
ficient.

Gilman believed that the architectural remedy she proposed would
have several benefits. First, it would make the home safer by eliminating the kitchen, the room that posed the greatest threat of accident,
fire, and illness; second, it would remove the most time-consuming
tasks from the home, particularly cooking and laundry, so that the house
could become a home "*while* the family are in it"; third, it would remove
the gender-based economic disparity from the home and propel women
into the work force, thereby alleviating the financial burden placed on
men; finally, it would place children into day care, which would ultimately yield brighter, cheerier children.

To demonstrate her vision of the "new" home, Gilman created a variety of fictional characters whose lives were dramatically improved when
their home environments were modified to eliminate domestic
bondage. She effected in her fictional world the changes she envisioned
and encouraged in the real world. In this way, Gilman was able to apply
her social theory to characters and circumstances in order to clearly
demonstrate the ideology she espoused. She used her fiction to show
that as women became productive members of the work force, and as
men and women worked together away from the home, the resulting
social evolution would strengthen family relationships by producing
happier husbands, happier wives, and happier offspring. Again and
again, Gilman preaches that breaking the chains that enslave women in
the home will free them to pursue meaningful work away from the
domestic arena. And through their repudiation of domestic work as their
only work, Gilman's fictional heroines become more productive and
more satisfied, ultimately serving the best interests of the entire family.
It was Gilman's hope that female readers would find the courage to
emulate the ideological models represented in her stories.

As Allen points out, Gilman uses architectural backdrops in her fiction to portray "very tangible ways of solving the problems of isolated,

overworked women" (Allen, 146). The stories in which Gilman advances this theme are numerous. In "The Cottagette," for example, she introduces her concept of the kitchenless home.[96] In the somewhat transparent plot, two women, Lois and Malda, arrange summer lodging at a beautiful mountain retreat for artists called High Court. The women move into a tiny but comfortable kitchenless cottage. Meals are taken at the central boardinghouse, less than a two-minute walk away, where, we are told, "the food was good . . . and the prices reasonable" (*CPG*, 48). The story revolves around Malda, who on the advice of her older friend Lois abandons her artistry to pursue cooking in an attempt to win the affection of an attractive literary man named Ford Mathews. Lois convinces Malda that a kitchen must be installed in the cottagette to allow Malda to win Ford's affection with her talent for preparing "delicious little suppers" (p. 52). Almost immediately after the kitchen is installed, however, Malda laments the loss of her freedom since her time becomes so consumed by domestic duties that she has to virtually abandon her artistic pursuits. "It interfere[d] with my work a good deal," she tells the reader. "It is astonishing how much work there is in the littlest kitchen" (p. 52). In the following weeks, the kitchen gradually grows smellier, noisier, and messier, and the cottagette loses its loveliness and becomes "just a bead on a string like other houses" (p. 53). But for love's sake, Malda continues to cook in her new kitchen. Eventually, Ford proposes marriage, but on one condition: that Malda stop cooking. Malda is surprised (and delighted) to learn that it is her artistic side (i.e., her nondomestic side) to which Ford is attracted. The artifice and pretense of feigning domesticity in order to secure the relationship is wholly unnecessary, which Ford makes clear to Malda. Thus the story ends with Gilman freeing her heroine from servitude while at the same time imbuing Ford Mathews with a liberality not often seen in her male characters. Gilman's goal, of course, is to encourage women to reassess the architectural dimensions of their subordination and to motivate them to consider alternative lifestyles that would result in greater autonomy and self-actualization.

Boardinghouse stories are also common in Gilman's oeuvre, both as fictional backdrops and in establishing scenarios that present investment opportunities for women seeking economic security. "Her Housekeeper" (1910), "Martha's Mother" (1910), "The Jumping-Off Place" (1911), and "The Boarder Bit" (1915), for example, all address, among other things, the advantages of boardinghouse living. In "Turned" (1911), it is a boardinghouse in which Mrs. Marroner takes refuge with her servant, Gerta, after learning of her husband's infidelity. Throughout her own life, Gilman resided on and off in boardinghouses and even assumed the management of one for a time in California in the early 1890s.[97]

"The time has come when it is better for the world that women be economically independent, and therefore they are becoming so," Gilman remarked in *Women and Economics* (p. 316). It was a short step from articulating theory to depicting in the fictional arena the benefits of economic autonomy. In addition to those works discussed here, several of Gilman's other short stories, including "Three Thanksgivings" (1909), "According to Solomon" (1909), "What Occupation?" (1911), "Old Mrs. Crosley" (1911), "Their House" (1912), "Mrs. Powers' Duty" (1913), "A Partnership" (1914), "The Pig of Gold" (1915), "A Surplus Woman" (1916), and "A Growing Heart" (1916), also underscore the theme of economic independence. Important elements of Gilman's advocacy of women's work outside of the home were not only the financial security it would engender but also the emotional well-being that would inevitably result: "Only as we live, think, feel, and work outside the home, do we become humanly developed, civilized, socialized," she insisted (*WE*, 222).

Social Problems and Human Rights

In addition to stories promoting economic self-reliance for women, Gilman wrote several stories exploring human rights and social problems. She constructed stories that addressed such issues as sexual harassment, blackmail, bribery, venereal disease, streetcar safety, tainted milk, social motherhood, and yellow journalism.

A story addressing the obsessive sexual pursuit by an older man toward a younger woman, "Old Water," was published in the *Forerunner* in 1911.[98] Although Gilman's didacticism remains intact in "Old Water," which intertwines the motifs of fantasy, obsession, and possession, this story is unconventional in its denouement, in which the villain dies.[99]

Gilman centers the action in "Old Water" around a prominent poet in pursuit of a beautiful young woman, Ellen Osgood, who repels his attempts at seduction. But his quest for mastery of Ellen compels him "madly, passionately, irresistibly" [*sic*] (*Yellow*, 128). Indeed, Gilman's poet, Pendexter, is a demonic character with an obsessive personality. When he meets Ellen for the first time, he is drawn to her beauty. "Her body is a poem!" he exclaims (p. 122). His subsequent transformation of

Ellen's body into a poem—a product over which he customarily has creative control—immediately reduces her to an object, a transfiguration that is further reinforced by his comparison of her to such mythological figures as Valkyr, Juno, and Atalanta. His obsession with Ellen escalates to the point where he desires to mold her into the kind of mythical woman he idealizes in his poetry. Ellen's recognition of the inherent superficiality in Pendexter's practice of writing poetry about "people who never existed anyhow" only fuels her dislike for him (p. 126). "What on earth does he want to make over those old legends for, anyway!" she complains to her mother (p. 126).

Pendexter's obsession with Ellen intensifies as she continues to resist his advances. His original fantasies about her elegant beauty metamorphose into a brutal quest to possess both her body and soul. He conceals "the storm of passion which was growing within him; a passion of such *seething intensity* as would have alarmed that gentle soul exceedingly.... His heart was *hot and dark* within him. The longer he pursued and failed the *fiercer* was his desire for her" (pp. 127–28; emphasis added). The demonic figure rages darker and fiercer as the object of his obsession continues to reject him.

Gilman's depiction of Ellen suggests that she resists Pendexter not only because of simple incompatibility—clearly the two have little in common—but also because she fears her own sexuality. Ellen has an irrational fear of water and dreams of "big beasts" that jump out at her (p. 124). She becomes alarmed by Pendexter's "mighty strokes" when he paddles her canoe. "Not so hard!" she cries. "You are stronger than I" (p. 126). And although "she did rather enjoy the well proportioned bulk of him," she "felt a real dislike for the heavy fell of black hair on his arms and hands" (p. 126). The beast of Ellen's dreams becomes an obvious metaphor for Pendexter, whose primordial, animalistic impulses threaten to destroy her innocence.

But the real focus of the story is on Pendexter's deformation of reality. He convinces himself that he and Ellen were paired in another life and that it is their fate to be together again: " 'Ah' he cried. 'It is your fate! Our fate! We have lived through this before! We will die together if we cannot live together!' " (p. 129). Through his distorted perception, Pendexter constructs another version of reality.

In the final scene, Ellen escapes a sexual assault by Pendexter, whose "blood [was] pounding in his veins, his voice shaken with the intensity of his emotions" (p. 128). Pendexter continues his pursuit, and as Ellen attempts to flee, the two end up struggling on the edge of a cliff. Pendexter's literal and figurative descent is completed as the two plummet into the lake below.

The ending of the story is ambiguous. Gilman presents at least the possibility that Pendexter has been murdered by Ellen: she survives; he does not. " 'It's pretty lucky I could swim,' said Ellen, as she hurried home, 'and he couldn't.' " We never see what actually transpires in the water, but it is unusual for Gilman's villains to meet their death. More often, the protagonist simply has the final word. In what appears as a postscript to the story, Ellen has escaped both an actual and a symbolic death at the hands of Pendexter. Gilman thus frees her protagonist and concludes the story with Ellen articulating the demonic nature of Pendexter's obsession: "He must have been crazy!" she remarks (p. 129).

"Being Reasonable" focuses on a bigamist and his two wives.[100] While the events of the story are far from plausible, "Being Reasonable" is as much about female bonding as it is about bigamy. Following a paradigm common in Gilman's fiction, the story centers on women combining their emotional resources to stand firm against their male oppressor. When his duplicity is discovered by the women who together confront him, the man refuses to acknowledge his moral responsibilities and ends up losing both wives. A story with a similar theme, "Turned,"[101] which addresses the issue of adultery and female camaraderie, is better constructed than "Being Reasonable." Gilman opens this story by juxtaposing descriptions of Mrs. Marion Marroner and her housekeeper, Gerta Petersen, both of whom are depicted in their respective bedrooms sobbing uncontrollably as a result of Mr. Marroner's deception. The middle-aged Mrs. Marroner "held a Ph.D." and "had been on the faculty of a college" (*CPG*, 89). Gerta is "ignorant and childish—a girl of eighteen" (p. 88). As the story unfolds, the reader learns that Gerta has been seduced and impregnated by Mr. Marroner, who is now away from home on an extended business trip lasting several months. When Mrs. Marroner discovers that Gerta is pregnant, she is initially sympathetic and vows to "stand by the poor, foolish thing till it's over" (p. 90). When she inadvertently learns, however, that it is her husband who has fathered Gerta's unborn child, the betrayed Mrs. Marroner confronts Gerta and immediately orders her out of the house. After the initial shock wears off, Mrs. Marroner begins to see Gerta for what she is: a helpless victim of her husband's exploitation. Although Gerta should "have resisted temptation ... Mrs. Marroner was wise enough to know how difficult temptation is to recognize when it comes in the guise of friendship and from a source one does not suspect" (p. 93). Moreover, Mr. Marroner "could fully foresee and measure the consequences of his act. He appreciated to the full the innocence, the ignorance, the grateful affection, the habitual docility, of which he deliberately took advantage" (p. 93). Once she acknowledges to herself that Gerta has been victimized by her husband, Mrs. Marroner comes to her aid, moves to another town, resumes teaching, and provides a home for Gerta and her new baby.

"The Chair of English," first published in the *Forerunner* in 1913, is constructed around the themes of deception, blackmail, and the misuse of power.[102] In this tale, the chair of a college English department, Dr. Irwin Manchester, is an unscrupulous sophist who fabricates an elaborate story about a colleague having an affair with the "undeniably attractive" wife of the college president (*Yellow*, 147). He then tells his colleague's wife about her husband's alleged infidelity, hoping to force his resignation and thereby secure the vacant post for a relative. Gilman imbues her protagonist, Mona Beale, with intelligence, wisdom, and grace. Although Dr. Manchester "was a practiced expert in the use of words," he meets his match in Mrs. Beale. When she has Dr. Manchester subpoenaed so he can testify to his statements under oath, "his nimble mind grasped with terrifying lucidity the consequences of his so testifying," and he recants his earlier statements (p. 152). But when Mrs. Beale confronts him with his previous account of the affair, secretly recorded on a dictagraph, the duplicitous Manchester is himself forced to resign his position. Gilman uses the story both to illustrate how deception is inherently dangerous and to underscore her own belief in "absolute truthfulness," which she tried to practice in her own life with "most meticulous accuracy" (*Living*, 59).

Deception and power struggles are dominant themes in "His Mother" (1914), a story focusing on a policewoman, Mrs. Martin, who is forced to arrest her own son for trafficking in prostitution.[103] A procurer of young prostitutes, the woman's son, Jack, epitomizes everything she despises, particularly since her work includes counseling victims of the white slave trade. When Jack preys on an attractive young store clerk with promises of marriage, he forces his mother's hand. After he drags the young woman, drugged and half-conscious, back to his room after a night on the town, he finds his mother waiting to arrest him. While the ending is melodramatic, Gilman's message is not: the story expresses her views about the exploitation of the innocent. Gilman saw an analogy, in fact, between women who were "exploited for the pleasure of men, not only in prostitution" but also in allowing themselves to be subjected to "helpless subservience in marriage."[104] The story also examines the issue of maternal guilt. Mrs. Martin originally entered police work to atone for the earlier sins of her son, who as a teenager had fathered a child out of wedlock. In the last scene, she is still trying to expiate his sins by spending "a long life in trying to do good enough to make up for her own share in his evil" (*Yellow*, 80).

"With a Difference (Not Literature)" (1914) also explores "the ruin of innocent girls" (pp. 29–30).[105] Dora Holcomb, a "sheltered flower" with a "romantic young heart," is deceived by "an attractive fellow, tall and good-looking, well-dressed and pleasant mannered," who spikes her beverage during a dinner date with a potent drug that leaves her "drowsy and . . . unresisting" (pp. 29, 30). He takes her back "to the apartment he occupied with whatever temporary companion or victim he chose," and the next morning, Dora awakens with the realization that "she was ruined" (p. 30). She manages to escape through a window, and "with the instinct of . . . a sorrowing child—she fled to her home" (p. 30). Her frantic mother takes Dora in her arms and "slowly, tenderly, with unbelieving horror . . . drew from her that dreadful story, and grasped its horror far more fully than the child in her arms" (pp. 30–31). When Dora's father arrives home and learns of the incident, he orders his "ruined" daughter out of his house, effectively blaming the victim. But then Gilman rewrites the ending to "the same old story," the narrator stating that "this is what happened in *this* story" (p. 31). Mrs. Holcomb confronts her husband and forcefully insists that their daughter be allowed to stay. Then Dora herself addresses her father, faulting him for failing to educate her about the dangers in the world. "I knew you were very strict about my speaking to strangers . . . but I didn't know *why*," she states. "If you had told me that there were that kind of men in the world—and the way they worked to trap young girls—*then* I'd have known what to look out for." (p. 31). The rest of the story, in effect, becomes a parabolic and sentimental tale, a kind of *Charlotte Temple* with a happy ending, in which "the father saw a great light," forgives his daughter, and chides himself for failing to educate her that "the world is not safe for girls, hardly anywhere" (p. 32). Although Dora goes on to lead a long, happy, and useful life educating young girls about the dangers inherent in society, "no man married her because his honor was putatively involved in her early disgrace" (p. 32). Nevertheless, she continued "working for a permanent enlightenment [for] all of us, such as had miraculously fallen upon her family" (p. 32).

Part of Gilman's philosophy of child-rearing, as she explained in detail in *Concerning Children* (1904) and briefly in her autobiography, was the importance of always pairing a reason with an action, "accustoming the young mind automatically to associate cause and effect" (*Living*, 155). "With a Difference" illustrates the disastrous results of the Holcombs' failure to inform Dora, as she reminds her parents when she remarks, "I was not taught what I needed to know" (*FR*, 32).

Another story exploring the theme of deception is "The Boys and the Butter," first published in the *Forerunner* in 1910.[106] With its Christian overtones, the story reflects Gilman's philosophy about the indignities that can be suffered by children at the hands of cruel and thoughtless adults. The simple plot centers on a superficially pious and meddlesome aunt, Jane McCoy, who bribes her two young nephews into going without butter for a year because, she insists, butter is "bad for the blood" and "self-denial is good for children" (*Yellow*, 67). With the promise of 50 dollars each as the reward for their sacrifice, the boys accept her proposition. The year passes and the "butterless boys" excitedly anticipate the delivery of their reward. Aunt Jane, however, breaches her promise and instead purchases two life memberships in her nephews' names in a Missionary Society. Upon learning of the circumstances under which the donation was made, however, the Missionary Society publicly repudiates the aunt for her sin and returns the money to the boys, "its rightful owners" (p. 72).

Also focusing on children's rights is "Joan's Defender," first published in the *Forerunner* in 1916.[107] The story opens with a description of Joan's mother, a frail and sickly woman whose "maternal instinct did not present that unbroken front of sterling courage, that measureless reserve of patience, that unfailing wisdom which we are taught to expect of it" (p. 96). Rather, Joan's mother is in broken health, and her "feeble nerves" are made worse by the constant bickering between her young son and Joan. Joan's mother unfairly places most of the blame on her, a petulant child whose long, curly hair provides endless temptations for brother Gerald's mischief. Although only nine years old, Joan "felt that life was not worth living," particularly when she was subjected to the "ignominious and unsatisfying punishment" from her father's whip (p. 97). "And then something pleasant happened," says the narrator. Enter Uncle Arthur, a "gentle and pleasant" man with "a nice voice, jolly but not loud" who comes for a week's visit (p. 97). A former physician, Uncle Arthur recognizes in Joan the signs of emotional abuse and requests permission to take her back to his home "for a long visit. It would be no trouble at all to us—we have eight, you know, and all outdoors for them to romp in," he tells his sister (p. 99). Moreover, he convinces her that her own health might recover if she only had the care of one child instead of two. Reluctantly, his sister agrees.

During the long train ride back to his ranch, Arthur cuts several inches off of Joan's long hair, much to her delight.[108] When they arrive at the ranch, Joan discovers that all her cousins wear their hair short and dress in "denim knickerbockers," and she has some difficulty distinguishing the boys from the girls (p. 101). In this gender-neutral environment, Joan thrives. She learns to ride ponies, climb hills, garden, and, most important, she becomes skilled in self-defense. The formerly whiny, whimpering, long-haired girl is transformed into a bright, independent, and cheerful child. When she returns home after two years under her uncle's care, brother Gerald greets her with mixed emotions: "She was certainly as big as he was now. With her curls gone she was not so easy to hurt" (p. 102). When Gerald finally does taunt her, she calmly knocks him down. She is no longer a helpless girl but a strong and self-sufficient equal.

Tainted milk is the subject of "A Personal Motive," a story that appeared in the May 1913 edition of the *Forerunner*.[109] Like many Americans, Gilman was outraged by the public health risk in the early part of the twentieth century caused by adulterated food that was distributed and sold. The "personal motive" in this story is the revenge by two parents who vow to "ruin every milkman in New York" after their baby dies from ingesting tainted milk. The story line is weak and implausible, but Gilman's point in writing "A Personal Motive" was to encourage women to "re-establish the health of the human race" by providing their infant offspring with "mother's milk" rather than subjecting them to "tuberculous milk" from "an animal foster-mother, a quadruped with split hooves, with horns and tails, a gramnivorous bovine beast."[110]

Another story examining a public health risk is "An Offender."[111] The president of a streetcar company, who wants to reconcile with his ex-wife, refuses to make his cars safer because of the expense involved in doing so. The safety issue is of paramount importance to the ex-wife, however, and she is reluctant to remarry him since he is not "a man who cared to give perfect service to his country" (p. 4) by installing safety fenders on his cars. After he witnesses the grisly death of a child who is hit by one of his streetcars, he vows to make them safer. But for his ex-wife, it is too late. "You must go. And you must never come back," she tells him. "I cannot bear to see your face again" (p. 6).

Venereal disease is the subject of several of Gilman's stories, including "Wild Oats and Tame Wheat" (1913), "Cleaning Up Elita" (1916), and "The Vintage" (1916).[112] While "Wild Oats and Tame Wheat" is a parable and "Cleaning Up Elita" shows how one town rids itself of prostitution houses, "The Vintage" examines the effects of venereal disease on just one family. It is a remarkable, deftly sketched story, and it succeeds admirably in achieving Gilman's goal of what "true" literature should do: "teach us life easily, swiftly, truly . . . not by preaching but by truly re-presenting."[113] The theme of the story is simple: it depicts a family devastated by the effects of syphilis, and it provides an effective, albeit moralizing, warning against the potential consequences of succumbing to romantic self-delusion. As the tale begins, the narrator remarks that "This is not a short story." Indeed, the impact of the disease "stretches out for generations" and "its beginning was thousands of years ago" (*Yellow*, 104). But the disease transcends class and income, and Gilman chooses as her victim/heroine a member of a proud aristocratic southern family, Leslie Vauremont Barrington Montroy. The villain is her husband, Rodger Moore, whose failure to confront the truth about himself ultimately destroys those he purports to love. Gilman simultaneously instructs the reader about the evils of sexually transmitted diseases and implicitly promotes monogamy and honesty in relationships. After Leslie bears a son who is "a hopeless cripple" and eventually dies "in the prime of her womanhood" (pp. 106, 107), Rodger decides with "grim determination" to "make up to the boy for his loss." But eventually, when his son is a grown man, "his father saw how all his days and nights of ceaseless devotion had in no way made up to the boy for losing the common things of life" (p. 110). When Rodger's son announces that a woman has fallen in love with him despite the fact that he is "different" (p. 110) and expresses the hope that he will marry her and have "a little boy of my own, some day, to love as you have loved me" (p. 110), Rodger is forced "to tell his son that he must never marry—and why" (p. 111). The ending is poignantly rendered; when the truth is revealed, the wronged son, rather than blaming his father, altruistically tries to console him instead.

Another issue that Gilman trumpeted in both her fiction and her nonfiction was ethical standards in journalism. Her interest in the subject began after her separation from her first husband, Charles Walter Stetson, in the early 1890s. News of their impending divorce was highly publicized, and Gilman was clearly upset not only by the invasion of privacy but also by the inaccurate and sensationalist newspaper accounts that followed the announcement.[114] Gilman opined that too many American newspapers and magazines, particularly those published by

William Randolph Hearst, epitomized the practice of yellow journalism. She argued that in its "endeavor to reach the largest number of readers," Hearst's vicious and sensational stories preyed on "the lowest average mind."[115] An eloquent champion of ethical journalism, Gilman offered a reason for the enduring popularity of the yellow press: "[It] frankly plays on the lowest, commonest of its traits; tickling it with salacious detail, harping on those themes which unlettered peasants find attractive, and for which most people retain an unadmitted weakness" (*FR*, 315).

Gilman promoted the practice of ethical journalism in several essays, in half a dozen poems, and in several short stories in the *Forerunner*, including two in which journalistic misconduct is the central theme. In the April 1916 issue, for example, Gilman featured a story titled "His Excuse" to not only reflect her contempt for the disreputable reporters who distorted facts about her personal life on numerous occasions but also to censure the abuses of freedom of speech, which she found wholly reprehensible.[116]

The central character in "His Excuse," Norman Parker, is a talented young reporter who "set forth boldly to face the apprenticeship for his Life Work" (*Yellow*, 92). Parker proved so competent, Gilman tells us, "that he was offered better pay to do similar work on one of the Hearst papers." The narrative continues: "Parker was not in favor of this grade of journalism, but, he told himself, a man must not let his prejudices hinder his advancement. . . . Spurred by his editors, praised and well-paid for his successes, insensibly lowering his standards as his work required it convincing himself by easy arguments and the press of opinion all around him that what he did was essential to the profession—and so quite justifiable, he became a star reporter" (pp. 92–93). Parker surrenders his integrity to obtain his stories, and before long he unwittingly injures the reputation of a woman he once loved. By the time he confronts his own baseness, however, the damage is done.

In another story, "An Unwilling Interview," the antagonist is clearly modeled on Hearst.[117] In this work, Gilman creates a plot in which the owner of a large newspaper exploits his power by printing an incriminating story about the marriage of the son of his fiercest competitor. The story, which is full of innuendos based solely on hearsay, causes a major rift in the family and wreaks havoc in the lives of the newlyweds. Gilman uses a visiting aunt as a mouthpiece to castigate the reporter, Jay Whitstone, who is responsible for writing the inflammatory article: "To injure a helpless woman is the work of a coward. To pry into private affairs is the work of a spy. To obtain a confidence and betray it is the work of a tell-tale. To publish what is not true is to lie. To do all this in perfect safety, shielded by a great public power like the Press, and then . . . to blame the outraged public for your infamy—this neither law nor language can touch," she writes (*FR*, 89). Gilman's characterization of "a helpless woman" might seem to be at odds with her social rhetoric vis-à-vis gender equality, but it accurately reflects the vulnerability she felt and the victimization she experienced when her own "name became a football for all the papers on the [west] coast" (*Living*, 143).

Reporters like the fictional Whitstone justified their journalistic tactics by virtue of the public's desire to know. "What if it does [desire to know]?" Gilman retorted. "A newspaper reporter has no more right to intrude upon a private family and demand information as to their private affairs than has the ice-man," she argued (*FR*, 316). "That a number of people have the instincts of Peeping Tom does not give them the right to intrude upon personal privacy, nor does it give that right to those papers which pander to a depraved taste, and seek continually to deprave further the taste to which it panders," she insisted (p. 316).

Near the conclusion of *Women and Economics*, Gilman discusses the inevitability of human progress. "To introduce conditions that will change humanity from within, making for better motherhood and fatherhood, better babyhood and childhood, better food, better homes, better society,—this is to work for human improvement along natural lines. . . . All we need do is to understand and help," she wrote (p. 317). Much of her *Forerunner* fiction was intended to help the reader understand how humanity might be changed from within and how existing social problems could be remedied and human rights restored.

Utopian Communities

Although her best-known utopian work is the novel *Herland*, first published in 1915, Gilman produced several short stories depicting utopian communities. Utopian fiction, particularly that showing cooperative communities, provided the perfect forum for illustrating her idealized vision of a world reformed.

Gilman's interest in utopian worlds can be traced back to when, at the age of 10, she constructed a fantastic tale about a "Prince and Princess of magic powers, who went about the world collecting unhappy children and taking them to a guarded Paradise in the South Seas" (*Living*, 23). While the propensity for constructing imaginary worlds is common in children, Gilman, significantly, began to envision utopian worlds where the female gender used its intelligence, strength, and coopera-tion to effect positive social change. As Carol Farley Kessler notes in her study *Charlotte Perkins Gilman: Her Progress Toward Utopia*, the works in Gilman's childhood notebook, "The Literary and Artistic Vurks of the Princess Charlotte" (dated 1870–71), show "the beginnings of parodic wit and the need to bolster self-esteem, [and] that her progress toward *Herland* has already begun."[118]

While Gilman's curiosity about utopianism had its origins in her youth, her experiences in later years would fuel her interest. When she moved to California in 1888, that "state peculiarly addicted to swift enthusiasms" (*Living*, 122), Gilman became deeply interested in Edward Bellamy's utopian romance *Looking Backward*. She was drawn to Bellamy's emphasis on political equality and quickly became a convert to Nationalism, the movement spawned by Bellamy's novel. Based on the principles of reform Darwinism, Nationalism reflected a belief in environmental determinism and embraced the view that society would evolve peacefully and progressively. Gilman was particularly interested in Bellamy's emphasis on women's rights, and actively advocated eco-nomic independence and social motherhood, themes that recur in her fictional utopias.

Along with Bellamy, English author and socialist Jane Hume Clapper-ton, whom Gilman met in the fall of 1896, helped to shape Gilman's utopian ideals. In *The Vision of the Future, Based on the Application of Ethical Principles* (1904), Clapperton argues that human beings can actively guide social evolution, particularly since "unconscious evolution has car-ried us forward from savagery through many transitions to a state of civilisation which, though grossly imperfect, contains within it an ele-ment of advance."[119] That "advance" is depicted in various stories by Gilman, including her short parable "Freed," which presents her vision of a utopian world in which the historical roots of oppression have been erased.[120] After a strange chemical obliterates any trace of "The Past," a new world emerges in which "new truths" and "beauty [were] given to the world" (*Yellow*, 207). Racial strife, class discrimination, and gender inequality are things of the past, and "there arose a new art, rich and wide, and literature was re-born, coming forth with glad breaths, as one released from beneath a mountain of rubbish" (p. 208).

The depiction of an ideal world is, of course, repeated frequently in Gilman's stories. Her idealism not only evolved from her belief in mat-rimonial and gender equality but, in a larger sense, grew out of a rejection of the emphasis on material wealth during the Industrial Revolution and the Gilded Age. During the later *Forerunner* years, which overlapped with the onset of World War I, Gilman's vision of an ideal world became even more pronounced. Gilman strove to preserve the basic ideas and beliefs inherent in idealism by demonstrating in her fictional world how equality and democracy could be effected.

Herland, for example, satirizes sexism and inequality, and Gilman effectively exposes the absurdities and limitations of patriarchal practices and institutions. One of the major thematic emphases of Gilman's idealism is that what we refer to as "masculine" traits are, as Ann J. Lane points out, "simply human traits, which have been denied to women and are thereby assumed to belong to men: traits such as courage, strength, creativity, generosity, and integrity."[121] *Herland* humorously carries the point to the extreme, but Gilman's purpose in doing so was to demonstrate an alternative social vision. While the representation of the ideal is obvious in *Herland* and in other works featuring utopian landscapes, the impact of Gilmanian idealism spills over, perhaps more subtly, into much of her short fiction as well. At the center of the majority of her short works, there is, in fact, an emphasis on the ideal, particularly through reeducating society about the benefits inherent in removing women from the exclusive (and exclusionary) realms of the domestic and the maternal and eliminating the roots of patriarchal oppression. While one could conceivably argue, in fact, that idealism and utopianism are one and the same (and hence, a utopian vision characterizes nearly all of Gilman's fictional works), for the purposes of this study, discussion will be limited specifically to Gilman's promotion of utopian communities.

Perhaps the story that best illustrates Gilman's ideas about the benefits of community living is "Her Memories" (1912).[122] The advantages of living in a high-rise apartment are elaborated on by a middle-aged woman, who corrects her unenlightened male companion's misconceptions. Through her reminiscences, she describes an environment that is a virtual utopia, where bluebirds and scarlet tanagers bathe in rooftop pools, and gardens grow thick with ferns, vines, shrubs, and an assortment of flowers. "There were day-nurseries and play-rooms and kindergartens and school-rooms—it was a kind of paradise," she tells her companion (p. 177). The idea of social motherhood has been perfected, and the children "grew up like sunbeams" under the proper care of a community mother (p. 178). The "pleasure resort" is, in effect, a self-contained community: it boasts gymnasiums, a bowling alley, swimming pools, baths, club rooms, and "big entertainment rooms—for dances and lectures" (p. 179). One of the most important features, the woman remarks, is the kitchenless apartments, with food sent up via a service elevator. This way, "Mamma goes to her work and papa goes to his work . . . and by and by they all come back—and then it's [a] home again" (p. 181). These are the same arguments Gilman advanced in *Women and Economics*, in which she advocated architectural remedies to the home. Like Olive Schreiner's world in "Three Dreams in a Desert," Gilman's utopias are not necessarily worlds in which men have no place; more often, men and women are given the opportunity to peacefully coexist as equal partners.

In another story, "Boone Farm" (1914), several brothers and sisters come together to transform their old homestead into a peaceful country resort featuring guest cottages.[123] Although financial security is their immediate concern, Gilman also demonstrates the benefits of cooperative ventures offering "a healthy place" that people will flock to for rest and recuperation. Each sibling has a particular talent, and when their resources are pooled, they all reap the rewards. Some are experienced in child care, some in cooking, and one is content "foreseeing steady work" (*FR*, 200). The youngest sibling, Alva, "roaming here and there, from the breezy pine-topped hill that crowned the place and showed the lovely world so wide and fair, to the cool green shade around the spring—that clear pool, paved and banked with big round stones, and set about with crowding ferns and long-stemmed violets; from the curving willow-darkened stretches of the placid river, to the broad silver of the lake; saw everywhere the lovely results of his unnoticed labor, and planned a richer, larger beauty for it all" (p. 200). His brother-in-law, Otto, "planned to invest his little capital as caterer for Boone Farm, and saw to it that the kitchen was both scientific and attractive" (p. 200). Sister Amanda demands that the guest cottages be comfortable: "Good towels, clean and plenty. Sheets that tuck in and turn over. . . . Blankets, light but woolly . . . closets—and bureaus" (p. 201). Together, the siblings realize their dream, and "from year to year Boone Farm grew in beauty, and in the wise blending of resources" (p. 201). In an earlier story, "Maidstone Comfort" (1912), Gilman likewise features kitchenless cottages and advocates shared resources as a way to implement change.

"Bee Wise" (1913) is a story about a group of enterprising women who establish two utopian communities in California.[124] As Kessler points out, "The story fully anticipates *Herland*" (p. 211). Indeed, the communities in "Bee Wise" contain many of the same amenities as those described in *Herland*, including sensible clothing, baby-gardens, and kitchenless homes. Some significant differences exist, however. First, the communities in "Bee Wise" are funded with 10 million dollars bequeathed to a young woman by her dying great-uncle. Second, unlike the women in *Herland*, the women of Beewise and Herways, a sister community, "had no objection to marrying on their own terms" (p. 217). Moreover, "the men were carefully selected. They must prove clean health—for a high grade of motherhood was the continuing ideal of the group" (p. 217). Gilman makes it perfectly clear, however, that the women are self-reliant and absolutely in control of their destinies. The story serves as yet another treatise-in-miniature of Gilman's life philosophy: that work is the "first duty of a human being" (*Living*, 42). The narrator of "Bee Wise" writes, "Everyone in Herways and Beewise worked, especially the women—that was the prime condition of admission," that they must be "valuable in social service" (*Progress*, 218). Gilman also has fun with the pun in the story's title. Not only is she encouraging the reader to "be wise," but the metaphorical association of "busy bees" underscores the extraordinary benefits of cooperative work in the utopian "hive."

After the unequivocal success of the initial two utopian communities, the women begin building "another rational paradise in another beautiful valley" (p. 219). "But far wider than their own immediate increase was the spread of their ideas, of the proven truth of their idea, that a group of human beings could live together in such wise as to . . . ensure health, peace and prosperity, and multiply human happiness beyond measure," says the narrator (p. 219). Perhaps anticipating skepticism from those who might point out that 10 million dollars to fund a utopian community is not available to the average person, Gilman has the narrator state that "The economic base might vary widely, but wherever there were a few hundred women banded together their combined labor could produce wealth, and their combined motherhood ensure order, comfort, happiness, and the improvement of humanity" (p. 219).

In "A Council of War" (1913), a group of women vote to establish "a world within a world" populated by a community of peaceful women (p. 228).[125] After realizing the extent to which "the evil results of male rule" have affected "the health, beauty, intelligence, prosperity, progress and happiness of humanity," the women decide to wage "war" to "establish a free and conscious womanhood for the right service of the world" (p. 223). This story is essentially a "how-to" guide; unlike some of the others, "A Council of War" merely recounts the steps necessary to effect change, and it ends with the women forming a committee to investigate further, "with the light of a new hope in their eyes" (p. 228).

Gilman's experience during the first two weeks of August 1897 at Summer Brook Farm in New York's Adirondack mountains may have shaped her ideas about the communities represented in her utopian short fiction. Summer Brook Farm, operated by *American Fabian* manager Prestonia Mann, was a "unique establishment" to which "interesting people of a progressive tendency" were invited (*Living*, 230). Gilman described Summer Brook Farm as a "*[l]ovely* place, way up at the head of Keene Valley," with a "most beautiful house, and glorious mountains" (*Diaries*, 1 August 1897). Like the patient in "Dr. Clair's Place," Gilman found the "bright and jolly" surroundings to be therapeutic, and spent part of each day walking, mountain climbing, and berry picking. "Two competent maids . . . did the cooking . . . but all the rest of the work was done by the guests" (*Living*, 230). Moreover, like the people who came to Dr. Clair's Place—"some teachers, some writers, some makers of various things"—Summer Brook Farm's inhabitants were "gallant college professors and high-minded poets" (p. 230).

Short Sermons

Approximately one-fourth of the 186 stories that Gilman published during her lifetime represent the genre that she classified as "short sermons."[126] Comprised of parables, fables, satirical pieces, and allegorical tales, Gilman used her short sermons, like her other fiction, to advance her position on everything from gender equality and social motherhood to hypocrisy and venereal disease. Some of the sermons are enigmatic; others are iconoclastic in their condemnation, and all are imbued with Gilman's social insights and crafted with insight and imagination. Gilman's earliest published story, "A Transparency" (mentioned earlier), a sermon on brotherhood, appeared in the December 1886 issue of *Alpha*.

While the number of short sermons far exceeds the scope of this study, several merit mention because of their effective expression of Gilmanian philosophy, particularly on controversial issues. "The Sensible Dead Man" (1911), for example, reflects Gilman's advocacy of cremation, her belief that headstones are nothing more than a wasteful extravagance, and her conviction that it makes more sense to venerate the living than the dead.[127] Presented as a conversation between a Dead Man and a group of Inquirers who have brought him back to the world of the living, though "how . . . no one knew" (*FR*, 106), the story reveals Gilman's views not only about society's fear of death but also about our blind adherence to various death rituals. While the Inquirers beg the Dead Man for knowledge "of The Beyond, of the Hereafter, of the Life After Death," the Dead Man is more interested in exploding social myths about death. While the Inquirers squirm at the "horrible" thought of cremation, insisting that they cannot bring their "delicate minds" to think about "what happens in the Oven," the Dead Man dismisses their views as "indefensible idiocies" (p. 106). Like Gilman, the Dead Man sees cremation as a practical measure, since "what you put in the ground" is eventually "turned into good potatoes and apples and wheat—maybe roses" (p. 106). The Dead Man's observation leaves the Inquirers "silent with pale disgust" (p. 106). When the Inquirers argue that they use headstones to honor the memory of the deceased, the Dead Man responds that "foolish stone piles" are a "waste [of] good money" (pp. 107, 106). "You never honored me when I was alive and useful," the Dead Man reminds them. He also makes the point that it is an "awful waste [to spend] good money on that solemn performance you call a Funeral" and suggests that the money might be better used by "the widows and orphans" still living (p. 107). "Why . . . spend all this money on The Remains?" he asks (p. 107). After all, if society believes "that the Soul goes on to Joy Eternal," then it seems inconsistent to "make such a fuss over losing him," the Dead Man reasons (p. 107). Gilman was herself cremated, as was her mother before her.[128] By directly confronting the reality of "what happens in the coffin" (p. 107), Gilman, the pragmatist, forces her readers to examine traditional death rituals, which she depicts as costly, wasteful, and highly impractical.

Motherhood is a topic that Gilman addressed frequently. In "Her Doll"(1911), a parable focusing on unfit mothers, Gilman uses a doll as a metaphor for an infant.[129] The story begins with the "pretty sight" of a "Little Girl" holding her doll to her bosom and "crooning lullabies." When her doll "was sick she was consumed with grief; . . . when it was well, she proudly walked with it in the street, wheeling it in a little carriage." The Little Girl enjoys dressing her doll and keeping it clean, but "she had also a Deep Concern for the Behavior of her Doll." Because the Little Girl had herself been "held rigidly to a narrow code of good behavior," which amounted to being "Imprisoned and Restricted," she "quite naturally required it of her Doll." When the Doll wet itself or soiled its fine garments, the Little Girl "was severe with her Doll," causing the narrator to speculate about the Little Girl's maternal proclivities and about her preparedness for motherhood. "I saw her punish it one day, and the Doll cried loud and long. I was much concerned. It did not seem to me quite right that she should be allowed to play as she liked with a Doll that was alive" (p. 183).

The story not only comments on the inadvisability of children having children but also implicitly makes a point about the impractical standards adults impose on children. They must be not only polite, obedient, and good but clothed in apparel that is not suited for their natural spontaneity, an issue Gilman addressed in *Concerning Children*, in her memoirs, and in various essays on the topic.[130] On the same page on which "Her Doll" appears, Gilman includes a poem as a companion to the story, titled "What Hope." "We may seek in a lap-dog intelligence high," Gilman writes, "But what training for life, either body or mind, / May be hoped for the doll of a doll?" (p. 183).

Gilman proposes a solution to the problem of maternal incompetence in "The Permanent Child" (1910), one of her strongest pleas for social motherhood.[131] "The Child does not need [maternal] sacrifice. It needs Wisdom and Freedom and Knowledge and Power. It needs Social Motherhood—the conscious, united Mother Love and Mother Care of the Whole World," she writes (p. 17). The story illustrates a mother's dawning awareness that to simply love her child is not enough. As Gilman argues in "The New Motherhood" (pp. 17–18), "child culture . . . requires high specialization" from those women who are "naturally fitted to it" (p. 17). Mothers who are also social servants are infinitely better for their children, Gilman maintains, in terms of both their own satisfaction and providing more positive role models.

Gilman's point is captured beautifully in the little tale "Two Storks" (1910), which playfully addresses women's multifaceted dimensions.[132] A young male stork thrilled by impending fatherhood assiduously helps his pregnant wife build a nest, and after their "downy wide-mouthed" hatchlings are born, he "devoutly" performs "his share of the brooding" and diligently assists in keeping them fed. When autumn arrives, however, and hunting becomes more difficult, the young male stork dreams of a warmer climate where ponds would be "teeming with fat frogs" (*Yellow*, 203). With each passing day, the imperative to fly to a land of "blue water and green land" becomes stronger, and one day he bids his wife and children adieu. When his wife announces that she and the children plan to accompany him, "He was shocked; grieved, astonished. 'Why, my Dear,' he said. 'How preposterous! You cannot go on the Great Flight! Your wings are for brooding tender little ones! . . . You cannot go!' " She ignores his protests, however, causing him to weep, "for his highest ideals were shattered" (p. 204). But the Mother Stork and the Precious Little Ones joyfully take flight. When the male stork catches up to them, he renews his objection. "But you are a Mother!" he reminds her, citing the impropriety of her flight from their home. " 'Yes!' she cried joyously, 'but I was a Stork before I was a Mother! and afterward!—and All the Time!' " (p. 204).

Similarly, in "The Lady Oyster" (1912), the Oyster's sole purpose is to fulfill the "law of her being, the process of maternity" (p. 210).[133] Although the Lady Oyster is largely immobile, unable to "creep, walk, run, jump, climb [or] fly," she "could and did produce Three Million Eggs" (p. 210). When a Captious Crab cynically notes that it has done the Lady Oyster no good to produce three million eggs, The Lady Oyster responds, "It is nothing to me what happens to them afterward. I have done my duty. . . . I am a Mother!" (p. 210). The same scenario is played out between a Mud-wasp and A Benevolent Bee, a Lady Sheep and a Skeptical Skunk, and a Lovely Lady and an Audacious Aunt. Like the others, the Lovely Lady "had fulfilled the law of her being, the process of maternity" (p. 211). When the Audacious Aunt points out that the Lovely Lady has brought into the world a child who "will grow up among deserts of ignorance, forests of prejudice; surrounded by dangers and temptations," and that perhaps the Lovely Lady should "rouse up and do something for your children," the Lady responds complacently that she has done her duty and she "now will rear a child. I am a mother," she repeats. "But the Audacious Aunt said, 'Huh! So is an Oyster!' " (p. 212). Gilman's point, of course, is that reproduction may be the natural law of the universe, but motherhood requires intelligence, wisdom, and proper training.

In "Improving on Nature" (1912), Mother Nature, having been asleep for "thousands of years" (p. 213), awakens suddenly to the sound of a screaming woman.[134] Like Irving's Rip Van Winkle, she discovers that during her slumber the world has dramatically changed. Man explains to her that "his female" is "behaving in an abominable and unheard-of manner" and "trying to be a man" (p. 213). When Man "exhibited with fond pride the female of the species," however, Mother Nature can only laugh at the sight of the "plump, pink little person; hobbled, stilted, and profusely decorated," who stands before her (p. 213). To each of Mother Nature's questions about her size and ridiculous appearance, the woman responds, "He likes us that way." She explains that man will marry only small, weak, impractically attired women who are willing to stay at home. Mother Nature is dismayed by what she learns, particularly after Man confirms that what the woman says is true. "The female must be small and weak and foolish and timid and ineffi- cient—because she is a female. 'That,' he said pompously, 'is the Law of Nature!' " (p. 214). Mother Nature becomes infuriated by his sexist assumptions and vows to remake the race of women. "Develop your brains and muscles; earn your own livings; be bought by no man; and choose the kind with which you wish to replenish the earth," she instructs the unenlightened women (p. 216). This is precisely the type of doctrine that Gilman spent a lifetime preaching.

Relationships between men and women are also explored in "Wild Oats and Tame Wheat" (1913), a short piece that examines the spread of venereal disease by a man who indiscriminately engages in sexual relations "freely, whereby he flattered himself that he learned to know women, and boasted thereof with his fellow scholars" (p. 218).[135] After "having sown his wild oats" and acquiring "one or two diseases" in the process, the man chooses to marry "a damsel young, innocent, in the bloom of maidenhood" (p. 218). Unlike the man, the woman has sown no wild oats, "but much tame wheat" (p. 218). She is the kind of woman Gilman describes in *Women and Economics* who engages in "eco- nomic beggary" (*WE*, 89) by learning to cook, clean, knit, mend, and sew, with the goal of "attaining her one hope—a husband" (*Yellow*, 218). Interestingly, Gilman uses this piece to implicate the woman and her upbringing every bit as much as the man. "In the shelter of the home she had lived; in walled gardens she had walked; in public she was veiled and guarded; the books allowed her told her little; her education was strictly limited; vice, license, and bad habits she but vaguely knew were in the world" (p. 218). Gilman concludes that for women to blindly accept the sowing of "tame wheat" as part of their socialization is not only stultifying but also dangerous.

That it is never too late to change one's attitudes is the message of a clever story titled "The Old Woman and The New Year"(1911).[136] The "old woman" is 60—not old by contemporary standards, to be sure, but she bemoans her lost youth, her stiff hands, her gray hair, her withered face, and her frail frame. "Why can I not die!" she wonders, only to be answered by the "small, cheerful voice" of an infant who allegorically represents the New Year. "You have to begin again like the rest of us, turn over a new leaf," he tells the self-pitying woman (*FR*, 19). The New

Year vows "to perform a surgical operation" on the old woman's soul so she can begin to enjoy life again. He breaks apart her "Custom and Convention," tears loose her "Stagnant Traditions," rips up "the bonds of Age-old Habit," and dislodges the "Inherited Ideas which had clogged her mind" (p. 19). The old woman experiences a rebirth and views life through newly awakened eyes. The ending of the story is somewhat ambiguous, failing to answer whether the woman has merely been dreaming or whether she has actually undergone a life-altering experience: "A heavy metal tongue boomed twelve in the clear winter's night, and a thousand deep-throated whistles, thin horns and every chiming bell in town burst into high rejoicing. It was the New Year" (p. 20).

A lesson in perspective is the subject of "On a Branch"(1913), a fable featuring a conversation between an ant and an eagle.[137] The ant is "an Observing Ant, studious as well as busy, and possessed of a scientific mind" (p. 46). The ant has studied the branch of a tall tree thoroughly, even counting the number of mites that inhabit it. When one day an Eagle alights on her branch, the Observing Ant points out the branch's "various qualities and attractions" (p. 46). When the Ant questions the Eagle about his observations of the world, he regales her with vivid descriptions of the forest, mountains, rivers, seas, deserts, and prairies. When he has finished, the Ant inquires about the mites. " 'The mites?' asked the Eagle. 'I do not understand.' 'I see,' said the Ant, sadly but firmly. 'What you know is after all only a smattering' " (p. 47). Gilman's discourse on vision and perspective is intended as a commentary on how a superficial view of the world provides a woefully inadequate understanding of nature.

A parable addressing dress reform, "A Poor Joke," was published in 1913.[138] A Devil, "seeking amusement," devises a way for men "to torment themselves" so that he might derive enjoyment from their pain. He enters the minds of the men who design clothing, and they begin to manufacture garments that "torture" the bodies of those who wear them. "More especially was all this done to women," the narrator reminds us (*FR*, 270). "The human body was desecrated, deformed, tormented, and made contemptible by the things they put upon it" (p. 270). Health was imperiled, purses were taxed, bodies exposed, but people kept wearing the uncomfortable clothing, the narrator says. More significant, they grew to like these torturous garments, much to the dismay of the Devil. "If all this ugliness and expense and labor and pain and care and gross discomfort are being enjoyed, it is a very poor joke indeed," the Devil reasons. "If I can make a woman into a grotesque, tottering cripple and she still thinks she is beautiful—and men think so, too—where is the fun?" (p. 271). But the Devil's disappointment is short-lived, since the garment makers continue to manufacturer and sell uncomfortable clothing, even "outdoing the Devil's devisers" (p. 271). This tale underscores Gilman's contempt for women's fashions, which, she held, were ridiculous and impractical.

Like her other fiction, Gilman's short sermons were avowedly didactic, and almost all of the topics she addressed had companion pieces in other genres. Her singular purpose was to get people to reenvision the world, to recognize hypocrisy, and to work toward progressive change. When the *Forerunner* ceased publication in 1916, Gilman's career as a fiction writer was effectively over. Her readership never approached the three thousand needed to make it self-sustaining, but she was still satisfied by her endeavor. In her autobiography, Gilman reports being "most agreeably surprised by the acceptance of so much of what I had to offer" (*Living*, 308). Moreover, she conceded that one cannot seek to change "the ideas, feelings and habits of the people and expect them to like it" (p. 308). Nevertheless, Gilman never gave up trying to do exactly that.

Notes to Part 1

1. Howells reprinted "The Yellow Wall-Paper" in his anthology *The Great Modern American Stories* (New York: Boni and Liveright, 1920).

2. *The Living of Charlotte Perkins Gilman* (New York: Appleton-Century, 1935; rpt. Madison: University of Wisconsin Press, 1990), 121. Hereafter, *Living*.

3. Mary A. Hill, ed., *Endure: The Diaries of Charles Walter Stetson* (Philadelphia: Temple University Press, 1985), 291. Hereafter, *Endure*.

4. Gilman to Caroline Hill, 4 December 1921, folder 143, Gilman Papers, Schlesinger Library, Radcliffe College. Quoted by permission.

5. Charlotte Perkins Gilman, "A Summary of Purpose," *Forerunner* 7 (November 1916): 286–90. Hereafter, "Summary."

6. Gilman to Houghton Gilman, 11 May 1897, folder 41, Gilman Papers, Schlesinger Library, Radcliffe College. Quoted by permission.

7. Gilman to Houghton Gilman, 22 May 1898, folder 51, Gilman Papers, Schlesinger Library, Radcliffe College. Quoted by permission. Charlotte Stetson married Houghton Gilman on 11 June 1900, at age 39.

8. Mary Austin, *Earth Horizon: Autobiography* (Boston: Houghton Mifflin Co., 1932), 326.

9. Gilman, "To My Real Readers," *Forerunner* 7 (December 1916): 327.

10. Gilman, "Coming Changes in Literature," *Forerunner* 6 (September 1915): 232.

11. *Topeka State Journal*, 15 June 1896.

12. Diary entry dated 9 November 1883. Denise D. Knight, ed., *The Diaries of Charlotte Perkins Gilman*, vol. 1 (Charlottesville: University Press of Virginia, 1994), 233. Hereafter, *Diaries*.

13. In a collection of miscellaneous notes titled "Thoughts and Figgerings, 1920–1935," Gilman makes two undated references to the painting "The Woman Against The Wall" in conjunction with her plans for writing her autobiography. In her notes for the chapter titled "The Breakdown," Gilman wrote: "The degree of weariness. Those *pictures*. The Woman by the Wall . . . & that ghastly photo." On another scrap of paper, she wrote herself a reminder: "To Put In [the autobiography] . . . Photographs—all the way up. If I can, find that picture of the Woman by the Wall." Folder 17, Gilman Papers, Schlesinger Library, Radcliffe College. Quoted by permission.

14. " 'The Yellow Wall Paper'—Its History & Reception." Undated typescript, box 17, folder 221, Gilman Papers, Schlesinger Library, Radcliffe College. Quoted by permission. Hereafter, "History."

15. Gilman's language in the undated typescript (cf. note 14) is somewhat different from the language in her memoirs. See part 2.

16. Gilman, "Why I Wrote 'The Yellow Wallpaper'?" *Forerunner* 4 (October 1913): 271. Hereafter, *FR*.

17. Elaine Hedges, " 'Out at Last'? 'The Yellow Wallpaper' after Two Decades of Feminist Criticism," in *The Captive Imagination: A Casebook on The Yellow*

Wallpaper, Catherine Golden, ed. (New York: Feminist Press, 1992), 319–33. Reprinted in *Critical Essays on Charlotte Perkins Gilman*, Joanne B. Karpinski, ed. (New York: G. K. Hall, 1992), 222–33. Reprinted in part 3 of this [Twayne] edition.

18. Amy Wellington, "Charlotte Perkins Gilman," in *Women Have Told: Studies in the Feminist Tradition* (Boston: Little, Brown, 1930), 118.

19. Gilman, "The Yellow Wall-Paper," *New England Magazine* (January 1892): 647–56; rpt., with an afterword by Elaine Hedges (Old Westbury: Feminist Press, 1973), 9. Page numbers in the text refer to the 1973 reprint edition. Hereafter, *YW.*

20. See for example Annette Kolodny's "A Map for Rereading: Or, Gender and the Interpretation of Literary Texts," *New Literary History* 11, no. 3 (1980): 451–67. Reprinted in *The Captive Imagination: A Casebook on The Yellow Wallpaper*, Catherine Golden, ed. (New York: Feminist Press, 1992), 149–67.

21. See Denise D. Knight, ed., *"The Yellow Wall-Paper" and Selected Stories of Charlotte Perkins Gilman* (Newark: University of Delaware Press, 1994) for the original manuscript version of the story. Hereafter, *Yellow.*

22. Kate Chopin, *The Awakening* (New York: Norton Co., 1976), 57.

23. William Veeder, "Who is Jane? The Intricate Feminism of Charlotte Perkins Gilman," *Arizona Quarterly* 44 (Autumn 1988): 40–79.

24. Ann J. Lane, *To "Herland" and Beyond: The Life and Work of Charlotte Perkins Gilman* (New York: Pantheon, 1990), 129.

25. In her diary entry for 5 February 1887, Gilman noted that she had resumed her "course of reading" after a two-week break, in order "to oblige" Walter. Stetson wrote in his diary on 9 February 1887 that "Charlotte of late has been so absorbed in the woman question—suffrage, other wrongs, that she has tired me dreadfully with it" (*Endure*, 331).

26. Martha Luther was Charlotte's longtime girlhood friend, with whom she "knew perfect happiness" (*Living*, 78). When Luther decided to marry Charles A. Lane, from Hingham, Massachusetts, Charlotte was devastated. "It was the keenest, the hardest, the most lasting pain I had yet known," she wrote (p. 80).

27. Gilman to Martha Luther Lane, 27 July 1890, Rhode Island Historical Society.

28. Significantly, in a poem titled "Locked Inside," first published in *Forerunner* 8 (January 1910) and later reprinted in *Woman's Journal* and *Suffrage Songs and Verses*, Gilman seems to concede that she possessed the power to effect change all along. The poem reads:

> She beats upon her bolted door,
> With faint weak hands;
> Drearily walks the narrow floor;

Sullenly sits, blank walls before;
Despairing stands.

Life calls her, Duty, Pleasure, Gain—
Her dreams respond;
But the blank daylights wax and wane,
Dull peace, sharp agony, slow pain—
No hope beyond.

Till she comes a thought! She lifts her head,
The world grows wide!
A voice—as if clear words were said—
"Your door, o long imprisoned,
Is locked inside!"

29. [Eliza D. Keith] Di Vernon, "Charlotte Perkins Stetson," *San Francisco News Letter* (28 March 1891): 5.

30. Since 1973 "The Yellow Wall-Paper" has been widely interpreted as a feminist text. Prior to that, it was regarded primarily, although not exclusively, as a gothic horror story, in part because of Gilman's allusions to such details as "ancestral halls," "a colonial mansion," and "a haunted house." William Dean Howells reports "shivering" over the story in his introduction to *The Great Modern American Stories* (1920), and Walter Stetson remarked that the story "beat Poe" (Stetson to Martha Luther Lane, 27 July 1890, Rhode Island Historical Society).

31. "The Giant Wistaria," *New England Magazine* 4 (June 1891): 480–85; rpt. with an introductory essay by Gloria A. Biamonte in *Legacy: A Journal of Nineteenth-Century American Writers* 5.2 (1988): 33–38. A critical essay by Gary Scharnhorst followed by a reprint of the story appeared in *Frontier Gothic: Terror and Wonder at the Frontier in American Literature*, David Mogen et al., eds. (Rutherford, NJ: Fairleigh Dickinson University Press, 1993), 156–174. Page numbers in the text refer to the 1891 edition. "The Rocking-Chair," *Worthington's Illustrated* 1 (May 1893): 453–59; rpt. *Boston Budget* (25 June 1893): 10. Page numbers in the text refer to the May 1893 edition. "The Unwatched Door" was published in 1894; cf. note 53. Gilman read Poe's tales in the 1880s. See, for example, her diary entries for 9 and 12 January 1885 and 21 March 1887.

32. *Diaries*, 4 and 11 March 1890.

33. Cf. note 31; Scharnhorst, 162.

34. Cf. note 31; Biamonte, 37.

35. *Diaries*, 26 August 1890.

36. Juliann E. Fleenor, "The Gothic Prism: Charlotte Perkins Gilman's Gothic Stories and Her Autobiography," in *The Female Gothic* (Montreal: Eden Press, Inc., 1983), 231.

37. The San Francisco *Examiner* published a sensational account of Gilman's impending divorce from Walter Stetson in 1892. That story was followed by several others over the next two years. In a diary entry dated 23 February 1893, Gilman's frustration with unscrupulous reporters is apparent: "The *Examiner* sends a man, Mr. Todd, to interview me on my views on the Marriage Question—the decrease of marriage [in society]. I refuse on the ground of the *Examiner*'s reputation—[I] will not write for the paper. He begs, he tries to fool me into conversation, he argues, he offers to pay me, he threatens covertly—I succeed in getting rid of him. Am exhausted by the contest, however."

38. "That Rare Jewel," *Woman's Journal* (17 May 1890): 158.

39. "The Unexpected," *Kate Field's Washington (*21 May 1890): 335–36; rpt. *Boston Budget* (29 June 1890): 10, *Forerunner* (November 1913): 281–84, and Knight, 115–21. Page numbers in the text refer to Knight's edition.

40. "My Poor Aunt," *Kate Field's Washington* (7 January 1891): 9–11; rpt. *Forerunner* (December 1913): 309–313. Page numbers in the text refer to the *Forerunner* edition.

41. "Society and the Philosopher," *Kate Field's Washington* (18 February 1891): 109; rpt. *Forerunner* (April 1914): 93–94. Page numbers refer to the reprint edition. "Society and the Baby," *Kate Field's Washington* (18 March 1891): 165–66; rpt. *Woman Worker* (London)(24 November 1909): 482. Page numbers refer to the original edition. "An Extinct Angel," *Kate Field's Washington* (23 September 1891): 199–200.

42. "A Walk for Two," *Pacific Monthly* (May 1891): 194–98.

43. "Their Dressmaker," *Woman's Journal* (25 June 1904): 202.

44. *Impress* 1 (6 October 1894): 4.

45. "Clifford's Tower," *Impress* (27 October 1894): 4–5. Portions of this discussion were drawn from my essay "such a hopeless task before her: Some Observations on Hawthorne and Gilman," in *Scribbling Women: Engendering and Expanding the Hawthorne Tradition*, John Idol and Melinda M. Ponder, eds. (Amherst: University of Massachusetts Press, 1997).

46. "Story Studies," *Impress* 1 (3 November 1894): 4.

47. The opening-night performance was staged on 1 January 1877. Gary Scharnhorst, ed., *The Critical Response to Nathaniel Hawthorne's The Scarlet Letter* (Westport, CT: Greenwood Press, 1992), xxv.

48. *Diaries*, 20 August 1882 and 25 December 1883.

49. Richard S. Brodhead, *The School of Hawthorne* (New York: Oxford University Press, 1985), 65.

50. "Story Studies," *Impress* 1 (3 November 1894): 4.

51. The Hawthornean themes of obsession, sin, and morality can be seen not only in "Clifford's Tower" but in the following pieces: "Her Beauty," *Forerunner* 4 (February 1913): 29–33; "His Mother," *Forerunner* 5 (July 1914): 169–73; reprinted in Knight, 73–80; and "The Vintage," *Forerunner* 7 (October 1916): 253–57; reprinted in Knight, 104–11.

52. Nathaniel Hawthorne, *The Scarlet Letter*, ed. Seymour Gross et al., 3rd ed. (New York: Norton, 1988), 177.

53. "The Unwatched Door," *Impress* (8 December 1894): 4–5.

54. "Story Studies," *Impress* (15 December 1894): 5.

55. I am grateful to Twain scholar Michael J. Kiskis for sharing with me his insights into "An Unpatented Process." Kiskis has brought to my attention several of Twain's domestic stories in which a clash between a clearheaded woman and a forgetful man is a central theme, including "Mrs. McWilliams and the Lightening" (1880) and "The McWilliamses and the Burglar Alarm" (1882).

56. "Story Studies," *Impress* (5 January 1895): 5.

57. "A Day's Berryin'," *Impress* (13 October 1894): 4–5; rpt. Knight, 195–98. Page numbers refer to the reprint edition. "Ad'line," *Impress* (3 November 1894): 4–5; rpt. Knight, 199–202. Page numbers refer to the reprint edition.

58. "Story Studies," *Impress* (20 October 1894): 5.

59. "Story Studies," *Impress* (10 November 1894): 5.

60. "Circumstances Alter Cases," *Kate Field's Washington* (23 July 1890): 55–56; rpt. *Boston Budget* (17 August 1890): 10, and *Forerunner* (April 1914): 85–88. Page numbers in the text refer to the *Forerunner* edition.

61. For several months in 1892, Gilman assumed the management of the Oakland, California, boardinghouse where she was living. Mary Westcott Perkins died at the boardinghouse in the early morning hours of 7 March 1893. In July 1893, Gilman ended an intense personal relationship with Adeline E. ("Delle") Knapp, a journalist for the *San Francisco Call*.

62. *Diaries*, 13 September 1892.

63. Portions of this discussion were drawn from my essay "The Reincarnation of Jane: 'Through This'—Gilman's Companion to 'The Yellow Wall-Paper,' " *Women's Studies* 20, no. 3/4 (1992): 287–302.

64. "Through This," *Kate Field's Washington* (13 September 1893): 166; rpt. *"The Yellow Wall-Paper" and Selected Stories of Charlotte Perkins Gilman*, Denise D. Knight, ed. (Newark: University of Delaware Press, 1994), 54–56. Page numbers in the text refer to the reprint edition.

65. Gilman, *Women and Economics. A Study of the Economic Relation Between Men and Women as a Factor in Social Evolution* (Boston: Small, Maynard & Co., 1898; rpt. New York: Harper & Row, 1966), 89. Hereafter, *WE*.

66. Gilman, *The Home: Its Work and Influence* (New York: McClure, Phillips, 1903; rpt., Urbana: University of Illinois Press, 1972). Hereafter, *Home*.

67. Conrad Shumaker, "Too Terribly Good to Be Printed: Charlotte Perkins Gilman's 'The Yellow Wallpaper,' " *American Literature* 57 (December 1985): 588–599.

68. "An Unnatural Mother," *Impress* (16 February 1895): 4–5. An abridged version appeared in *Forerunner* 4 (June 1913): 141–43. The original version of the story was reprinted in *Forerunner* 7 (November 1916):281–85, under the title "The Unnatural Mother." It was reprinted in *Charlotte Perkins Gilman*

Reader, ed. Ann J. Lane (New York, Pantheon, 1980), 57–65. Page numbers in the text refer to Lane's edition. Hereafter, *CPG*.

69. Gilman to Houghton Gilman, 25 December 1899, Schlesinger Library. See also *Living*, 275–76.

70. Ann J. Lane, *To Herland and Beyond: The Life and Work of Charlotte Perkins Gilman* (New York: Pantheon, 1990), 324.

71. Harriet Howe, "Charlotte Perkins Gilman—As I Knew Her," *Equal Rights: Independent Feminist Weekly* (5 September 1936): 211–16.

72. Austin, 293.

73. "The Lake of Mrs. Johnsmith," *The Criterion* (22 October 1898): 3–4.

74. "Mary Button's Principles," *Forerunner* (July 1912): 169–72; rpt. Knight, 57–61. Page numbers in the text refer to the reprint edition.

75. American poet Edwin Markham (1852–1940) achieved fame with "The Man with the Hoe," published in 1899.

76. "The Hypnotizer," *Forerunner* (October 1914): 253–56; rpt. Knight, 81–87. Page numbers in the text refer to the reprint edition.

77. "Spoken To," *Forerunner* (February 1915): 29–33.

78. Until her marriage to Stetson in 1884, Charlotte Anna Perkins lived at home with her mother. For much of that time, her aunt Caroline resided with them, as did her older brother Thomas until 1879. Gilman's father moved out of the house when she a child.

79. Gilman was instrumental in garnering support for the Providence Ladies Gymnasium. See *Living*, 66–67. The correct date for the opening of the gymnasium in *Living* is fall 1881 rather than 1891.

80. In her diary entry for 26 March 1879, Gilman reports that she read *Daisy Miller* that day, but she did not record her impression of the work.

81. James's Mr. Giovanelli is described as a "low-lived foreigner" with a "wonderful moustache," "a handsome face . . . a brilliant smile," an "intelligent eye," and "an artfully poised hat" that he waves "with a too emphatic flourish."

82. "Dr. Clair's Place," *Forerunner* (June 1915): 141–45; rpt. Knight, 177–84. Page numbers in the text refer to the reprint edition.

83. For a discussion of Gilman's animosity toward Hearst, see Denise D. Knight, "Charlotte Perkins Gilman, William Randolph Hearst, and the Practice of Ethical Journalism," *American Journalism* 11, no. 4 (Fall 1994): 336–47.

84. *Forerunner* 1–7. Reprint, with an introduction by Madeleine B. Stern (New York: Greenwood, 1968).

85. *Forerunner* 1 (November 1909): 32.

86. Gilman's *Women and Economics* was published in 1898 by Small, Maynard, and Co.

87. "Mrs. Beazley's Deeds," *Woman's World* (27 March 1911): 12–13, 58; rpt. *Forerunner* (September 1916): 225–32 and Knight, 163–76. Page numbers in the text refer to Knight's edition.

88. Mary E. Wilkins Freeman, "The Revolt of Mother," in *Selected Stories of Mary E. Wilkins Freeman*, ed. Marjorie Pryse (New York: Norton, 1983), 293.

89. "Mrs. Elder's Idea," *Forerunner* (February 1912): 29–33; rpt. Knight, 138–45. Page numbers in the text refer to the reprint edition.

90. "Mrs. Mann's Clothes," *Forerunner* (May 1914): 113–17.

91. Gilman attended the Woman's Suffrage Convention in Washington, D.C., in January 1896. In her coverage of the event, New York *World* correspondent Nellie Bly [Elizabeth Cochrane Seaman] reported that Gilman [then Stetson] had "a large vocabulary, a good voice, an attractive smile and magnificent thinking faculties." But "as I looked at Mrs. Stetson I mourned. She has an ideal face, clear cut and poetic. She parts her hair and combs it smoothly back over her ears. . . . But oh, how she dresses! I fear she is daft on dress reform or some other abomination. She was decidedly wider at the waist than she was below it. We did not need to be told that she was corsetless, and, I fear, petticoatless! Her suit was a mud-colored cloth, the waist being low-necked and double-breasted, and the short scant skirt hung every way but prettily" ("Nellie Bly With the Female Suffragists," New York *World* [26 January 1896]: 4).

92. Gilman, "Why Women Do Not Reform Their Dress," *Women's Journal* (23 October 1886): 338.

93. Gilman, "The New Motherhood," *Forerunner* 1 (December 1910): 17.

94. "Making a Change," *Forerunner* (December 1911): 311–15; rpt. Lane, 66–74. Page numbers in the text refer to Lane's edition.

95. Polly Wynn Allen, *Building Domestic Liberty: Charlotte Perkins Gilman's Architectural Feminism* (Amherst: University of Massachusetts Press, 1988), 6.

96. "The Cottagette," *Forerunner* (August 1910): 1–5; rpt. Lane, 47–56. Page numbers in the text refer to Lane's edition.

97. See *Living*, 137–38.

98. "Old Water," *Forerunner* (October 1911): 255–59; rpt. Knight, 122–29. Page numbers in the text refer to the reprint edition.

99. The discussion of "Old Water" is drawn from my essay " 'such a hopeless task before her': Some Observations on Hawthorne and Gilman," in *Scribbling Women: Engendering and Expanding the Hawthorne Tradition*, John Idol and Melinda M. Ponder, eds., (Amherst: University of Massachusetts Press, 1997).

100. "Being Reasonable," *Forerunner* (August 1915): 197–201; rpt. Knight, 185–192. Page numbers in the text refer to the reprint edition.

101. "Turned," *Forerunner* (September 1911): 227–32; rpt. Lane, 87–97. Page numbers in the text refer to Lane's edition.

102. "The Chair of English," *Forerunner* (March 1913): 57–61; rpt. Knight, 146–53. Page numbers in the text refer to the reprint edition. Gilman made substantial revisions to the story sometime after 1922, when she was living in Norwich Town, Connecticut, and changed the title to "A Reliable Witness." She was apparently unsuccessful in placing the revised story for publication. The original manuscript of "A Reliable Witness" is among the collection of Gilman Papers at the Schlesinger Library.

103. "His Mother," *Forerunner* (July 1914): 169–73; rpt. Knight, 73–80. Page numbers in the text refer to the reprint edition.

104. Gilman, "Feminism" (in typescript), folder 175, Gilman Papers, Schlesinger Library. Quoted by permission.

105. "With a Difference (Not Literature)," *Forerunner* (February 1914): 29–32.

106. "The Boys and the Butter," *Forerunner* (October 1910): 1–5; rpt. Knight, 65–72. Page numbers in the text refer to the reprint edition.

107. "Joan's Defender," *Forerunner* (June 1916): 141–46; rpt. Knight, 96–103. Page numbers in the text refer to the reprint edition.

108. Gilman frequently expressed the view that long hair on women is purely a matter of sex decoration, worn by women to attract men at the expense of their own comfort and ease. See for example "Her Hair," *Forerunner* 5 (July 1914): 175–76; and "Women's Hair and Men's Whiskers," *Forerunner* 7 (March 1916): 64–65.

109. "A Personal Motive," *Forerunner* (May 1913): 113–18.

110. Gilman, "Milk, Motherhood and Morality," *Forerunner* (April 1913): 99–102.

111. "An Offender," *Forerunner* (February 1910): 1–6.

112. "Wild Oats and Tame Wheat," *Forerunner* (May 1913): 130–31; rpt. Knight, 218–19. "Cleaning Up Elita," *Forerunner* (January 1916): 1–4. "The Vintage," *Forerunner* (October 1916): 253–57; rpt. Knight, 104–11. Page numbers in the text refer to the reprint editions.

113. Gilman, *The Man-Made World; Or, Our Androcentric Culture* (New York: Charlton Co., 1911), 101.

114. Cf. note 37.

115. Gilman, "Newspapers and Democracy," *Forerunner* 7 (December 1916): 315.

116. "His Excuse," *Forerunner* (April 1916): 85–89; rpt. Knight, 88–95. Page numbers in the text refer to the reprint edition.

117. "An Unwilling Interview," *Forerunner* (April 1912): 85–89; rpt. *Woman's Journal* (29 March 1913): 98–99. Page numbers in the text refer to the *Forerunner* edition.

118. Carol Farley Kessler, *Charlotte Perkins Gilman: Her Progress Toward Utopia with Selected Writings* (Syracuse: Syracuse University Press, 1995), 85. Hereafter, *Progress*.

119. Jane Hume Clapperton, *The Vision of the Future, Based on the Application of Ethical Principles* (London: Sean Sonnenschein, 1904), 328.

120. "Freed," *Forerunner* (March 1912): 65–66; rpt. Knight, 206–9. Page numbers in the text refer to the reprint edition.

121. Ann J. Lane, introduction to Gilman's *Herland* (1915; rpt. New York: Pantheon, 1979), xi.

122. "Her Memories," *Forerunner* (August 12): 197–201; rpt. Kessler, 174–81. Page numbers in the text refer to the reprint edition.

123. "Boone Farm," *Forerunner* (August 1914): 197–201.

124. "Bee Wise," *Forerunner* (July 1913): 169–73; rpt. Kessler, 211–19. Cf. note 116. Page numbers refer to the reprint edition.

125. "A Council of War," *Forerunner* (August 1913): 197–201; rpt. Kessler, 220–28. Page numbers in the text refer to the reprint edition.

126. The term "short sermon" is Gilman's; she used it in advertising the *Forerunner*.

127. "The Sensible Dead Man," *Forerunner* (April 1911): 106–7.

128. Gilman was cremated following her death, and her ashes were scattered by her daughter, Katharine, in the Sierra Madre mountains in California. Gilman's mother's remains were cremated following her death in 1893; see *Living*, 152.

129. "Her Doll," *Forerunner* (July 1911): 183.

130. See, for example, "Children's Clothing," *Harper's Bazaar* 44 (January 1910): 24, and "The Dress of Women," serialized in the *Forerunner* in 1915.

131. "The Permanent Child," *Forerunner* (December 1910): 15–17; rpt. *LaFollette's* 1 (April 1911): 10, and *Pasadena Star* 3 (May 1911): 2. Page numbers in the text refer to the *Forerunner* edition.

132. "Two Storks," *Forerunner* (February 1910): 12–13; rpt. *Woman's Journal* (26 February 1910): 33; *Public* (13 January 1911): 38–39; *Life and Labor* (March 1913): 76–77; *Woman's Voice: An Anthology*, ed. Josephine Conger (Boston: Stratford Co., 1918), 280–83; and Knight, 203–205. Page numbers in the text refer to Knight's reprint edition.

133. "The Lady Oyster," *Forerunner* (May 1912): 131–32; rpt. Knight, 210–12. Page numbers in the text refer to the reprint edition.

134. "Improving on Nature," *Forerunner* (July 1912): 174–76; rpt. Knight, 213–17. Page numbers in the text refer to the reprint edition.

135. "Wild Oats and Tame Wheat," *Forerunner* (May 1913): 130–31; rpt. Knight, 218–19. Page numbers in the text refer to the reprint edition.

136. "The Old Woman and the New Year," *Forerunner* (January 1911): 19–20.

137. "On a Branch," *Forerunner* (February 1913): 46–47; rpt. *Public* (24 October 1914): 1024–25. Page numbers in the text refer to the reprint edition.

138. "A Poor Joke," *Forerunner* (October 1913): 270–71.

Part 2

THE WRITER

Introduction

"If I can learn to write good stories," Charlotte Perkins Gilman wrote in 1893, "it will be a powerful addition to my armory. I have written some good stories—therefore, I know I can."[1] The means by which Gilman measured the success of her forays into fiction, however, marks a clear departure from standards typically applied in the evaluation of literature. Gilman's assessment of a "good" story had little to do with skillful execution or aesthetic elements; rather, her main concern was whether she had successfully demonstrated how society might be reformed. With few exceptions, Gilman wrote her stories hastily and without revision; her purpose was to illustrate tangible solutions to existing social problems.

"I have never made any pretense of being literary," Gilman admitted in her autobiography (*Living*, 284). Neither was she inclined to be particularly introspective about her writing. "As far as I had any method in mind, it was to express the idea with clearness and vivacity, so that it might be apprehended with ease and pleasure," she remarked (pp. 284–85). Indeed, there is little that can be said about Gilman's "method." As her friend and fellow writer Amy Wellington noted, Gilman was not "given to the luxury of self-expression."[2]

Of the nearly two hundred stories that Gilman produced, the only one about which she commented publicly was "The Yellow Wall-Paper." Even then, her discussion was limited by her flat, factual reporting of the background and purpose of the story. Unlike many fiction writers, Gilman failed to submit to interviews that might shed light on factors influencing her writing or strategies governing her composing process.

In the first selection reprinted here, "Apropos of Literature," published in 1890, Gilman condemns the proliferation of popular literature as a profit-driven "disease" generated by people "writing for money and not because they have anything to say." The mass of publications that are "thrown out from the flying presses day by day" are designed "to allure and attract and stimulate an evil curiosity," she contends. When the law of supply and demand enables business to benefit from "the feverish appetite" of the book-buying public, "how can we expect literature to escape the blight?" she asks.

The three selections that follow, "Why I Wrote The Yellow Wallpaper?" " 'The Yellow Wall Paper'—Its History & Reception," and excerpts from her autobiography, offer Gilman's reflections on her chronic depression, her experiences in undergoing the rest cure, her objectives in writing the famous story, and its reception. In each of these narratives, Gilman notes that Dr. S. Weir Mitchell, the specialist who treated her for neurasthenia in 1887, altered his methods after reading her story. She also credits work, "without which one is a pauper and a parasite," as the most significant factor in restoring her sanity following her breakdown.

Significantly, each of these pieces implicitly refutes the early characterization of "The Yellow Wall-Paper" as a gothic horror story; rather, they reinforce Gilman's long-held conviction that work was the "first duty of a human being" and that it was essential in maintaining her emotional health (*Living*, 42). Forbidden to work as part of the rest cure therapy, Gilman's already marked predisposition to melancholia only intensified, as she graphically describes in the excerpt from *The Living of Charlotte Perkins Gilman*.

The brief selections from "Thoughts and Figgerings," Gilman's informal collection of miscellaneous notes, illustrate the shift in her purpose in fiction writing, from urging individual reform (as in the case of Dr. Mitchell) to advocating the transformation of society in general. In addition to providing Gilman with some much-needed income, the production of "good stories" would "serve for practice for larger work," she wrote in 1894. Thirty years later, at age 64, Gilman expressed the fear that she would soon "drift into a helpless old age" unless she kept intellectually active. Writing "some good stories," she concluded, "would be a permanent form of occupation—and income." Regrettably, although Gilman continued to dabble in fiction and even produced a full-length detective novel in her later years, there were "no takers" (*Living*, 332). Her career as a fiction writer effectively ended when the *Forerunner* ceased publication in 1916.

The chapter "Masculine Literature," from *The Man-Made World* (1911), is reprinted here in its entirety. In this work and in the excerpts from "Coming Changes in Literature" (1915), Gilman argues that most fiction had focused primarily on the influence of the androcentric culture and that literature "is far too great a thing to be wholly governed by one dominant note." Fortunately, she writes, "the art of fiction is being re-born," and the "humanizing of women" will offer fresh perspectives to the fiction writer. "When our women writers emerge from the smothering pressure of literary tradition, and recognize their distinctive place and power, we shall have a new portent—the woman, as an artist," Gilman observes.

In the next piece, "Instead of a Story," Gilman focuses her rhetorical commentary on the atrocities of World War I. She conceded in the December 1915 issue of the *Forerunner* that with the "Nightmare in Europe" demanding public attention, "there seems to be no room for stories now." In place of a story, Gilman produced a sketch in which the "commonplace melodrama," featuring the submissive and obedient woman character, is replaced by an assertive wage-earning wife and mother who defies her husband's authoritarian rule. "What a difference it would make," Gilman concluded, if women placed more value on their maternal responsibilities than on their matrimonial vows.

Part 2 concludes with a brief study by Gilman's close friend the writer Amy Wellington, who cites Gilman's recognition of "women's subordinate and cruel position" as the force that "move[d] her powerfully" to write about "their narrow deadening circumstances" and "their pitiful economic dependence." "Originality," Wellington argues, was Gilman's "most outstanding quality." Indeed, the selections that follow betray not only Gilman's distinctive originality but also her profound conviction that existing literature must be modified to represent the "other half" of the human species.

Notes

1. This quotation, dated 26 March 1894, is from folder 16, titled "Thoughts & Figgerings," the Gilman Papers, Schlesinger Library. Gilman often wrote her thoughts, her objectives, and her long-term plans on odd scraps of paper that she collected and saved over the years. Quoted by permission.

2. Amy Wellington, *Women Have Told: Studies in the Feminist Tradition* (Boston: Little, Brown, 1930), 123.

From "Apropos of Literature"

Charlotte Perkins Stetson [Gilman]

There are certain features in the current literature of the day, not the big magazine especially, but in the mass of publications thrown out from the flying presses day by day, which show a great deal to the student. There are plenty who can read the lesson forward, who can see the results, good and bad, of their innumerable volumes; but there are few who look backward and see their causes. But you must find causes always, before you can prevent disease. And there is no cure but prevention. In a book-store the other day I glanced over the great counter in the middle piled high with "popular literature." It must be popular because there is so much of it. I am not so certain of its being literature. The exact definition of that form of art is yet unattained. We can tell the difference between music and noise quite sharply; but in the art of painting and the art of writing it is a difficult task to define limit. But the counter I speak of was covered with books, and they were what the sales-woman called "the newest books." What has newness to do with one's buying a book? Why should we buy a book that is a day or a week or a month fresher from the press than another? Think that out, you who can think at all. The first thing that struck me in this feast of reason was the brilliancy of the covers. All were pictorial, all were more or less gaudy, and the scenes thereon were such as we see on the boardings around cheap theatres.

On "Miss Mephistophele" stood an alluring figure in scarlet tights and a black mask. What was in this book I do not know, so those who would look for it because of this mention may be disappointed! Still they need not lose heart, where so much is bad a book with that cover can hardly be good.

On "The Evil That Men Do" was some kind of a lurid drowning scene; and on "The Pace That Kills" a sheeted skeleton clawing about most dangerously.

I'm not an old person but I can remember well when book covers carried only a title, with more or less decoration. Decorative art in brass

From "Apropos of Literature," *Pacific Monthly* 2 (July 1890), 123.

and stripes and zigzags, all more or less abominable. But now it is pictorial art, and more and more abominable.

To catch the eye, of course; to allure and attract and stimulate an evil curiosity. And all on the same principle as the rest of our business life. To sell. Not to sell to meet a demand, but to create and sustain a demand in order to feed it. It is not that we are all so bad, or so anxious to be bad. We do not hunger and thirst after these books before we see them. And if we hunger and thirst for them, why that is but human. When you see a plump young person in scarlet tights and a black mask you naturally wonder what mischief she is up to. Old ones who know all about the mischief are almost as much interested as young ones who keep the ball rolling, very largely.

There is lots of imitation in these pretty books. They are vastly improving to the mind and soul. And it all comes down to a money basis after all, to the fact of the people who write, writing for money and not because they have anything to say; and to the publishers standing in that conscienceless middle position which is too much for human nature always. Their living depends on selling; the more they sell the more they get, and how can you expect a man to consider peoples [*sic*] digestion when he keeps a restaurant? The caterer just cates—that is his business. And he says soothingly to himself[,] "They needn't buy if they don't want to—I dont [*sic*] make 'em buy!"

Ah but he does though! The popular publisher finds out weak spots in humanity—he doesn't have to look far!—and works through them. He tickles the weak spots, he salves and irritates at the same time, he keeps the feverish appetite well fed and yet eager. They don't have to buy—O no! but he means that they shall! Well: He must live, or at least he thinks he must; and we can't blame him for that.

And when "business" creates a demand in order to supply it, when thousands, yes millions of men, get their whole subsistence off artificial wants—just thrive on the public weakness—the public disease—why how can we expect literature to escape the blight?

Nothing escapes it. Nothing will escape it while present economic conditions hold. It is all very well to preach, and struggle, but the just law of nature is self-preservation and "man must live." So let us be a little patient with these wicked bright-colored blossom, [*sic*] until we can reach their innocent looking roots.

Why I Wrote The Yellow Wallpaper?

Charlotte Perkins Gilman

Many and many a reader has asked that. When the story first came out, in the *New England Magazine* about 1891, a Boston physician made protest in *The Transcript*.[1] Such a story ought not to be written, he said; it was enough to drive anyone mad to read it.

Another physician, in Kansas I think, wrote to say that it was the best description of incipient insanity he had ever seen, and—begging my pardon—had I been there?

Now the story of the story is this:

For many years, I suffered from a severe and continuous nervous breakdown tending to melancholia—and beyond. During about the third year of this trouble I went, in devout faith and some faint stir of hope, to a noted specialist in nervous diseases, the best known in the country. This wise man put me to bed and applied the rest cure, to which a still good physique responded so promptly that he concluded there was nothing much the matter with me, and sent me home with solemn advice to "live as domestic a life as far as possible," to "have but two hours' intellectual life a day," and "never to touch pen, brush or pencil again as long as I lived." This was in 1887.

I went home and obeyed those directions for some three months, and came so near the border line of utter mental ruin that I could see over.

Then, using the remnants of intelligence that remained, and helped by a wise friend, I cast the noted specialist's advice to the winds and went to work again—work, the normal life of every human being; work, in which is joy and growth and service, without which one is a pauper and a parasite; ultimately recovering some measure of power.

Being naturally moved to rejoicing by this narrow escape, I wrote *The Yellow Wallpaper*, with its embellishments and additions to carry out the ideal (I never had hallucinations or objections to my mural decorations) and sent a copy to the physician who so nearly drove me mad. He never acknowledged it.

"Why I Wrote The Yellow Wallpaper?" *Forerunner* 4 (October 1913): 271.

The little book is valued by alienists and as a good specimen of one kind of literature. It has to my knowledge saved one woman from a similar fate—so terrifying her family that they let her out into normal activity and she recovered.

But the best result is this. Many years later I was told that the great specialist had admitted to friends of his that he had altered his treatment of neurasthenia since reading *The Yellow Wallpaper*.

It was not intended to drive people crazy, but to save people from being driven crazy, and it worked.

Note

1. *Editor's note:* There is nothing to corroborate the identity of the writer as a "Boston physician." Gilman is apparently assuming that the "M.D." who signed the letter in the *Boston Evening Transcript* was a medical doctor, when it is more likely that the writer was simply using his or her initials.

"The Yellow Wall Paper"
—Its History & Reception

Charlotte Perkins Gilman

"*The Yellow Wallpaper*" was written in two days, with the thermometer at one hundred and three—in Pasadena, Cal.

It was put in the hands of an agent, and offered to the Atlantic Monthly. Mr. Horace Scudder, then the editor, declined it in these terms: I am returning herewith the manuscript of "The Yellow Wallpaper". I should never forgive myself if I made other people as miserable as reading your story has made me.

A Boston physician wrote a protest in The Transcript,[1] asserting that such a story should not be allowed to appear in print—that it was enough to drive people mad to read it.

A western physician, one Dr. Brommell Jones,[2] wrote to the author that the story was "the best study of incipient insanity I have ever seen, and, begging your pardon, have you been there?"

The story is well known among alienists, and in one case, caused an eminent specialist in that field to state that he had changed his treatment of neurasthenia since reading it.

In some cases it is used in college rhetoric courses.

Following its first publication, a man wrote to inquire if it was founded on fact. He knew of a woman, similarly affected, and treated in the same mistaken manner by her friends. When satisfied as to the basis of the story, he gave it to these friends to read, and it so alarmed them that they forthwith altered their methods and the woman got well.

Notes

1. *Editor's note:* Cf. note 1 of "Why I Wrote The Yellow Wallpaper?" reprinted in this edition.

2. *Editor's note:* In *The Living of Charlotte Perkins Gilman*, Gilman identifies her correspondent as Dr. Brummel Jones.

Undated typescript left by Gilman, box 17, folder 221, Gilman Papers, Schlesinger Library, Radcliffe College. Quoted by permission.

From *The Living of Charlotte Perkins Gilman*
Charlotte Perkins Gilman

Besides [the poem] "Similar Cases" the most outstanding piece of work of 1890 was "The Yellow Wallpaper." It is a description of a case of nervous breakdown beginning something as mine did, and treated as Dr. S. Weir Mitchell treated me with what I considered the inevitable result, progressive insanity.

This I sent to Mr. Howells, and he tried to have the *Atlantic Monthly* print it, but Mr. Scudder, then the editor, sent it back with this brief card:

> DEAR MADAM,
> Mr. Howells handed me this story.
> I could not forgive myself if I made others as miserable as I have made myself!
> Sincerely yours,
> H. E. SCUDDER

This was funny. The story was meant to be dreadful, and succeeded. I suppose he would have sent back one of Poe's on the same ground. Later I put it in the hands of an agent who had written me, one Henry Austin, and he placed it with the *New England Magazine*. Time passed, much time, and at length I wrote to the editor of that periodical to this effect:

> DEAR SIR,
> A story of mine, "The Yellow Wallpaper," was printed in your issue of May, 1891. Since you do not pay on receipt of ms. nor on publication, nor within six months of publication, may I ask if you pay at all, and if so at what rates?

They replied with some heat that they had paid the agent, Mr. Austin. He, being taxed with it, denied having got the money. It was only forty dollars anyway! As a matter of fact I never got a cent for it till later publishers brought it out in book form, and very little then. But it made a tremendous impression. A protest was sent to the Boston *Transcript*, headed "Perilous Stuff"—[1]

TO THE EDITOR OF THE TRANSCRIPT:

In a well-known magazine has recently appeared a story entitled "The Yellow Wallpaper." It is a sad story of a young wife passing the gradations from slight mental derangement to raving lunacy. It is graphically told, in a somewhat sensational style, which makes it difficult to lay aside, after the first glance, til it is finished, holding the reader in morbid fascination to the end. It certainly seems open to serious question if such literature should be permitted in print.

The story can hardly, it would seem, give pleasure to any reader, and to many whose lives have been touched through the dearest ties by this dread disease, it must bring the keenest pain. To others, whose lives have become a struggle against an heredity of mental derangement, such literature contains deadly peril. Should such stories be allowed to pass without severest censure?

Another doctor, one Brummel Jones, of Kansas City, Missouri, wrote me in 1892 concerning this story, saying: "When I read 'The Yellow Wallpaper' I was very much pleased with it, and now that I have read it again I am overwhelmed with the delicacy of your touch and the correctness of portrayal. From a doctor's standpoint, and I am a doctor, you have made a success. So far as I know, and I am fairly well up in literature, there has been no detailed account of incipient insanity." Then he tells of an opium addict who refused to be treated on the ground that physicians had no real knowledge of the disease, but who returned to Dr. Jones, bringing a paper of his own on the opium habit, shook it in his face and said, "Doctor, you've been there!" To which my correspondent added, "Have you ever been—er——; but of course you haven't." I replied that I had been as far as one could go and get back.

One of the *New England Magazine's* editors wrote to me asking if the story was founded on fact, and I gave him all I decently could of my case as a foundation for the tale. Later he explained that he had a friend who was in similar trouble, even to hallucinations about her wallpaper, and whose family were treating her as in the tale, that he had not dared show them my story till he knew that it was true, in part at least, and that when he did they were so frightened by it, so impressed by the clear implication of what ought to have been done, that they changed her wallpaper and the treatment of the case—and she recovered! This was triumph indeed.

But the real purpose of the story was to reach Dr. S. Weir Mitchell, and convince him of the error of his ways. I sent him a copy as soon as it came out, but got no response. However, many years later, I met some one who knew close friends of Dr. Mitchell's who had told them that he had changed his treatment of nervous prostration since reading "The Yellow Wallpaper." If that is a fact, I have not lived in vain.

A few years ago Mr. Howells asked leave to include this story in a collection he was arranging—*Masterpieces of American Fiction*. I was more than willing, but assured him that it was no more "literature" than my other stuff, being definitely written "with a purpose." In my judgment it is a pretty poor thing to write, to talk, without a purpose. (*Living*, 118–21)

Such writing as I have done in those years of free delivery was easy work. An average article, about three thousand words, took three hours to do, a day's work. Sometimes I would have to copy it, or change a little, but usually it was written and sent—like a letter. This is not, in the artistic sense, "literature." I have never made any pretense of being literary. As far as I had any method in mind, it was to express the idea with clearness and vivacity, so that it might be apprehended with ease and pleasure.

I had a little talk once with Mary Austin, the beauty of whose writing is well known, in which I disclaimed any pretension to literature, but said I thought I had "a style of my own." She demurred, hardly thought it style, but granted distinction, adding kindly, "I do think, however, that if you gave your mind to it, you could write." This was certainly encouragement. (*Living*, 284–85)

As years passed and continuous writing and speaking developed the various lines of thought I was following, my work grew in importance but lost in market value. Social philosophy, however ingeniously presented, does not command wide popular interest. I wrote more and sold less.

Theodore Dreiser, then on the *Delineator*, as I remember, looked gloomily at me over this desk, and said, "You should consider more what the editors want." Of course I should have, if I had been a competent professional writer. There are those who write as artists, real ones; they often find it difficult to consider what the editor wants. There are those who write to earn a living, they, if they succeed, *must* please the editor.

The editor, having his living to earn, must please his purchasers, the public, so we have this great trade of literary catering. But if one writes to express important truths, needed yet unpopular, the market is necessarily limited.

As all of my principal topics were in direct contravention of established views, beliefs and emotions, it is a wonder that so many editors took so much of my work for so long.

But as time passed there was less and less market for what I had to say, more and more of my stuff was declined. Think I must and write I must, the manuscripts accumulated far faster than I could sell them, some of the best, almost all—and finally I announced: "If the editors and publishers will not bring out my work, I will!" And I did. In November, 1909, I started the *Forerunner*.

This was a small monthly magazine, written entirely by myself. There have been other one-man magazines, but smaller and confined to one kind of writing as a rule. Mine was not very big, ten-by-seven pages, twenty-eight of them, seven hundred and fifty words to a page, made some twenty-one thousand to the issue. It equaled four books a year, books of thirty-six thousand words.

Each issue included one instalment [*sic*] of a novel, also of a book published serially; a short story, articles of various length; poems, verses, allegories, humor and nonsense, with book reviews and comment on current events. . . .

The cost of publishing this work was $3,000 a year; its price, a dollar. If I could have achieved three thousand subscribers then I would cheerfully have done the work for nothing, but I never had sense enough—business sense, that is, to get them. About fifteen hundred was our income, and the rest of the expense I met by doing extra work in writing . . . and as usual, lecturing. . . .

However, regardless of difficulties, I wrote and published the *Forerunner* for seven years. . . . In regard to the general attitude of hearers, readers and editors, toward my work, I have met a far wider and warmer welcome than I ever expected. Not aiming in the least at literary virtuosity, still less at financial success, I have been most agreeably surprised by the acceptance of so much of what I had to offer. One cannot undertake to alter the ideas, feelings and habits of the people and expect them to like it. (*Living*, 303–6, 308)

Note

1. *Editor's note:* The original publication of "Perilous Stuff" in the 8 April 1892 issue of the *Boston Evening Transcript* contains some slight variations from the version Gilman included in her autobiography. In addition to the occasional use of variant punctuation and spelling, the most significant differences in the original are the inclusion of the word "through" in "passing through the gradations," "nearest ties" rather than "dearest ties," and the inclusion of the words "without protest" preceding the words "without severest censure."

From "Thoughts and Figgerings"
Charlotte Perkins Gilman

[31 May 1893]

Stories

If I can learn to write good stories, it will be a powerful addition to my armory.

I have written some good stories—therefore I know I can.

"If you want to draw, draw."

"Practice makes perfect."

If I can do this little call work at even [$]5.00, it ought to mean at the end of the year and a half $350.00—no mean addition.

One crisp sharp little sketch per week, 70 of them.

If I can write seventy 1000 word stories that are even decent, it ought to help me amazingly. Say one day of my five a week for a short story. . . .

I surely ought to be able to write one such trifling tale a week—with such large results before me.

It will all serve for practice for larger work. Suppose I make them character sketches—bits of scenery—preliminary drawings for great future compositions. That would be well worth while.

[8 April 1894?]

Help me to work! To really do the things I have in mind. To write—write—write. . . . Help me to see the way and follow it. Whatever else may come or go this is my clear straight path—to work. What needs now is to place things. Keep my mind clear and my heart strong! pour in—pour in—give me more and more of the great stream of life. Let me feel

Between 1883 and 1935, Gilman often jotted her thoughts, her objectives, and her philosophy on little scraps of paper that she collected in a folder. In her later years, she titled the collection "Thoughts and Figgerings." The collection is located in box 2, folders 16 and 17, Gilman Papers, Schlesinger Library, Radcliffe College. Quoted by permission.

it and give it out in all the ways I know. This means health and power and all good. Help me O God!

[25 August 1924]

It is absurd that I should not be able to launch out and earn far more than I do now.

Unless I do it—write, review, lecture, and do it soon—I shall drift into a helpless old age.

Well then. What have I still to say?

Nothing further that is new. I have made my discoveries and urged them with ability. Unless I manifest new abilities I can do no more.

How about stories?

If I could do some good stories, they would be a permanent form of occupation—and income. . . .

Have a try!

"Masculine Literature" from
The Man-Made World;
Or, Our Androcentric Culture (1911)

Charlotte Perkins Gilman

When we are offered a "woman's" paper, page, or column, we find it filled with matter supposed to appeal to women as a sex or class; the writer mainly dwelling upon the Kaiser's four K's—Kutchen, Kinder, Kirche, Kleider.[1] They iterate and reiterate endlessly the discussion of cookery old and new, of the care of children, of the overwhelming subject of clothing, and of moral instruction. All this is recognized as "feminine" literature, and it must have some appeal, else the women would not read it. What parallel have we in "masculine" literature?

"None!" is the proud reply. "Men are people! Women, being 'the sex,' have their limited feminine interests, their feminine point of view, which must be provided for. Men, however, are not restricted—to them belongs the world's literature!"

Yes, it has belonged to them—ever since there was any. They have written it and they have read it. It is only lately that women, generally speaking, have been taught to read; still more lately that they have been allowed to write. It is but a little while since Harriet Martineau[2] concealed her writing beneath her sewing when visitors came in—writing was "masculine"—sewing, "feminine."

We have not, it is true, confined men to a narrowly constructed "masculine sphere," and composed a special literature suited to it. Their effect on literature has been far wider than that, monopolizing this form of art with special favor. It was suited above all others to the dominant impulse of self-expression, and being, as we have seen, essentially and continually "the sex;" they have impressed that sex upon this art overwhelmingly; they have given the world a masculized literature.

It is hard for us to realize this. We can readily see, that if women had always written the books, no men either writing or reading them, that would have surely "feminized" our literature; but we have not in our minds the concept, much less the word, for an overmasculized influence.

116

Men having been accepted as humanity, women but a side-issue; (most literally if we accept the Hebrew legend!), whatever men did or said was human—and not to be criticized. In no department of life is it easier to controvert this old belief; to show how the male sex as such differs from the human type; and how this maleness has monopolized and disfigured a great social function.

Human life is a very large affair; and literature is its chief art. We live, humanly, only through our power of communication. Speech gives us this power laterally, as it were, in immediate personal contact. For permanent use speech becomes oral tradition—a poor dependence. Literature gives not only an infinite multiplication to the lateral spread of communion but adds the vertical reach. Through it we know the past, govern the present, and influence the future. In its serviceable common forms it is the indispensable daily servant of our lives; in its nobler flights as a great art no means of human inter-change goes so far.

In these brief limits we can touch but lightly on some phases of so great a subject, and will rest the case mainly on the effect of an exclusively masculine handling of the two fields of history and fiction. In poetry and the drama the same influence is easily traced, but in the first two it is so baldly prominent as to defy objection.

History is, or should be, the story of our racial life. What have men made it? The story of warfare and conquest. Begin at the very beginning with the carven stones of Egypt, the clay records of Chaldea, what do we find of history?

"I, Pharoah, King of Kings! Lord of Lords!" (etc. etc.), "went down into the miserable land of Kush, and slew of the inhabitants thereof an hundred and forty and two thousands!" That, or something like it, is the kind of record early history gives us.

The story of Conquering Kings, whom and how many they killed and enslaved, the grovelling adulation of the abased, the unlimited jubilation of the victor, from the primitive state of most ancient kings, and the Roman triumphs where queens walked in chains, down to our omnipresent soldier's monuments; the story of war and conquest—war and conquest—over and over, with such boasting and triumph, such cock-crow and flapping of wings as show most unmistakably the natural source.

All this will strike the reader at first as biased and unfair. "That was the way people lived in those days!" says the reader.

No—it was not the way women lived.

"Oh, women!" says the reader, "Of course not. Women are different."

Yes, women are different; and *men are different!* Both of them, as sexes, differ from the human norm, which is social life and all social development. Society was slowly growing in all those black, blind years. The arts, the sciences, the trades and crafts and professions, religion, philosophy, government, law, commerce, agriculture—all the human processes were going on as well as they were able, between wars.

The male naturally fights, and naturally crows, triumphs over his rival and takes the prize—therefore was he made male. Maleness means war.

Not only so; but as a male, he cares only for male interests. Men, being the sole arbiters of what should be done and said and written, have given us not only a social growth scarred and thwarted from the beginning by continual destruction; but a history which is one unbroken record of courage and red cruelty, of triumph and black shame.

As to what went on that was of real consequence, the great slow steps of the working world, the discoveries and inventions, the real progress of humanity—that was not worth recording, from a masculine point of view. Within this last century, "The woman's century," the century of the great awakening, the rising demand for freedom, political, economic, and domestic, we are beginning to write real history, human history, and not merely masculine history. But that great branch of literature—Hebrew, Greek, Roman, and all down later times, shows beyond all question, the influence of our androcentric culture.

Literature is the most powerful and necessary of the arts, and fiction is its broadest form. If art "holds the mirror up to nature" this art's mirror is the largest of all, the most used. Since our very life depends on some communication, and our progress is in proportion to our fullness and freedom of communication, since real communication requires mutual understanding; so in the growth of the social consciousness, we note from the beginning a passionate interest in other people's lives.

The art which gives humanity consciousness is the most vital art. Our greatest dramatists are lauded for their breadth of knowledge of "human nature," their range of emotion and understanding; our greatest poets are those who most deeply and widely experience and reveal the feelings of the human heart; and the power of fiction is that it can reach and express this great field of human life with no limits but those of the author.

When fiction began it was the legitimate child of oral tradition, a product of natural brain activity; the legend constructed instead of remembered. (This stage is with us yet as seen in the constant changes in repetition of popular jokes and stories.)

Fiction to-day has a much wider range; yet it is still restricted, heavily and most mischievously restricted.

What is the preferred subject matter of fiction?

There are two main branches found everywhere, from the Romaunt of the Rose to the Purplish Magazine;—the Story of Adventure, and the Love Story.

This Story-of-Adventure branch is not so thick as the other by any means, but it is a sturdy bough for all that. Stevenson and Kipling have proved its immense popularity, with the whole brood of detective stories and the tales of successful rascality we call "picturesque." Our most popular weekly shows the broad appeal of this class of fiction.

All these tales of adventure, of struggle and difficulty, of hunting and fishing and fighting, of robbing and murdering, catching and punishing, are distinctly and essentially masculine. They do not touch on human processes, social processes, but on the special field of predatory excitement so long the sole province of men.

It is to be noted here that even in the overwhelming rise of industrial interests to-day, these, when used as the basis for a story, are forced into line with one, or both, of these two main branches of fiction;—conflict or love. Unless the story has one of these "interests" in it, there is no story—so holds the editor; the dictum being, put plainly, "life has no interests except conflict and love!"

It is surely something more than a coincidence that these are the two essential features of masculinity—Desire and Combat—Love and War.

As a matter of fact the major interests of life are in line with its major processes; and these—in our stage of human development—are more varied than our fiction would have us believe. Half the world consists of women, we should remember, who are types of human life as well as men, and their major processes are not those of conflict and adventure, their love means more than mating. Even on so poor a line of distinction as the "woman's column" offers, if women are to be kept to their four K's, there should be a "men's column" also, and all the "sporting news" and fish stories be put in that; they are not world interests, they are male interests.

Now for the main branch—the Love Story. Ninety per cent of fiction is in this line; this is pre-eminently the major interest of life—given in fiction. What is the love story, as rendered by this art?

It is the story of the pre-marital struggle. It is the Adventures of Him in Pursuit of Her—and it stops when he gets her! Story after story, age after age, over and over and over, this ceaseless repetition of the Preliminaries.

Here is Human Life. In its large sense, its real sense, it is a matter of inter-relation between individuals and groups covering all emotions, all processes, all experiences. Out of this vast field of human life fiction arbitrarily selects one emotion, one process, one experience, as its necessary base.

"Ah! but we are persons most of all!" protests the reader. "This is personal experience—it has the universal appeal!"

Take human life personally, then. Here is a Human Being, a life, covering some seventy years, involving the changing growth of many faculties; the ever new marvels of youth, the long working time of middle life, the slow ripening of age. Here is the human soul, in the human body, Living. Out of this field of personal life, with all of its emotions, processes, and experiences, fiction arbitrarily selects one emotion, one process, one experience, mainly one of sex.

The "love" of our stories is man's love of woman. If any dare dispute this, and say it treats equally of woman's love for man, I answer, "Then why do the stories stop at marriage?"

There is a current jest, revealing much, to this effect:

The young wife complains that the husband does not wait upon and woo her as he did before marriage; to which he replies, "Why should I run after the street-car when I've caught it?"

Woman's love for man, as currently treated in fiction is largely a reflex; it is the way he wants her to feel, expects her to feel. Not a fair representation of how she does feel. If "love" is to be selected as the most important thing in life to write about, then the mother's love should be the principal subject. This is the main stream, this is the general underlying, world-lifting force. The "life-force," now so glibly chattered about, finds its fullest expression in motherhood; not in the emotions of an assistant in the preliminary stages.

What has literature, what has fiction to offer concerning mother-love, or even concerning father-love, as compared to this vast volume of excitement about lover-love? Why is the search-light continually focused upon a two or three year space of life "mid the blank miles round that?" Why indeed, except for the clear reason, that on a starkly masculine basis this is his one period of overwhelming interest and excitement.

If the beehive produced literature, the bee's fiction would be rich and broad, full of the complex tasks of comb-building and filling, the care and feeding of the young, the guardian-service of the queen; and far beyond that it would spread to the blue glory of the summer sky, the fresh winds, the endless beauty and sweetness of a thousand thousand flowers. It would treat of the vast fecundity of motherhood, the educative and selective processes of the group mothers, and the passion of loyalty, of social service, which holds the hive together.

But if the drones wrote fiction, it would have no subject matter save the feasting, of many; and the nuptial flight, of one.

To the male, as such, this mating instinct is frankly the major interest of life; even the belligerent instincts are second to it. To the male, as such, it is for all its intensity, but a passing interest. In nature's economy, his is but a temporary devotion, hers the slow processes of life's fulfillment.

In humanity we have long since, not outgrown, but overgrown, this stage of feeling. In Human Parentage even the mother's share begins to pale beside that ever-growing Social love and care, which guards and guides the children of to-day.

The art of literature in this main form of fiction is far too great a thing to be wholly governed by one dominant note. As life widened and intensified, the artist, if great enough, has transcended sex; and in the mightier works of the real masters, we find fiction treating of life, life in general, in all its complex relationships, and refusing to be held longer to the rigid canons of an androcentric past.

That was the power of Balzac—he took in more than this one field. That was the universal appeal of Dickens; he wrote of people, all kinds of people, doing all kinds of things. As you recall with pleasure some preferred novel of this general favorite, you find yourself looking narrowly for the "love story" in it. It is there—for it is part of life; but it does not dominate the whole scene—any more than it does in life.

The thought of the world is made and handed out to us in the main. The makers of books are the makers of thoughts and feelings for the people in general. Fiction is the most popular form in which this world-food is taken. If it were true, it would teach us life easily, swiftly, truly; teach not by preaching but by truly re-presenting; and we should grow up becoming acquainted with a far wider range of life in books than could even be ours in person. Then meeting life in reality we should be wise—and not be disappointed.

As it is, our great sea of fiction is steeped and dyed and flavored all one way. A young man faces life—the seventy year stretch, remember, and is given book upon book wherein one set of feelings is continually vocalized and overestimated. He reads forever of love, good love and bad love, natural and unnatural, legitimate and illegitimate; with the unavoidable inference that there is nothing else going on.

If he is a healthy young man he breaks loose from the whole thing, despises "love stories" and takes up life as he finds it. But what impression he does receive from fiction is a false one, and he suffers without knowing it from lack of the truer, broader views of life it failed to give him.

A young woman faces life—the seventy year stretch remember; and is given the same books—with restrictions. Remember the remark of Rochefoucauld, "There are thirty good stories in the world and twenty-nine cannot be told to women."[3] There is a certain broad field of literature so grossly androcentric that for very shame men have tried to keep it to themselves. But in a milder form, the spades all named teaspoons, or at the worst appearing as trowels—the young woman is given the same fiction. Love and love and love—from "first sight" to marriage. There it stops—just the fluttering ribbon of announcement—"and lived happily ever after."

Is that kind of fiction any sort of picture of a woman's life? Fiction, under our androcentric culture, has not given any true picture of woman's life, very little of human life, and a disproportioned section of man's life.

As we daily grow more human, both of us, this noble art is changing for the better so fast that a short lifetime can mark the growth. New fields are opening and new laborers are working in them. But it is no swift and easy matter to disabuse the race mind from attitudes and habits inculcated for a thousand years. What we have been fed upon so long we are well used to, what we are used to we like, what we like we think is good and proper.

The widening demand for broader, truer fiction is disputed by the slow racial mind; and opposed by the marketers of literature on grounds of visible self-interest, as well as lethargic conservatism.

It is difficult for men, heretofore the sole producers and consumers of literature; and for women, new to the field, and following masculine canons because all the canons were masculine; to stretch their minds to a recognition of the change which is even now upon us.

This one narrow field has been for so long overworked, our minds are so filled with heroes and heroes continually repeating the one-act play, that when a book like David Harum is offered the publishers refuse it repeatedly, and finally insist on a "heart interest" being injected by force.[4]

Did anyone read David Harum for that heart interest? Does anyone remember that heart interest? Has humanity no interests but those of the heart?

Robert Ellesmere was a popular book[5]—but not because of its heart interest.

Uncle Tom's Cabin appealed to the entire world, more widely than any work of fiction that was ever written;[6] but if anybody fell in love and married in it they have been forgotten. There was plenty of love in that book, love of family, love of friends, love of master for servant and servant for master; love of mother for child; love of married people for each other; love of humanity and love of God.

It was extremely popular. Some say it was not literature. That opinion will live, like the name of Empedocles.[7]

The art of fiction is being re-born in these days. Life is discovered to be longer, wider, deeper, richer, than these monotonous players of one tune would have us believe.

The humanizing of woman of itself opens five distinctly fresh fields of fiction: First, the position of the young woman who is called upon to give up her "career"—her humanness—for marriage, and who objects to it. Second, the middle-aged woman who at last discovers that her discontent is social starvation—that it is not more love that she wants, but more business in life: Third, the inter-relation of women with women—a thing we could never write about before because we never had it before: except in harems and convents: Fourth, the interaction between mothers and children; this not the eternal "mother and child," wherein the child is always a baby, but the long drama of personal relationship; the love and hope, the patience and power, the lasting joy and triumph, the slow eating disappointment which must never be owned to a living soul—here are grounds for novels that a million mothers and many million children would eagerly read: Fifth, the new attitude of the full-grown woman, who faces the demands of love with the high standards of conscious motherhood.

There are other fields, broad and brilliantly promising, but this chapter is meant merely to show that our one-sided culture has, in this art, most disproportionately overestimated the dominant instincts of the male—Love and War—an offense against art and truth, and an injury to life.

Notes

1. *Editor's note:* Kaiser Wilhelm II (1859–1941) believed women should remain within the domestic sphere of "kitchen, children, church, clothing."

2. *Editor's note:* Harriet Martineau (1802–1876) was an English novelist and economist; her works include *Illustrations of Political Economy* (1832–34), *Deerbrook* (1839), *The Hour and the Man* (1840), and *Letters on the Laws of Man's Nature and Development* (1851).

3. *Editor's note:* François de La Rochefoucauld (1613–1680) was a French writer of such works as *Réflexions ou Sentences et Maximes Morales* (1665) and *Les Mémoires sur la Régence d'Anne d'Autriche* (1662).

4. *Editor's note: David Harum, A Story of American Life*, by American author Edward Westcott (1846–98), was published posthumously in 1898.

5. *Editor's note: Robert Elsmere*, by English novelist Mary Augusta Ward (1851–1920), was first published in 1888. The novel was a spiritual romance envisioning a vigorous Christianity that fulfilled the social gospel.

6. *Editor's note: Uncle Tom's Cabin*, by Gilman's great-aunt Harriet Beecher Stowe, was first published serially in the *National Era* in 1851–52.

7. *Editor's note:* Empedocles was a Greek philosopher and statesman of the fifth century B.C., who, according to tradition, hurled himself into the crater of Mt. Etna in order that his sudden disappearance might convince people he was a god.

From "Coming Changes in Literature"

Charlotte Perkins Gilman

If literature is the mirror of life, then any general change in life must change its literature; if it is a personal expression, then any general change in personality will alter it again. Both the conditions of human life and its personality are altering vitally and rapidly to-day; and if art keeps pace with events, we are on the brink of a new literature.

This change is not merely a question of degree, of the rate of progress, of the varying environment; the main characters in the drama are being altered; that is what marks the new era. To broadly generalize: All previous literature has been androcentric; written by men for men, by men to please their women, or by their women to please men. The coming literature commands a new field and deals with the new characters. It recognizes women as full citizens of the world, and treats of their relations to the world; both entirely new subjects.

Hitherto, viewed from the man's position, the world was his world, to be striven with, fought against, overcome or vanquished by, according to the cult of masculine destructiveness. Now we are beginning to look at it as also woman's world, to be nursed and cared for, fed, protected, educated and improved, according to the cult of feminine productiveness. Hitherto, viewed from man's position, women were his women; classed with children, forming his family; to be desired, pursued, conquered and kept; to be worshipped or despised; to be valued always in personal relations, primarily as his mother, secondarily as his sister, thirdly as his wife, fourthly as his daughter—always and exclusively as a female relative. Now we shall begin to look at women as persons, and measure them in relation to other persons, and to the world at large.

Hitherto, in this purely relative position we have quite overlooked the most distinctive feature of woman as such—motherhood. We have talked and written about it to be sure; especially when women showed any signs of wanting to become more broadly developed human beings; we have used it as our strongest appeal, our heaviest deterrent, in seeking to check this progress; but what we spoke of was not in truth moth-

From "Coming Changes in Literature," *Forerunner* 6 (September 1915): 230–36.

erhood; but a department of matrimony, of matrimony most patently androcentric. Of real motherhood, of its overwhelming power and responsibility, the world has so far known nothing, literature has said nothing, women themselves have no faintest inkling.

Yet it is, second to the law of progress, the major process of life. Life's first governing law is that of improvement, of evolution. In this work, reproduction is the main subsidiary process, and in reproduction motherhood is the principal factor. Yet so blind has been our art, so wholly one-sided, that it has exalted Eros, the god of man's desire, and built whole literatures upon his field of action; ignoring the great goddess of mother-love in whose service young Eros is but a running footman.

In social evolution, men and women serve as human beings, and should serve equally; in physical evolution heredity is the most important process, and in heredity motherhood is the main power. The work of the mother is to improve the race; first through the transmission of personal efficiency, and second through her essential prerogative of choice. From the lowest life forms where sexes are found, this law obtains; the males vary widely and compete fiercely; the females select the victors, so continually transmitting the best qualities and lifting the race type. . . .

In human history, with the female treated as the property of the male, she could neither be the best, nor choose the best, and motherhood became a secondary matter. Therefore it is that in all the length and breadth of literature, you do not find one case in a thousand where the woman's real business is given its true place. We have "the love story" for ever and ever; the romance of the pre-marital struggle, a matter of essentially masculine interest; but the mother-love story—nature's endless serial—has had practically no notice. . . .

The love story of literary commerce is in its very nature limited, having but two endings—she will or she won't. Because of its limitations we tire of it; because we tire of it, does the wearied writer resort to every fair artifice and foul allurement to make his wares attract. The mother-love story is as unlimited as life itself, the oldest, deepest, widest, longest, truest passion; varying as people vary, growing forever as life brings new wisdom to the tasks of child-rearing. . . .

Hitherto, when mentioned at all, the mother's love was so subordinated to her love for man, that she is spoken of as "bearing him a son." Even her child she valued most as a "man-child." With motherhood fairly seen, a woman-child is respected as a great world servant, both through her womanhood and her personality.

Literature, entering here, has a world outlook. Stories of the growing girl, looking forward to her mother-power with highest ambition, tenderest hope, profoundest joy; with the consecration of soul and body; with the splendid pride of the world-maker. To such a girl, reared on such literature, the complications of the "love-story" would have a new application; and the whole fabric change. We have described the devoted daughter marrying an inferior, defective or vicious man "to save him." The woman who appreciates motherhood will not do that. Marriage is not a reformatory. Its dominant purpose is the improvement of the human stock, the main functionary is the mother, and literature should show us this—and soon will.

As it is, the young man reads fiction which dwells forever on his natural emotions and sensations, both the primitive and those later developed, and the young woman reads it too. Her emotions and sensations are all in relation to him, with some faint decorous hint of coming hopes. But there is nothing to portray her deeper feelings; the feelings that are hers by right and hers by duty; the instincts and demands of selective motherhood, under which she would refuse a never-so-attractive wooer if he seemed unfit for noble fatherhood.

So, after marriage, if aught befell to vitiate the true relation, instead of the pictures so long given us of patient, faithful women, with husbands, drunken, immoral, or diseased; we should have conscientious women, refusing from maternal duty to remain with such husbands; meeting poverty, loneliness, and even disgrace, rather than so sin against this vital law of motherhood.

Then follows even wider range of subject matter, as yet scarce touched. The story of the child. This not the occasional revelation of some self-conscious genius, nor the "child-story" of current fiction (though that points often in the right direction), but serious treatment of the universal drama of personality, the young soul's entrance upon life. Dickens has given us something of this, and countless readers have felt its charm. Many an author has touched it more or less; but it is almost always as mere preliminary—an introduction to "the love story," which furnishes the main interest. There is room—world room—for deeper work.

When our women writers emerge from the smothering pressure of literary tradition, and recognize their distinctive place and power, we shall have a new portent—the woman, as an artist, studying and writing about children; using her special sympathy and knowledge to voice for the world more clearly than ever before the story of its first twenty years. . . .

Look at this as a subject for literature. See the field for dramatic action; the personal romance involved—the world interest, the studies of changing souls. At the present time the opportunity is specially dazzling; for now we have fresh in our minds and still prominent among us the old type of woman, and at the same time the rapid emergence of the new. There was never such an overturning. It is so strangely sudden—in one lifetime it confronts her; she who was reared in the dark ages finds herself at once in the twentieth century; she who has for so long cared only for her own small brood, finds her heart swell with longing to help the world.

In these first stumbling steps she is hampered at every turn by the limitations of her earlier state. As her time-honored skirts impede her bodily steps, so do conventions, prejudices, habits of thought, impede her social progress. She may be wholly blind to the true import and value of what she is doing; she may disapprove entirely of the new position forced upon her, yet it is forced upon her by the resistless march of social development.

The excessive femininity developed in her by long ages of harem life, makes her new steps at once perilously easy and cruelly hard. If love is with her or before her, all goes on wings; if love stands aside or behind, then she must "choose," "renounce," "decide between marriage and a career."

Of all dramatic figures the world has never seen one more appealing than this. The woman, the feeble, timid, foolish woman—made so by long restriction; now forced willy nilly into the humanity that belongs to her; and the man, the lover, the father, the tender husband, beating her down with every weapon at his command.

He has opposed every step, each in turn. He refused her equal education, but she has won it—in large measure. He has resisted violently her demand for political equality—and is still resisting. He is now greatly concerned over what he terms "woman as a business competitor" (perhaps if he said "assistant" instead of competitor it would look more attractive) and he opposes her economic progress as far as possible.

Most women, siding with most men, oppose it also. Nevertheless, in spite of herself, her sisters and mankind, the position of woman changes with impressive speed. While it is going on is the time to study it at first hand, for such portrayal as is possible to us.

Here is the young woman reader. She forms a large proportion of the reading public. She herself is the acting heroine in the world drama.

Why does not the writer give her a true picture of what is going on, both within her and without, the tumult of new emotions, the confusion between the ultra-feminine background of inherited feeling and the waxing power of honest thought?

Here is the changed environment, the world no longer a howling wilderness to be feared and avoided, the home no longer the safest place to hide in—and hiding no longer a worthy act. Here are the calls of life—all life, rousing in her new ambitions, new hopes, a new conscience. Then comes Love—and the conflict.

So far our story-writers have seen something of this, have tried a little to present it, but how? Almost to a man—and to a woman—they assume that the problem is merely one of decision, that the girl must give up one thing or the other—and that "Love is best." Over and over they present the girl choosing a husband as being happy; or choosing a career and being unhappy.

What she wants is both the husband and the career—and still to be happy. We need wiser, more far-seeing treatment. We need to see that it is not a question of choice, but a far harder one—one of combination and adjustment. Let literature wake up and study the facts, new ones as well as old.

Beyond this; leaving the girl and her affairs far behind, there is still another market, another subject for literature, hitherto quite overlooked. This is the woman. Not the girl, marriageable or unmarriageable, marrying or unmarrying; but the woman; married long since or recently, demarried, remarried, or not married at all—just the woman as a human creature.

No wonder she has no place in art—she has had no existence before. Women as persons, human beings, treated in their social relation solely, are quite new to us. We persist in measuring them by the marital or maternal possibility alone. We have stories about men, short stories and whole novels, in which no woman enters, no love-motive is used, but they are regarded and exhibited in their relation to one another and to society. "The Man Without a Country" is a famous instance of this treatment. We have long since seen that there were other interests than those of sex, for men. We must learn that these exist for women as well.

Here again our hindrance lies in the traditions of the androcentric cult. Because, so far, the most distinctive human interests were monopolized by men, therefore we have called such interests masculine, and the worker goes forth to his task, as Browning so briefly puts it—"a man in a world of men."

This attitude is changing. The growing crowds of women who start out when business hours begin, almost tempt us to reverse the phrase; but it is not reversal we are approaching, it is an equal combination, men and women in a world of men and women, co-workers in a common sphere of action. . . .

Here is scope for the writer. Here is the human soul in a new position altogether, wrestling with new forces, learning to see life in a totally different perspective; bursting in one generation from a larval state of development into the winged freedom of full humanity.

And it was Mr. Howells who spoke years ago of the woman's movement as "that cause so lacking in picturesqueness!" Lacking! No more picturesque, more vividly dramatic subject was ever offered to the artist. Here is the world-mother, long the great uplifting power in physical evolution; then subverted, enslaved, oppressed, but working nevertheless through all the crushing pressure, and modifying the race to evil ends because her own position was so false. Then the awakening—the time of stress and anguish, of weariness, conflict and doubt, of rising ambition and waxing power; and the emergence at last of that unknown figure—the Human Woman.

In this vexed period every feature of comedy and tragedy is found; humor, pathos, patience, despair, and a silent grandeur both of failure and success which ought to inspire the dullest soul. Ibsen caught vague glimpses of this movement and gave us what he saw. Shaw sees it as one turning somersaults before a kaleidoscope—and flickers and scintillates for us in endeavoring to present it. One after another catches some glimpse of vast upheaval and overturning, and shows forth his vision as he may.

But the veil of ignorance, the false light of prejudice, and all the trammels of age-old tradition prevent our seeing clearly. We catch faint glimpses and misrepresent the fragments we have seen. When the scope and bearing of this mighty change are fairly grasped it will be seen as a world epoch second to none, of importance unrivalled save by that prehistoric cataclysm, that huge race-tragedy which underlies all ancient cultures, and which gave rise to the universal myth of the fall of man, that unnatural crime of a subjugated motherhood—the fall of woman.

Quite beyond such immediate issues as have been discussed, come the widening, deepening results in the utmost reaches of art, in the attitude of science, in the whole poise and conduct of the world.

The human mind will make great strides in development when at last it has a full-grown mother. That triviality which so disfigures life, the vulgar curiosity for personal detail which makes the market alike for sensational memoirs of the past and sensational news of the present, will pass with these little-minded women and their little-minded sons. The demand for continuous harping on "the heart interest" will pass when this great rearguard of the world comes forward to full social life and finds it has more interests than one.

The state of mind of the whole world is changing with this change. The poet need no longer so persistently feel of his feelings, the novelist no longer harp on strings worn to a thread by constant fingering. This new womanhood brings not only a fresh field for literature, but a fresh market. Already it is here—unheralded and unsupplied.

Our newsstands are smothered with publications for women—so-called—which are not truly for women at all, but only for dressmakers, cooks, nurses, houseservants, and those who need books on etiquette. The publisher is conscious of a new demand and tries to meet it by a flood of old material. These housekeeper's manuals are not the literature for the new woman.

What she needs as a human creature, she can find in the publications meant for people, unlabelled male or female. What she needs as a woman is clear portrayal of the tremendous issues of the transition period, stories that treat of the girl's struggle for independence, struggle with parental love, struggle with filial duty, struggle with domestic limitations—these would be eagerly read by innumerable women. Are there no women who can write them?

We need stories of the married woman who is vaguely dissatisfied, not with her husband, but with the clumsy mechanism of her life. The novelist tries vainly to satisfy her with quarrel and reconciliation with her husband; rewards years of patience by providing another and superior husband, or punishes her rebellion by the loss of husband, children, or both.

Let us rub our eyes, consider the case of this woman—her name is legion—and work out the problem on new lines. These numerous and pathetic *femmes incomprise*—if they would branch out and use their human faculties in human work, would find their feminine needs much less clamorous. They would find that their husbands would do very well after all—perhaps better than well; that what they wanted was not another man or a change in this one, but larger occupation. This is a field of infinite variety, interesting to men as well as women.

The man himself, in this new association, offers another subject refreshingly novel. Man married to reason as well as love; man befriended instead of waited on; met by a cheerful intelligence, a wise good will, an affection that has understanding; instead of helpless innocence, pathetic dependence, and all the dragging selfishness of the pretty, greedy childish thing, who is one of the by-products of the woman's false position. Kipling and young Burne-Jones have given us a piercing picture of this Vampire. But she is no product of nature. Man made her—and fears his Frankensteina.

The freedom and happiness of men, when mothered, sistered and wived by adequate normal women, is itself a subject to occupy many pens for many years.

Art is not great unless it is true. The crusting encroachments of convention and tradition constantly threaten, and it must steadily face life with open eyes and a brave heart, if it is to be alive and free.

The extent of the reading world of to-day gives a power to literature greater than any art of any age before us. If literature be true it can keep in the public mind the swift moving changes of time; show forth their power and purpose; hold us to a knowledge of new truth; and this not in didactic form, but in the freest fiction. Truth in fiction is as true—and as necessary—as in sermon or lecture, and far wider in its reach.

A young school of writers is coming forward now, who feel this, and who are working grandly to show us social movement, and their interaction with personality; but none as yet has grasped this radical change of base that foreshadows such wide upheaval in our novels, stories, poems; in essay and article, in memoir, biography and history itself.

The world of letters will be another world when the long-arrested woman-half has come forward to an equal, even place; in fact, and in that more than fact—general recognition.

Instead of a Story

Charlotte Perkins Gilman

There seems to be no room for stories now, in *The Forerunner*, at any rate. There is the temporary end of "Benigna Machiavelli," of course (she is not even married yet, much less ended), but no other fiction is forthcoming.

The Nightmare in Europe is the Nightmare of the World. It is upon us all, and every thought, every feeling, is needed to urge us to such action as will not only end this immediate horror, but makes its recurrence impossible.

But if anyone wants here some suggested grouping of imaginary people whose actions amuse and interest, here is the framework of a story— left to that blessed resource of last century writers—the reader's imagination.

* * *

Characters:
  A Man, Husband and Father;
  A Woman, Wife and Mother;
  An Impeccable Young Daughter;
  An Extremely Peccable Young Son.

* * *

The Son is a sorry character. His early escapades grow into serious misdemeanors. His Sister shields and aids him most devotedly. Finally, he pawns his Mother's valuable jewels, is discovered, and is open to arrest as a thief.

Then uprises Mr. Father and performs the melodramatic act of "disowning" him. He casts him off. He swears he is no longer a son of his— which is a futile denial of fact. He proclaims: "Leave my house forever!"

Old stuff this, isn't it? Commonplace melodrama.

But here comes in the new part of the story.

Mrs. Mother rises up, too.

"Instead of a Story" appeared in *Forerunner* 5 (December 1915): 309.

"I beg your pardon for correcting you, John," she says, "but this is my house. You will remember my father gave it to me for a wedding present—it is held in my name, it and all the furnishings."

"Woman!" he thunders. "Do you dare oppose me?"

"I do," she replies calmly. "The first duty of a mother is to her children. If we both had done better by our boy he would not be in this trouble now. But I mean to stand by him now that he is in trouble. That is what mothers are for. I make no charges against him. He is quite welcome to the jewels; I freely give them to him."

Then the Enraged Father cries: "If you defy me to my face I will leave you."

To which she replies:

"I shall miss you sorely, John, and you will be welcome back to your comfortable home as soon as you wish to return. My son, my daughter and I can earn quite enough to support ourselves in your absence."

* * *

What a difference it would make in stories, nearly all of them, if women saw that Mother Duty is higher than Wife Duty, and if they earned their own livings.

From "Charlotte Perkins Gilman"

Amy Wellington

Charlotte Perkins saw more clearly, with more imaginative insight, than any other New England girl of her day, the crippled lives of housewives and mothers, their narrow deadening circumstances; above all, their pitiful economic dependence. "In Duty Bound," one of her earliest printed poems, written when she was about twenty-one, expresses eloquently, not only the limitations of her own young life, but of all New England girlhood in that generation.

One counts it, therefore, an historic date when, on New Year's Day, 1887, Charlotte Perkins Stetson, then a young wife and mother, a busy artist and writer, went to the Public Library in Providence, Rhode Island, and, getting a new card, filled it with the names of books on women. The contemplation of women's subordinate and cruel position in life had begun to move her powerfully. . . .

Charlotte Stetson could communicate the thrill of horror in both prose and verse, an uncanny art, used infrequently, with a purpose, and finding its most startling expression about this time in "The Yellow Wall Paper," the story of a nerve-sick young mother's hallucination caused by loneliness and inactivity. The figure of a woman creeps from the paper of the room in which the patient is most tenderly confined, and haunts her with a secret and growing power until the day comes when she completely identifies herself with the creeping form and is mad. "The Yellow Wall Paper" has been placed by critics with the weird masterpieces of Hawthorne and Poe; but this is only a lazy classification for a story which stands alone in American fiction. For originality, both as thinker and writer, was Charlotte Stetson's outstanding quality, except, perhaps, the inspirational beauty of her thought and its joyousness, which rose from her profound perception of reality. . . .

"Modern society is no society," Ibsen had said in his justice to women; "it is merely a masculine society." In "The Man-made World, or Our Androcentric Culture," Charlotte Gilman analyzes our masculine

From Amy Wellington, "Charlotte Perkins Gilman," in Wellington, *Women Have Told: Studies in the Feminist Tradition* (Boston: Little, Brown, 1930), 115–31.

civilization with startling results. . . . But it is in literature, the chief art of humanity . . . that Charlotte Gilman finds this predominance of masculine traits most subtly injurious. For men have written and men have read the world's literature. . . . Most hurtful of all is the "perverted sex philosophy of Freud and his followers," this "belated revival of phallic worship," which now distorts our literature. . . .

Part 3

The Critics

Introduction

Until recently, virtually all of the criticism on Charlotte Perkins Gilman's short fiction focused, not surprisingly, on her most popular story, "The Yellow Wall-Paper." Because essays on that story are both abundant and accessible—and because I wish to correct the critical neglect of her other short works—I have chosen to reprint only two. Also included as reprints are an essay on "The Giant Wistaria" and an excerpt from an essay on Gilman's utopian fiction. Three new essays focusing on several of Gilman's lesser-known works appear in this section. They include an examination of Gilman's "Studies in Style," an assessment of masculine roles in several works, and a discussion of lesbian overtones in selected stories.

Elaine Hedges's fine historical retrospective of the critical response to "The Yellow Wall-Paper" opens this section. Working from a primarily feminist perspective, Hedges traces the evolution of the often-contradictory interpretations engendered by the story and offers a response to the "trajectory of literary criticism" that has resulted. In her reading of "The Yellow Wall-Paper," Catherine Golden explores the dichotomy between text and subtext by examining the story's linguistic features. Golden concludes that "The Yellow Wall-Paper" can best be read as a double palimpsest through which the narrator ultimately achieves a "dubious victory."

"The Giant Wistaria" is the subject of Gary Scharnhorst's critical essay, in which he observes that the work "is, in its most elementary sense, a formulaic ghost story, a terrifying diptych about an unwed mother, tormented by Puritan patriarchy, whose spirit haunts a decaying mansion." Scharnhorst probes the intricate layers of the story, and concludes that it is "not merely a tract in the gothic mode" but a complex work that paradoxically borrows elements from frontier mythology and from Gilman's biography to form a story that "compels the reader to sift through the fragments of debris and puzzle over the sequence of episodes." Scharnhorst contends that in the final analysis, " 'The Giant Wistaria' is a type of open-ended riddle . . . an alternative fiction which reaches across the frontier of expression."

Kenneth Huntress Baldwin attempts to repair the critical neglect of Gilman's "Studies in Style," which appeared in the short-lived literary weekly the *Impress* in 1894–95. Nearly 10 percent of her short fiction was published in "Studies in Style." Baldwin examines "Gilman's sophisticated performance as imitator, originator, and experimenter" and maintains that "the lack of critical attention is a result of [the] radical inaccessibility" of the series. As Baldwin observes, "[T]he *Impress* remains the last major known" work by Gilman "yet to be issued in a format that would make it readily available to students and scholars."

Monika M. Elbert's reading of several stories supports Gilman's contention that she was more a humanist than a feminist. Drawing on Gilman's theoretical tracts in *The Home*, *The Man-Made World*, and *Women and Economics*, Elbert argues that the fiction depicts "the masculine sense of overdeveloped familial duty and allegiance to a mercenary business system [that] brutalizes and desensitizes men to the point where they themselves are . . . caught in the stultifying web of domesticity as surely as [women]." Among the stories that Elbert examines are "Making a Living," "Her Beauty," "His Excuse," "Mrs. Elder's Idea," "Mr. Peebles' Heart," "Joan's Defenders," "Her Housekeeper," and "The Cottagette."

Barbara A. White questions the "almost universal" reading of Gilman as a heterosexual writer and discusses several stories that she maintains are "unmistakably 'Lesbian texts.'" White argues that while Gilman failed to emphasize "lesbian possibilities" in her fiction because it "would have contradicted her major reason for writing," several stories nevertheless betray evidence of sexual attraction between women. The stories that White examines include "My Poor Aunt," "Lost Women," "Mrs. Power's Duty," "The Boarder Bit," "Turned," and "Being Reasonable."

In her study of Gilman's utopian fiction, Carol Farley Kessler argues that in her fictional world, "Gilman 're-presented' her ideas clothed as characters" and that her utopian stories were "'thought experiments' which extrapolate possibilities from present-day society." Kessler maintains that the stories perform "cultural work" by providing explicit models to show "how Gilman's readers might go about realizing their utopian visions."

Until now, there has been a widespread tendency among critics to label Gilman's oeuvre as "social reform" fiction, a term that is both arbitrary and limiting. Collectively, the essays in this section challenge the popular assumptions by arguing that Gilman's literary style was much more diverse—and her ideas far more complex—than critics have generally allowed.

Elaine R. Hedges

"I've got out at last," said I ... "And I've pulled off most of the paper, so you can't put me back!"

Since 1973, when I wrote the Afterword to the Feminist Press edition, "The Yellow Wallpaper" has become the Press's best-selling volume and one of the best-selling works of fiction by university presses in the United States. It has been reprinted in England, France, Spain, the Netherlands, Germany, Sweden, and Iceland, and it has inspired several film and dramatic versions, a television adaptation, and even an opera. It is of course regularly assigned in women's studies and literature courses and is by now firmly established in the literary canon, appearing in all of the major anthologies. Together with *The Awakening* it is probably the most well-known rediscovered work by a nineteenth-century American woman.

Since the story's republication, there have been more than two dozen critical studies of it, including biographical, genre, reader response, discourse theory, psychoanalytic, and new historicist and cultural studies readings. Collectively they offer a dazzling and significantly disparate array of interpretations. The wallpaper, as the story's key metaphor, has been read as inscribing the medical, marital, maternal, psychological, sexual, sociocultural, political, and linguistic situation of its narrator-protagonist; as an image of the situation of the woman writer and hence a way of understanding the dilemmas of female authorship; as revealing the relations between gender and reading and gender and writing; and as a description of the problems of female self-representation within both the Lacanian world of the Symbolic and the capitalist world of the United States in the late nineteenth century. Analyses of the story's formal and stylistic features have variously argued for it as a realistic story, a feminist Gothic tale, and one of the earliest modernist texts. The end-

---

"'Out at Last'? 'The Yellow Wallpaper' after Two Decades of Feminist Criticism." From *The Captive Imagination: A Casebook on 'The Yellow Wallpaper,'"* Catherine Golden, ed. (New York: The Feminist Press, 1992), 319–33. Reprinted by permission.

lessly debated ending has been interpreted as the narrator's triumph and/or her defeat, with positions ranging along a spectrum that, at one end, sees her madness as a higher form of sanity and her search for meaning in the paper as successful and liberating, to the other end, that sees her as fatally retreating to a condition of childishness, or infantilism, or animalhood, or even inanimateness. Her crawling, thus, is either a sign of rebirth or of regression; and her husband's fainting proof either that she has outwitted him or that, by becoming unconscious, he's outwitted her, by refusing to listen to her. Finally, critics have argued that Gilman's contemporaries could not read the story because they lacked the necessary reading conventions, and, on the other hand, that they in fact had such conventions but would not read it, for very fear of discovering what it really said.

Such a synopsis might suggest that "The Yellow Wallpaper" has become our white whale, or, as some recent critics would have it, our feminist albatross, for by now not only the story's once roughly agreed-upon meaning, but its privileged status as an exemplary text and a feminist critical touchstone are being challenged. At the same time, however, the story has been adopted by new historicist critics as one of *their* exemplary texts, so that its continuing visibility and critical viability seem assured. This would seem, then, to be a good moment for a backward glance and a reconnoitering. What do the story's changing interpretations, and the recent challenges to the earliest interpretations, tell us about the trajectory of literary criticism, and particularly of feminist literary criticism, over the last twenty years?

The earliest studies of the story—and I'm referring to four that are frequently grouped together—my Afterword, Sandra Gilbert and Susan Gubar's treatment in *The Madwoman in the Attic*, Annette Kolodny's "A Map for Rereading: Or, Gender and the Interpretation of Literary Texts," and Jean Kennard's "Convention Coverage or How to Read Your Own Life"—read it, sympathetically, as the narrative of a woman's efforts to free herself from the confining social and psychic structures of her world, with the wallpaper interpreted as encoding those oppressive structures. The extent to which she was seen as succeeding was moot, with my arguing that she achieves temporary insight but is at the end defeated, totally mad, and Kolodny similarly concluding that she manages only to reencode her own unacceptable reality within herself. The readings of Gilbert and Gubar and Kennard showed the greatest investment in the narrator's success, with the former seeing her as "mad" only by society's standards but in fact moving into "the open spaces of . . .

[her] own authority" (91), and the latter arguing that her madness could be seen as a higher form of sanity or truth. Other early, briefer, analyses were similarly split, with Loralee MacPike and Beate Schöpp-Schilling describing the narrator's insanity as, respectively, a creative act and a successful defiance, and Mary Beth Pringle on the other hand arguing that all she accomplishes is to shape the wallpaper into "the only thing she knows: a cage" (21). Despite what is roughly a fifty-fifty division here, the idea that its earliest critics saw an essentially or largely triumphant conclusion to the story, a victory for the narrator, has prevailed, with critical consequences that will be apparent later.

Although these studies, from 1973 to 1981, tended to read the wallpaper primarily in terms of the narrator's social situation, broadly defined, interest in describing her dilemma through reference to issues of textuality, language, and discourse was early evident, since, of course, the narrator in the story is crucially engaged both in writing—she tries to record her experience in her journal—and in reading—she tries to decipher the patterns in the paper. However, whose text she was reading—whether her own or her husband's—and how she read it, soon became as problematical as the degree of her success or failure. For Gilbert and Gubar, concerned as they were in *The Madwoman in the Attic* with the anxiety of female authorship, the wallpaper was "the facade of the patriarchal text" (90), which, by releasing the woman inside it, the narrator escapes, becoming ready to author her own. But for Kolodny the wallpaper was the narrator's own text, the text of herself, which could not get read or recorded. In 1985 Paula Treichler approached the story as a struggle over woman's right to author her own sentences, in opposition to her doctor-husband's medical "sentencing" of her, and found that the narrator did so, at least temporarily, through an "impertinent" language that defied male control, and through her relation to the wallpaper, which Treichler saw as a metaphor for women's discourse, "thick with life, expression, and suffering" (75, 73). The following year Judith Fetterley, also concerned with male control of textuality—of the scripts or stories through which women must try to define and understand themselves—found the narrator temporarily achieving the authority of her own script, but the wallpaper, as patriarchal text, eventually strangling the women who try to get through—a conclusion with which two other critics, Karen Ford and Carol Neely, who had written brief rejoinders to Treichler, generally agreed.

By 1986 this approach to the story, in terms of textuality and language, was producing readings that seemed to offer less and less autonomous or expressive space to the narrator. Two articles appeared that year that read the wallpaper, in Lacanian psychoanalytic terms, as the site of the narrator's struggle with self-representation through language. In "Monumental Feminism and Literature's Ancestral House: Another Look at 'The Yellow Wallpaper,' " Janice Haney-Peritz, arguing, as Treichler had, that the story should be approached not in terms of oppressive social structures, as earlier interpretations had approached it, but in terms of the oppressive structures of male discourse, could find less room for even the partial victory that Treichler and Fetterley, like most earlier critics, had tried to negotiate. For Haney-Peritz, once the narrator perceives a *real* woman as opposed to the *symbol* of a woman in the paper, she has surrendered all access to the Symbolic realm, the linguistic realm in which her identity as a speaking and writing subject must be constructed, and retreated into the realm of the pre-Oedipal Imaginary, where she becomes infantilized and hopelessly encrypted in fantasy. And Mary Jacobus, in her book, *Reading Woman*, by focusing on the narrator as an hysteric, saw her as engaged in a process of figuration, an hysterical overreading of the wallpaper, that trapped her in a maze of signs, where she becomes totally lost.

These readings, and especially Haney-Peritz's, were in turn given additional currency in a 1988 article by Diane Herndl, for whom the narrator is also an hysteric who, after failing in the Symbolic realm to find self-representation, retreats to the hallucinatory realm of the Imaginary. When, in that hallucinatory realm, she endows the wallpaper with life, she becomes herself an object, "just another of the indecipherable furnishings in her husband's house" (74). Although in 1988 in *Writing Beyond the Ending* Rachel Blau DuPlessis could suggest both possibilities—that the narrator's madness might be seen as "divinest Sense" or, from the "perspective of normalcy," as irrational and delusive behavior (92–93), and in 1989, in volume two of *No Man's Land*, Gilbert and Gubar could envision the narrator not only out on the garden paths beyond the house but "fleeing towards the . . . gardens of *Herland*" (77), Gilman's utopian world of liberated women, it was apparent that a new critical period had begun.

The new readings depended to a significant degree on foregrounding elements in the story that, Jacobus argued, earlier critics had left unexamined: the disturbing yellow color of the wallpaper, and its smell. In her interpretation Jacobus had importantly relied on these elements, reading the yellow "stain" and the odor that the narrator ascribes to the paper as symbols of her repressed sexuality, denied representation by her culture. Embodied in her hysteric posture and erupting in her defensive and anxiety-induced overreading of the paper, this repression reduces her, at the story's end, to a creeping animal, "all body" (241), repugnant and terrifying to her fainting husband.

By the time of Jacobus's essay the wallpaper's yellow color and smell had in fact already begun to be examined, by Juliann Fleenor in 1983, and Jeffrey Berman in 1985. Both of these critics had also read the yellow color and smell as representing the narrator's sexuality, specifically her sexual fear and disgust. For Fleenor, the yellow color implied "something strange and terrible about ... female procreation, and about female physiology" (123), and for Berman the color and the smell also suggested fears of "uncontrolled reproduction" and "sexual defilement" (56). Three more recent readings have concurred. In 1988 William Veeder associated the yellow color and smell with the narrator's inability to handle adult sexuality; in 1989 Marianne deKoven saw the paper as "bloated" with denied sexual desire, its "waddling," "sprawling," "wallowing" qualities (31, 32), as well as its smell, symbolizing the narrator's sexual self-disgust; and in the same year Linda Wagner-Martin also found the story conveying the "disgust ... [the narrator] feels for herself as a sexual, procreative woman" (60).

As the quotations from Fleenor, Berman, and Wagner-Martin suggest, critics were also relating the narrator's sexual difficulties to her experience and attitudes as a new mother—another aspect of the story that its earliest critics had not extensively explored. Berman, who offered a Freudian interpretation of the story based on Gilman's own life—her unsatisfactory first marriage and her troubled childhood relationship to her parents—emphasized the narrator's fascination with the wallpaper's frightening ability to sprout into uncontrolled new growths—toadstools, seaweed, fungi—and found her projecting on to the paper her morbid fears of motherhood and reproduction. Veeder, reading the story in the light of psychological models taken from boundary and object relations theory and also using the facts of Gilman's own life, similarly found the narrator unable to deal with motherhood and, as a result, retreating to an infantile state, with the paper's repugnant yellow stain and smell becoming the infant's urine.

Meanwhile, the interpretations of Haney-Peritz and Jacobus not only disputed what they saw as the hegemonic reading of the story in my Afterword, and in Gilbert and Gubar, Kolodny, and Kennard; they also importantly challenged the interpretive practices on which those readings were based. Early interpretations, Haney-Peritz charged, citing

especially Gilbert and Gubar's and Kolodny's, were essentialist: gener-
alizing from the situation of one nineteenth-century woman, they read
the story as "the" woman's story, as having some essential " 'female
meaning' " (121, 122); and, she also argued, by encouraging readers to
identify with the narrator, especially through a belief in the possibilities
of her liberation, the critics had created and perpetuated an erroneous
feminist critical assumption—namely, that women's literature contains
"a really distinctive body" of meaning that can be discovered through
such identification (123). Questioning whether we should identify with
a narrator who may be reading her husband's text rather than her own,
she therefore also warned against the assumption that such identification is necessarily liberating.

In 1990, in "Feminist Criticism, 'The Yellow Wallpaper,' and the Politics of Color in America," Susan Lanser reiterated and extended these
charges. She, too, questioned the story's canonical status, the essentialist readings of some of its earliest critics, and their encouragement of
reader identification with the narrator, while adding the observation that
its interpreters have all been white academics, who have perhaps simply
repeated the reading practice of the story's narrator, pursuing and finding in the text, as the narrator does in the wallpaper, only our own image
reflected back. Emphasizing that both the story and its author are the
products of their culture, Lanser urged us to recognize that not only
men's writings, as feminist critics have long recognized, but women's,
and feminist criticism as well, are all "collusive with ideology" (422),
likely, that is, to embody and reflect the biases and prejudices of their
times. In the light, especially, of current concern with differences among
women, she therefore reads—or as she admits, provocatively overreads—
the wallpaper, not, or not only, as either the patriarchal text or the
woman's text, but as the culture's text. The result is that she finds in the
paper's yellow color and smell and in its imagery a reflection of the
nation's obsession, at the turn of the century, with issues of race, due to
the massive immigration at the time from southern and eastern Europe
and from Asia, an obsession which Gilman, as shown in her nonfictional
writings, shared, and one which, according to Lanser, the word "yellow"
came to convey, as connoting strangeness, ugliness, uncleanness, and
inferiority. Where the wallpaper, for Jacobus, was the site of the sexual
unconscious, it is now the site of the "political unconscious" (429), and
what is found there is equally unsettling.[1]

But if some recent feminist critics are rejecting "The Yellow Wallpaper" as a paradigmatic or exemplary text, preferring to see it as at best

(Jacobus) a "minor classic of female Gothic" (235) and at worst (Haney-Peritz) a "memento mori" (123), it seems to have found a new home among the new historicists, who, moreover, like Lanser, are interested in the text's complicitousness with ideology.[2] Two new historicist studies of the story that appeared in 1987 focus, as Jacobus and Herndl do, on the narrator's hysteria, but with hysteria now seen as a disease of capitalism. Walter Benn Michaels uses the story as the introduction to his study of the relation of late-nineteenth-century literary texts to American capitalism, *The Gold Standard and the Logic of Naturalism*, explicitly calling it his exemplary text. What it exemplifies now is the genesis of the marketplace, or the birth of the culture of consumption. In Michaels's reading, which is based on the Derridean idea of the self as an effect of writing, the narrator's nervous breakdown is "a function of her involvement in a certain political economy of selfhood" (27). Determined to produce herself through writing, she consumes herself in the process—a turn of affairs that of course undermines the gospel of production that Gilman preached, but that makes the narrator, as combined producer and consumer, the "efficient scene of [market] circulation" (13). Michaels's reading is extended and refined by Gillian Brown in "The Empire of Agoraphobia," which similarly sees the narrator as engaged in circulation—in, out, and around the walls of her room. But for Brown, such circulation, in both parodying that of the marketplace and protesting the immobility of domestic confinement, succeeds in making the story a feminist critique, one that anticipates Gilman's feminist redefinition of the home and women's role in her later, nonfictional works.

Where, then, are we, after almost two decades of reading "The Yellow Wallpaper," with its narrator described now as a "post-partum psychotic" or "schizophrenic" (Veeder, 63, 64), a child or infant, a disgusting body, a dead object; or, what may not be much better, a politically compromised but quite efficient member of the world of capitalism? To state the critical situation thus is of course to overstate it, since most of the newer critical interpretations still read the story as a feminist text. But it highlights what has been a major shift: the diminishment or even disavowal of the narrator's status as a feminist heroine.

What accounts for this shift are of course changes in the intellectual and critical climate since the story's first republication in the early 1970s. In her 1981 essay Kennard ably described much of that climate out of which the earliest readings emerged, especially the literary and extraliterary circumstances that enabled and encouraged us to read madness as a kind of sanity, or insight; to see the narrator as on a quest for her identity, or, as I described her, as "fighting for some sense of independent self" (51); and to see her husband as representing the patriarchal forces with which she had to contend. I should like now simply to elaborate a bit on what Kennard said, to talk in somewhat more detail about a few aspects of that intellectual climate.

Certainly the prior rediscovery and publication of Kate Chopin's *The Awakening* centrally mattered. The story of a woman who was questioning marriage and motherhood in the interest of her need for some greater fulfillment, its thematic appeal was strong at a time when we were posing the same questions about our own lives. "The Yellow Wallpaper" carried the same theme, with its important additional emphasis on the narrator's yearning for what she calls "congenial work" (Hedges 10). And both stories, of course, posed similarly problematic endings: whether the narrator's madness, like Edna Pontellier's drowning, was to be read as a victory or a defeat. To the extent that there was an early critical investment in finding some degree of triumph in the endings of both works, it was, I think, due not only to the textual clues that could support such readings, but also to our concern, in those years when the history of women's lives was being newly recovered, that that history not be read merely as one of victimization, the passive acceptance of subordination and suffering. As Elaine Showalter has noted, the image of "awakening" carried special resonance for women at the time (40), and so the narrator's growing awareness of her situation, her efforts to decipher, understand, and then question it—quite apart from the degree of her ultimate success or failure in changing it—were given important thematic weight. Kennard found "a sort of triumph" in the narrator's "understanding of her situation" (77), and I found her "heroism" residing "in her perceptivity and in her resistance" (53).

To a significant degree that resistance took the form of anger, as expressed for example in her defying both her husband's and the housekeeper's orders, or in tearing the paper, and this was important at a time when we were discovering, and wondering how to deal with, our own. Two years before the republication of "The Yellow Wallpaper" the poet Adrienne Rich had delivered a talk that would become one of her most influential pieces of writing. In "When We Dead Awaken: Writing as Re-Vision"—and the title's use of the image of awakening is of course further proof of its power in the early 1970s—she had linked women's anger to their victimization, encouraging its release into creative expression, thus validating what was considered an "unfeminine" emotion and supporting its discovery in women's texts.

In "The Yellow Wallpaper" the narrator's husband was also a doctor, important of course in many interpretations of the work. His occupation was yet another aspect of the story that in the 1970s carried a special force as we absorbed the implications of the discoveries then being made about the medical profession's treatment of women in the nineteenth century. Those reactions were best captured in the title of a later work on nineteenth-century medical attitudes toward women, G. J. Barker-Benfield's *The Horrors of the Half-Known Life* (1976). Yet the work of researchers like Barbara Ehrenreich and Deirdre English in *Complaints and Disorders: The Sexual Politics of Sickness* and of Ann Douglas Wood in " 'The Fashionable Diseases': Women's Complaints and Their Treatment in Nineteenth-Century America," both published the same year as The Feminist Press edition of "The Yellow Wallpaper," provided a context that further committed us to the story's narrator in her struggle against a husband who could be seen as a doubly powerful antagonist. In the words of the title of the book published in 1971 by the Boston Women's Health Book Collective, at the beginning of the women's health movement, we, like the narrator, were trying to reclaim "our bodies, ourselves."

Finally, one cannot discount the political climate of the time. The year that saw the republication of "The Yellow Wallpaper" was the year of the *Roe v. Wade* Supreme Court decision, which climaxed a decade of legislative victories for women, from the Equal Pay Act of 1963 to Title VII of the Civil Rights Act to Title IX of the Education Act. This record of accomplishment created a sense of hope and expectation that could infuse the reading of women's texts, since their recovery, after years, decades and sometimes centuries of silence and neglect, was itself a "political" achievement. As Rich said in 1971, and as we believed, "hearing our wordless or negated experiences affirmed" in literature could have "visible effects on women's lives" (34).

In August 1973, shortly after The Feminist Press edition of "The Yellow Wallpaper" was published, I received a letter from writer Joanna Russ that described her experience teaching the story to her students. "I found myself emphasizing to the class (I'm not sure why) that although the protagonist is, of course, defeated at the end . . . some really extraordinary kind of positive things come out at the same time. Rage is one of them. And that lovely statement, 'Life is much more exciting now than it used to be.' And a genuinely eerie, ironic over-playing of her role into caricature, acting out (almost) the kind of questions her husband keeps asking her: But darling, what's *wrong?* Do be sensible! Her behavior in the last scene is a marvelously witty, wicked, loony way of doing the same to him, with its mock naivete, its addressing him as 'young man' (silly goose) and its triumphantly ghastly question, 'Now why should that man have fainted?' "

In asking why, in 1973, she found herself emphasizing the comic-triumphant aspects of "The Yellow Wallpaper," and clearly rooting for its heroine, Joanna wondered if it was "just a matter of temperament." I think it was more: our living in a historical moment when, as Kennard recognized, there was a community of readers sharing the same literary conventions, the same expectations of women's literature, and, I would add, the same political hopes. So Joanna found the story "wonderful to teach and the class loved it."[3]

The newer interpretations of "The Yellow Wallpaper" come out of a drastically changed intellectual and political climate and out of a myriad of new schools of critical thought whose methods and governing assumptions importantly differ, as Haney-Peritz, Jacobus, and Lanser make clear, from those that informed the story's earliest readings. If my Afterword appeared in the same year as *Roe v. Wade,* recent interpretations are appearing in the years that have seen increasing attacks on that decision, the failure of the Equal Rights Amendment, the erosion of affirmative action, and renewed, virulent racism, all leading to a skepticism or disillusionment about women's power to create and sustain significant political and social change, or at least to the recognition that change will be slower and more difficult to achieve. The new schools of critical thought are consonant with, although not the direct outgrowth of, this climate of reduced expectations. Post-structuralist, deconstructionist, psychoanalytic, and cultural studies critical theories—all of which have been brought to bear on "The Yellow Wallpaper"—newly problematize terms or concepts that were important to the thinking of the story's earliest critics and to the political activism of the time, such as "identity," "autonomy," and "liberation." Especially in retheorizing "identity"—seeing it as culturally or linguistically or textually constructed, and as fragmented and alienated from itself, even as fictitious—and in focusing on the narrator's unconscious, the new theories, from a pre–post-structuralist point of view, diminish her potential for understanding her situation, displace her from the heroic center of her tale, and drastically reduce the extent to which she can be seen as in control of the telling. Unconscious feelings, be they sexual, maternal, or racial, damage or even destroy her; her efforts to find her identity or subjectivity within the masculine signifying system of the Symbolic, the male realm of language, are almost always, given the sheer difficulty for all women of inserting themselves into that realm, likely to fail; and the story she tells unconsciously reveals meanings of which she is unaware, and which undermine faith in what Kennard had called the "triumph" of her understanding.

The story continues to be read as a feminist text. Many of its critics continue to find its narrator achieving a temporary insight into the nature of her oppression or a momentary victory over it; indeed, this tension between the degree of her success or her failure, dramatically unresolved in the narrative, continues to be the dynamic propelling many of the new readings. And in interpretations that see the narrator as defeated, the text itself still triumphs, makes its feminist point. For Jacobus, for example, the narrator's hysteria, and for Veeder her infantilization, are to be read as compelling critiques of her society's sexual or marital arrangements. For Jacobus the repugnant body to which the narrator is reduced becomes a figure for the repressions imposed both on representations of sexuality and on women's writing in the Victorian period; for Veeder, the story is a feminist cautionary tale that brilliantly exposes the inadequacies and infantilization of both men and women in Victorian marriage. While we may have lost a feminist heroine, we have retained a feminist text.[4]

To say that in their diminishment of the protagonist these new feminist readings are less empowering than earlier ones would probably be to misplace the locus of concern, implying that newer readings of the story should do for their time what our earlier readings did for ours. Critics like Haney-Peritz, for example, or Lanser, in warning against the tendency of earlier critics to identify with a narrator whom they see as seriously flawed or embedded in fantasy, are concerned, still, with the need for political and social change. Haney-Peritz's concluding argument is that only radical changes in "the material conditions of social life" will ultimately liberate the delusioned protagonist (124); and Lanser's caveat against assuming that the situation of one white woman can stand for the situation of all women reflects the greater sensitivity to issues of racial and ethnic diversity that has characterized the women's movement in the last decade, as well as her sense that feminism's identity today is more "precarious and conflicted" (425) than it was in the 1970s.

But warnings against essentializing the story of "The Yellow Wallpaper" and against identifying with its protagonist—if indeed she is allowed an identity to identify with—can also run the risk of depoliticizing it, stripping it of some of its imaginative—and political—power. Current suspicion or rejection of "essentializing" or "totalizing" words like "woman," as others have observed, seriously risks denying the existence of commonalities among women and of their group identity, rooted in subordination, whose recognition is essential to political action.[5] "The Yellow Wallpaper" is a story about a nineteenth-century white, middle-class woman, but it addresses "woman's" situation in so far as women as a group must still contend with male power in medicine, marriage, and indeed most, if not all, of culture. In so far as its earliest critics "identified," we identified, I believe, with that situation. As Diana Fuss has recently observed, the post-structuralist project to problematize and displace identity is difficult to reconcile with the feminist project to reclaim it (70). Whether newer readings of "The Yellow Wallpaper," as they continue to nuance both its narrator and her story, may help achieve that reconciliation remains to be seen.

Notes

1. Barbara Johnson in 1989 also deals briefly with the race and class aspects of the story, arguing that "[t]he very equation of the woman's body with the blank page implies that the woman's body is white," and noting that "there are many other invisible men and women trapped in the wallpaper of the Western canon ... that neither psychoanalytic nor feminist theory has taken sufficiently into account...." (267, 268).

2. For Veeder, the story is still a major text, "one of the premier women's texts" (40).

3. Quoted by permission of the author.

4. Michaels would be an exception. In arguing that the narrator's commitment to work produces her madness he is not reading the story as a feminist text but seems, as a reviewer of his book has observed, "treacherously close to blaming a victim." Christopher P. Wilson, "Containing Multitudes: Realism, Historicism, American Studies," *American Quarterly* 41, no. 3 (September 1989): 475. Richard Feldstein, on the other hand, in an article published in 1989, argues for retrieving the protagonist as a feminist heroine by reading her regression ironically, as a "cunning craziness, a militant, politicized madness" (273), but he notes that this is, by then, a minority view.

5. See, for example, the article by Susan Bordo in Works Cited for an excellent discussion of this and related issues.

Works Cited

Berman, Jeffrey. "The Unrestful Cure: Charlotte Perkins Gilman and 'The Yellow Wallpaper.' " In *The Talking Cure: Literary Representations of Psychoanalysis.* New York: New York University Press, 1985.

Bordo, Susan. "Feminism, Postmodernism, and Gender-Skepticism." In Linda J. Nicholson, ed., *Feminism/Postmodernism.* New York: Routledge, 1990.

Boston Women's Health Book Collective. *Our Bodies, Ourselves: A Book by and for Women.* New York: Simon and Schuster, 1971.

Brown, Gillian. "The Empire of Agoraphobia." *Representations* 20 (Fall 1987): 134–57.

DeKoven, Marianne. "Gendered Doubleness and the 'Origins' of Modernist Form." *Tulsa Studies in Women's Literature* 8, no. 1 (Spring 1989): 19–42.

DuPlessis, Rachel Blau. *Writing Beyond the Ending: Narrative Strategies of Twentieth-Century Women.* Bloomington, Ind.: Indiana University Press, 1985.

Feldstein, Richard. "Reader, Text, and Ambiguous Referentiality in 'The Yellow Wall-Paper.' " In Richard Feldstein and Judith Roof, eds., *Feminism and Psychoanalysis.* Ithaca, N.Y.: Cornell University Press, 1989.

Fetterley, Judith. "Reading About Reading: 'A Jury of Her Peers,' 'The Murders in the Rue Morgue,' and 'The Yellow Wallpaper.' " In Elizabeth A. Flynn and Patrocinio P. Schweickart, eds., *Gender and Reading: Essays on Readers, Texts, and Contexts.* Baltimore, Md.: Johns Hopkins University Press, 1986.

Fleenor, Juliann Evans. "The Gothic Prism: Charlotte Perkins Gilman's Gothic Stories and Her Autobiography." In Sheryl L. Meyering, ed., *Charlotte Perkins Gilman: The Woman and Her Work.* Ann Arbor, Mi.: UMI Research Press, 1989.

Ford, Karen. " 'The Yellow Wallpaper' and Women's Discourse." *Tulsa Studies in Women's Literature* 4 (Fall 1985): 309–14.

Fuss, Diana. *Essentially Speaking: Feminism, Nature and Difference.* New York: Routledge, 1989.

Gilbert, Sandra, and Susan Gubar. *The Madwoman in the Attic: The Woman Writer and the Nineteenth-Century Literary Imagination.* New Haven, Conn.: Yale University Press, 1979. pp. 89–92.

———. *No Man's Land: The Place of the Woman Writer in the Twentieth Century.* Vol. 2. New Haven, Conn.: Yale University Press, 1989.

Haney-Peritz, Janice. "Monumental Feminism and Literature's Ancestral House: Another Look at 'The Yellow Wallpaper.' " *Women's Studies* 12, no. 2 (1986): 113–28.

Hedges, Elaine. Afterword. *The Yellow Wallpaper.* (New York: The Feminist Press, 1973).

Herndl, Diane. "The Writing Cure: Charlotte Perkins Gilman, Anna O., and 'Hysterical Writing.' " *NWSA Journal* 1, no. 1 (1988): 52–74.

Jacobus, Mary. "An Unnecessary Maze of Sign-Reading." In *Reading Women: Essays in Feminist Criticism.* New York: Columbia University Press, 1986.

Johnson, Barbara. "Is Female to Male as Ground Is to Figure?" In Richard Feldstein and Judith Roof, eds., *Feminism and Psychoanalysis.* Ithaca, N.Y.: Cornell University Press, 1989.

Kennard, Jean E. "Convention Coverage or How to Read Your Own Life." *New Literary History* 13 (Autumn 1981): 69–88.

Kolodny, Annette. "A Map for Rereading: Or, Gender and the Interpretation of Literary Texts." *New Literary History* 11, no. 3 (1980).

Lanser, Susan S. "Feminist Criticism, 'The Yellow Wallpaper,' and the Politics of Color in America." *Feminist Studies* 15, no. 3 (Fall 1989): 415–41.

MacPike, Loralee. "Environment as Psychopathological Symbolism in 'The Yellow Wallpaper.' " *American Literary Realism 1870–1910* 8 (Summer 1975): 286–88.

Michaels, Walter Benn. *The Gold Standard and the Logic of Naturalism.* Berkeley: University of California Press, 1987.

Neely, Carol Thomas. "Alternative Women's Discourse." *Tulsa Studies in Women's Literature* 4 (Fall 1985): 315–22.

Pringle, Mary Beth. " 'La Poetique de L'Éspace' in Charlotte Perkins Gilman's 'The Yellow Wallpaper.' " *The French American Review* 3 (1978): 15–22.

Schöpp-Schilling, Beate. " 'The Yellow Wallpaper': A Rediscovered 'Realistic' Story." *American Literary Realism 1870–1910* 8 (Summer 1975): 284–86.

Showalter, Elaine. "Women's Time, Women's Space: Writing the History of Feminist Criticism." In Shari Benstock, ed., *Feminist Issues in Literary Scholarship.* Bloomington, Ind.: Indiana University Press, 1985.

Treichler, Paula. "Escaping the Sentence: Diagnosis and Discourse in 'The Yellow Wallpaper.' " *Tulsa Studies in Women's Literature 3* (1984): 61–77.

———. "The Wall Behind the Yellow Wallpaper: Response to Carol Neely and Karen Ford." *Tulsa Studies in Women's Literature* 4 (Fall 1984–5): 323–30.

Veeder, William. "Who is Jane? The Intricate Feminism of Charlotte Perkins Gilman." *Arizona Quarterly* 44 (1988): 40–79.

Catherine Golden

The first-person narrative of "The Yellow Wallpaper" unfolds as a diary written by a woman undergoing a three month rest cure for a postpartum depression.[1] Judith Fetterley has argued that the wallpaper functions as a text through which the narrator expresses herself; its pattern becomes the dominant text and the woman behind the pattern the subtext with which the narrator identifies.[2] To recall the terminology of *The Madwoman in the Attic,* the yellow wallpaper thus can be perceived as a "palimpsest." Similarly, Charlotte Perkins Gilman's story itself can be read as a palimpsest. The hallucinations and dramatic actions of tearing the wallpaper and creeping on the floor comprise the dominant text, but the writing comprises the second muted text, informing the narrator's final characterization. This muted text shows how the narrator fictionalizes herself as the audience of her story. Forbidden to write but continuing to do so in secret, the narrator comes to express herself by writing her own text. As she comes to see the wallpaper as a palimpsest, she presents herself on paper in a way that suggests that, although mad, she is not completely "destroyed"[3] by her patriarchal society. As the story unfolds, the narrator's writing ceases to match her thoughts and actions or to convey a cohesive characterization of a timid oppressed figure. The increased use of "I" and her syntactical placement of the nominative case pronoun within her own sentences demonstrate a positive change in self-presentation precisely at the point when her actions dramatically compromise her sanity and condemn her to madness.[4]

The narrator records her stay in a country ancestral hall through twelve diary-like entries, each undated and separated only by several lines of blank space. The separateness of these units can be seen as a spatial indication of the narrator's own fragmented sense of self.[5] As Walter Ong notes, the audience of a diarist is oneself "encased in fictions. . . . The diarist pretending to be talking to himself has also, since he is writing, to pretend he is somehow not there. And to what self is he talking? To the self he imagines he is? Or would like to be?"[6] Although the narrator may in fact be writing for a fictional self, the way she imag-

"The Writing of 'The Yellow Wallpaper': A Double Palimpsest." From *The Captive Imagination: A Casebook on 'The Yellow Wallpaper,'* Catherine Golden, ed. (New York: The Feminist Press, 1992), 296–306. Reprinted by permission.

ines this self to be changes as the entries continue. The writing in her early entries matches the dominant text of her thoughts and actions. In the opening sentence the narrator introduces her husband before herself: "It is very seldom that mere ordinary people like John and myself secure ancestral halls for the summer."[7] Rarely used for self-expression, the reflexive case more effectively emphasizes an antecedent rather than replaces a subject. The narrator who claims she wants very much to write also hides her own belief that writing is "a great relief to my mind" (p. 10) by placing this insight in parentheses. Punctuation marks eclipse the forcefulness of this belief, which directly confronts the opinion of those who prescribe her rest cure: her physician-husband John, who "hates to have [her] write a word" (p. 13); her physician brother; the socially prominent nerve specialist S. Weir Mitchell, who is "just like John and [her] brother, only more so!" (p. 19); and even John's sister Jennie, an "enthusiastic housekeeper" who "thinks it is the writing which made [her] sick!" (pp. 17–18). At this point in the story the self-consciousness displayed through punctuational subordination keeps the narrator in a subordinate place within her sentences. The muted text matches the dominant text of her actions, which at this point reveals the narrator as fanciful and fearful. Even though her room initially repulses her, she rests in the former nursery because John chose it for her. The narrator prefers a room "that opened on the piazza and had roses all over the window, and such pretty old-fashioned chintz hangings!" (p. 12), yet she does not pursue her softly expressed conviction: " 'Then do let us go downstairs' " (p. 15). Asserting herself only through her secret act of writing, she hides her journal when she senses John's entry. Fear of detection restricts the amount she writes; she remains aware of her larger social reality at this point in the story and does not perceive of her private journal as a place for self-expression or a safe domain.

The dominant text of her actions and the muted text of her writing no doubt initially concur, in part, because the narrator is not only oppressed by those who forbid her to write but by language itself.[8] The language through which the narrator writes is imbued with a social, economic, and political reality of male domination of the late nineteenth-century that governs the way the narrator perceives language. The doctors pronounce the narrator "sick!" (p. 10). There is no escaping the words through which the doctors deliver their diagnosis, their prescription of a rest cure, or the language itself which the narrator must produce to maintain her sanity.

In the initial entry the narrator refers frequently to "Dear John" as well as what "John says" (p. 16). "John" appears four times on the opening page, the last three of which successively introduce a new paragraph:

> John laughs at me, of course, but one expects that in marriage.
> John is practical in the extreme. He has no patience with faith, an intense horror of superstition, and he scoffs openly of any talk of things not to be felt and seen and put down in figures.
> John is a physician, and *perhaps*—(I would not say it to a living soul, of course, but this is dead paper and a great relief to my mind)—*perhaps* that is one reason I do not get well faster. (pp. 9–10)

Her husband appears ten times as "John" and eleven times as the forceful nominative "he" within the initial entry of thirty-nine short paragraphs. Reference and deference to her husband keep John firmly the subject of her sentences that describe how he "scoffs" and "laughs" at her and loses "patience" with her. Within her own journal of "dead paper" meant to be read by no "living soul" (except, of course, the narrator), she privileges the man who laughs at her, misunderstands her nature, and calls her, albeit affectionately, his "blessed little goose" (p. 15).

While she calls John by his proper name, the narrator elects to remain nameless until the very end of the story, where she hints that her name may be Jane.[9] Moreover, she rarely presents herself through "I." To recall the opening sentence of the story, "It is very seldom that mere ordinary people like John and myself secure ancestral halls for the summer" (p. 9). Herein "like" functions as a preposition meaning "similar to." Usage favors "me" rather than "myself" after a preposition; the reflexive case is heavier and more cumbersome in English than in other languages.[10] In introducing "myself" and "John," the narrator intensifies her awkward positioning in her sentence and society; she is not even on par with "ordinary people like John." Since the muted text of her writing initially concurs with her actions, it is not surprising that the narrator concludes at the end of the first entry: "There comes John, and I must put this away,—he hates to have me write a word" (p. 13). Using "I" becomes not an act of assertion but rather of acquiescence determined by John's authority. The blank space confirms that the narrator has put away her writing in compliance to John's prescription.

The narrator also elects to present herself anonymously as "one," "a kind of disguised *I*."[11] The narrator disguises her autonomy when she begins to question John's authority: "You see he does not believe I am sick! And what can one do?" (p. 10). "One" dominates the second page of the first entry (it occurs three times in close proximity). The syntactic positioning calls further attention to this pronoun. The expression "what is one to do" (p. 10) semantically conveys the narrator's helplessness and perceived inability to change her uncomfortable situation; the repetition of "one" creates a haunting echo of anonymity throughout this entry and the entire story.

As the entries unfold, the narrator comes to write for a different self hinted at on the opening page through her three-fold presentation of self as "I" (one time hidden in parentheses). To recall Ong once again, the narrator comes to write for the more forceful self she "would like to be." Simply by writing and exercising grammatical options within her patriarchal language, she writes in a way that questions and ultimately challenges the authorities that confine and oppress her. Her visible expansion on the sentence level[12] shows the muted text diverging from the dominant text. Learning to read the subtext of the yellow wallpaper, the narrator gives way to fancy and loses sight of her larger social reality. However, she concomitantly fictionalizes an identity overriding the fragmentation inherent within the discrete units of language she produces and the fragmentation she feels as a woman within her society. The narrator's greater self-awareness, emerging through her self-presentation beginning in the fourth entry, undermines her original compliance to John's orders to "lie down ever so much now" and "to sleep all [she] can" (p. 26).

When the narrator begins to cry uncontrollably at "nothing" (p. 19), to obsess with her reading of the shapes of the wallpaper's dominant and muted pattern, and to perceive that the muted text "is like a woman stooping down and creeping about behind that [dominant] pattern" (p. 22), she begins to write for a forceful fictionalized self, beginning successive sentences with "I":

> I don't know why I should write this.
> I don't want to.
> I don't feel able.
> And I know John would think it absurd. But I *must* say what I feel and think in some way—it is such a relief! (p. 21)

The contents of the "I" sequence records the narrator's vacillation and questioning of her own prescription of writing to improve her nervous condition. Janice Haney-Peritz even suggests that "such contradictions

. . . betray the narrator's dependence on the oppressive discursive structure we associate with John."[13] But the clustering of "I," the italicized
emphatic "must," and the exclamation point following "relief" convey
an emerging sense of self and conviction precisely when she begins to
have delusions leading to her final actions of tearing the wallpaper from
the walls in order to free the woman and that part of herself trapped
behind the restrictive bars of the dominant pattern of the wallpaper.

Appearing a total of seven times in this sequence, "I" introduces each
of four consecutive sentences, three of which begin a new paragraph.
No longer deferring to "John" or the social authority he represents, she
conspicuously positions "I" in a configuration suggestive of a stronger
albeit fictionalized self. The positioning and four-fold use of "I" most
noticeably recalls the four-fold repetition of John on the opening page.
However, in the fourth entry the narrator dramatically inverts her original pattern; by beginning the first three rather than the last three paragraphs with "I," the narrator gives heightened emphasis to self. The
introductory positioning of the subject connotes power, and her use of
"I" demonstrates a reversal of the dynamics of power between the narrator and John.

The narrator occasionally reverts to the reflexive case, such as within
the sixth entry when she writes about solving the wallpaper's pattern:
"I am determined that nobody shall find it out but myself!" (p. 27). In
this sentence, however, the weight of the reflexive gives added force to
her assertion, further accentuated through the surrounding words and
the punctuation. A coordinating conjunction of contrast placed directly
in front of the reflexive, "but" underscores her conviction and calls
attention to "myself"; an exclamation mark reiterates this force. In the
tenth, eleventh, and twelfth entries, the narrator uses "I" for self-
presentation as well as to initiate short direct sentences, such as in the
final entry when she tells John she cannot open the door to her room:
" 'I can't,' said I" (p. 36). "I" becomes the first and the last word. The
narrator syntactically occupies the two most powerful positions within
her own sentence.

The choice and positioning of pronouns suggest a forceful sense of
self complicating the narrator's final characterization. Independent of
the muted text, the dominant text of her actions incrementally reveals
her destruction. The later entries in which the narrator also comes to
creep by daylight and to gnaw her bed in anger (pp. 34–35) demonstrate her delusional actions, which become increasingly dominant. In
fact, "a slight hysterical tendency" (p. 10) grows into eventual madness

as she gets in to the muted text of the yellow wallpaper. Given to fancy
from the start, she begins to see the wallpaper come to life as she cries
"at nothing . . . most of the time" (p. 19) and cannot sleep. Within the
wallpaper she sees "strangled heads and bulbous eyes and wadded fungus growths" (p. 34). Personified midway through the second entry
("This paper looks to me as if it *knew* what a vicious influence it had!"
[p. 16]), the muted side of the wallpaper assumes a human shape as the
narrator sees within it "a strange, provoking, formless sort of figure"
(p. 18). The muted figure within the wallpaper increasingly gains more
definition for her. Although in the fourth entry she qualifies that the figure looks "like a woman" (p. 22), she confirms this perception in the
sixth entry when she claims "now I am quite sure it is a woman" (p. 26).
As the muted pattern becomes dominant to the narrator, her delusions
translate into actions of madness that become most apparent during the
final four entries. She sees the woman behind the wallpaper creeping
and begins to creep herself, at first secretively just as she begins her
writing: "I always lock the door when I creep by daylight. I can't do it at
night, for I know John would suspect something at once" (p. 31). The
dominant wallpaper pattern becomes prison bars, and the woman
locked behind "just takes hold of the bars and shakes them hard" (p. 30).
Sympathizing with the muted text, she writes more forcefully but acts
more madly. She begins to peel the wallpaper from the walls to release
that part of herself trapped by her own social condition as mirrored by
the barred pattern of the wallpaper. The muted woman behind bars
becomes a symbol and a message for women as the narrator sees outside
the window "so many of those creeping women, and they creep so fast"
(p. 35); in fact, she begins to "wonder if they all come out of that wall-
paper as I did?" (p. 35).

Born of an hallucination, her identification leads the narrator to free
herself from the restrictive pattern of her own society, and this liberation
is conveyed on paper through her pronoun choice. Particularly the opening of the twelfth entry celebrates the narrator's fusion of identity with
the subtext of the wallpaper: "I pulled and she shook, I shook and she
pulled, and before morning we had peeled off yards of that paper" (p.
32). But following her dramatic freeing of the woman behind the wallpaper, the narrator emerges independent and forceful. Hiding the key to
her room under a plantain leaf, she seals herself in her room so that she
can "creep around as I please!" (p. 35). The narrator tells her husband
where he can find the key. Unlike the initial entry in which she senses

John's entrance and puts away her journal, she does not allow his intrusion to disrupt her creeping in the finale. The narrator, mad, is no longer timid in her action. Echoing her use of "one" to avoid self-confrontation, the narrator now speaks with detachment of her husband: "Now why should that man have fainted? But he did, and right across my path by the wall, so that I had to creep over him every time!" (p. 36).

More than the tone of writing or pronoun usage, the placement of pronouns in this closing paragraph reveals the narrator's growing sense of awareness of her former submissive state and a reversal of the power dynamics of gender. Relegating John to a modifying phrase following an intransitive verb, the narrator assumes the subject position within the final clause. This sentence, in fact, exchanges the grammatical positions the narrator originally elected for each to occupy in a grammatically similar sentence on the opening page of "The Yellow Wallpaper": "John laughs at me, of course, but one expects that in marriage" (p. 9). In selecting an intransitive verb to convey John's abuse, the narrator in her early writing undeniably isolates herself from his emotional cruelty. The verb "to laugh" can only function intransitively and thus cannot possess or envelop the narrator, "me," as its object.[14] But, in doing so, the narrator relegates herself (and later John) to a weak position within the formal bounds of the sentence. Not a basic or essential sentence part, the prepositional phrase "at me" functions as a modifier embellishing the sentence (in this case adverbially).[15] Governed only by the preposition "at," the narrator in the first entry can be dropped from her sentence, which would thus read grammatically: "John laughs . . . , of course, but one expects that in marriage" (p. 9). With such a revision her presence would remain only through a disguised reference to self ("one"). However, by changing positions with John in the grammatically similar sentence in the twelfth entry, the narrator now sends John—who has fainted to the floor—to a nonessential, powerless, syntactical place. Governed only by the preposition "over," John can be dropped from her final clause, which would thus read grammatically: "I had to creep . . . every time!" (p. 36). The narrator's actions are outside the realm of sanity, but the syntactic position she comes to occupy conveys her emerging sense of defiance against one of the forces in her patriarchal society that has fragmented her.

Other examples, particularly in the final four paragraphs of the twelfth entry, join with this exchange of grammatical positions to affirm the narrator's newly imagined self:

"What is the matter?" he cried. "For God's sake, what are you doing!"

I kept on creeping just the same, but I looked at him over my shoulder.

"I've got out at last," said I, "in spite of you and Jane. And I've pulled off most of the paper, so you can't put me back!"

Now why should that man have fainted? But he did, and right across my path by the wall, so that I had to creep over him every time! (p. 36)

John's name seems conspicuously absent from these paragraphs. Four times the narrator substitutes the nominative case for John's name ("he cried" and "he did" within her narration and "you" twice in her dialogue). Within these paragraphs she thrice substitutes the objective case for John and further reduces his status by making each pronoun an object of a preposition ("at him," "of you," and "over him"). In the final paragraph she also uses the demonstrative pronoun "that" in "that man," a detached and generic reference to John. Unlike the demonstrative "this," "that" points the reader to something or someone who is respectively farther away in a spatial sense and thus works to distance the reader and the narrator from John and his authority, to which she once readily adhered. Used to direct the reader to a preceding rather than a subsequent reference, "that man" also orients the reader to the previous rather than the two future references to him, occurring in the final sentence; the wording anticipates John's disappearance from the final dramatic clause and close of "The Yellow Wallpaper," which leaves the narrator creeping flamboyantly in the daylight as she desires.

The narrator presents herself as "I" six times in the final four paragraphs, twice forcefully beginning her own paragraphs. She displays her growing sense of self, power, and confidence at the point at which she has uncoded the text of the yellow wallpaper and liberated its muted side. In addition, an exclamation point at the end of both the last and the penultimate paragraphs gives emphasis to her final sentences, in which she moves into the subject place initially reserved for John.[16] When referring to self, she uses the possessive case twice and the objective case once, but she no longer positions the objective case reference for self in a precarious place. Importantly, in the sentence "can't put me back," "me" functions as a direct object of the transitive verb "put." Securely positioned, "me" becomes essentially connected to the action verb. The use of negation in this sentence subtly undermines the contents of earlier sentences containing transitive verbs, such as "John gathered me up in his arms, and just carried me upstairs and laid me on the bed" (p. 21); while in both sentences "me" carries the force of her male oppressor, the negation in the later sentence equally negates his force and matches the writing in the finale, where the narrator is able to write a sentence that can function grammatically without "John."

Examining the muted text of the narrator's writing within this palimpsest in relation to the dominant text of her delusional actions permits the narrator a dubious victory. Her widening use of "I" and grammatical repositioning of "I" and "John" hint at a degree of personal liberation for her fictionalized self recorded within this tale of a woman's breakdown. The muted text of her writing comes to reflect her growing self-awareness as she moves beyond the prescription of healthy eating, moderate exercise, and abundant rest and chooses literal madness over John's prescription for sanity. As the narrator tears the paper to free the woman and that part of herself trapped within the story's mirrored palimpsest and creeps over her husband, she acts in a way that implies a cogent madness, rid of the timidity and fear that punctuate her earlier entries. Only at the point at which she acts out of madness does she find a place within the patriarchal language she uses, although not yet within her larger social reality. Creeping deeper into madness and her fictionalized self, the narrator writes in a defiant voice, circumvents John's force, and banishes "him" to the outer boundaries of her own sentence.

Notes

1. In "Monumental Feminism and Literature's Ancestral House: Another Look at 'The Yellow Wallpaper,' " *Women's Studies*, 12, No. 2 (1986), 113–28, Janice Haney-Peritz calls the ten sections "diary-like entries" (p. 114). See also Paula A. Treichler's essay, "Escaping the Sentence: Diagnosis and Discourse in 'The Yellow Wallpaper,' " in *Feminist Issues in Literary Scholarship*, ed. Shari Benstock (Bloomington: Indiana Univ. Press, 1986), p. 63.

2. Judith Fetterley, "Reading About Reading: 'A Jury of Her Peers,' 'The Murders in the Rue Morgue,' and 'The Yellow Wallpaper,' " in *Gender and Reading: Essays on Readers, Texts, and Contexts*, ed. Elizabeth A. Flynn and Patrocinio P. Schweikart (Baltimore: Johns Hopkins Univ. Press, 1986), pp. 147–64. Fetterley advances that "blocked from expressing herself *on* paper, she seeks to express herself through paper" (p. 162). Although my reading concurs with and draws upon Fetterley's analysis, I would argue that the narrator does not experience writer's "block." While writing less and less frequently, she, in fact, writes more forcefully as she expresses herself through the paper and gets in to the subtext.

3. Elaine R. Hedges, "Afterword," *The Yellow Wallpaper* (New York: Feminist Press, 1973), p. 55. Hedges praises the late nineteenth-century work because it authenticates the experience of women restricted by a patriarchal society, but she concludes that the narrator's final actions confirm her destruction.

4. The relationship between language and the mental and social condition of the narrator has not gone undetected in previous literary and biographical criticism. See Hedges, pp. 48–49, on paragraphing and mental state; Annette Kolodny, "A Map for Rereading: Or, Gender and the Interpretation of Literary Texts," *New Literary History*, 11 (1980), 458–59, on pronouns and identity; and Treichler, p. 75, on the narrator as language user. These observations suggest a need for a systematic examination of the way the narrator writes to herself and for herself in her patriarchal society. Verb usage, discussed only briefly in this article, remains a rich field for systematic examination.

5. Akin to diary writing, the epistolary form divides writing into separate entities with discrete beginnings and endings and so accentuates the gaps inherent within all language. For more discussion, see Christina Gillis, *The Paradox of Privacy* (Gainesville: Univ. of Florida Press, 1984); Janet Altman, *Epistolarity: Approaches to a Form* (Columbus: Ohio Univ. Press, 1982).

6. Walter Ong, "A Writer's Audience Is Always a Fiction," *PMLA*, 90 (1975), 20.

7. Charlotte Perkins Gilman, *The Yellow Wallpaper* (New York: Feminist Press, 1973), p. 9. Further references will be included in the text and cited by page number.

8. For discussion of the relationship between language and social reality, see, for example, Robin Lakoff, *Language and Woman's Place* (New York: Harper & Row, 1975) and two useful collections: Barrie Thorne, Chris Kramarae, and Nancy Henley, eds., *Language, Gender, and Society* (Rowley: Newbury House, 1983); Sally McConnell-Ginet, Ruth Borker, and Nelly Furman, eds., *Women and Language in Literature and Society* (New York: Praeger, 1980).

9. Hedges, pp. 62–63. The narrator's reference to "Jane" at the end of the story may be a printer's error, but it equally can be the narrator referring to her respectable and socially defined "Jane" self, of which she is also free at the end of the story. However, "Jennie" can also be a nickname for "Jane" and thus suggests she has freed herself despite John and Jennie.

10. For more explanation of the reflexive see Otto Jespersen, *Essentials of English Grammar* (University: Univ. of Alabama Press, 1981), p. 112.

11. Jespersen, p. 150.

12. For further discussion of deep surface structure, see Scott Soames and David Perlmutter, "Meaning and Underlying Structure," in *Syntactic Argumentation and the Structure of English* (Berkeley: Univ. of California Press, 1979), pp. 533–36.

13. Haney-Peritz, p. 116.

14. Although "laugh" is an intransitive verb, Jespersen points out that the sentence "everybody laughed at Jim" can be interpreted in two ways. Jim is governed by the preposition "at" and thus may be considered the object of the preposition. But "laughed at" can equally be considered a transitive verb phrase having Jim as its object. This latter interpretation explains the possibility of passivization for the sentence "Jim was laughed at by everybody" (pp. 122–23). This same reasoning can be applied to the sentences the narrator constructs in "The Yellow Wallpaper."

15. For more discussion of the roles of the prepositional phrase in sentence structure (passivization), see Soames and Perlmutter, pp. 552–68, and Jespersen, p. 121.

16. The narrator undeniably places an exclamation point following John's statement of outrage at her actions of tearing down the wallpaper, but her consecutive two-fold usage of this forceful punctuation mark weights the attention in favor of her own declaration.

Gary Scharnhorst

Charlotte Perkins Gilman, a socialist, sociologist, and "the leading intellectual in the woman's movement in the United States" early in the twentieth century,[1] first rose to public prominence as a poet and writer of fiction during the last decade of the nineteenth. Gilman "has made a place of her own," W. D. Howells announced in 1896, though he feared her work was mostly appreciated by "fanatics, philanthropists and other Dangerous Persons."[2] Such has been the case, it seems, with two gothic tales Gilman published early in the 1890s in the *New England Magazine*. The second of these stories was "The Yellow Wallpaper," a harrowing and "macabre postpartum fantasy"[3] which, after long neglect, has been disinterred from the moldering pages of bound periodicals and widely circulated. The first of Gilman's works in the *New England Magazine*, however, is virtually unknown to modern readers. "The Giant Wistaria," a forgotten tale remarkable for its adaptation of frontier mythology to the tradition of the female gothic, deserves to be resurrected in its own right.

"The Giant Wistaria" is, in its most elementary sense, a formulaic ghost story, a terrifying diptych about an unwed mother, tormented by Puritan patriarchy, whose spirit haunts a decaying mansion. In the first section of the story, set sometime in the late eighteenth century, the unnamed woman suffers disgrace for bearing a child upon her arrival in the wilderness of the New World. Her father physically abuses her and insists that she marry a cousin, a "coarse fellow" whose proposals she had "ever shunned."[4] He also demands that she return with him to England, abandoning her child, and that she be locked in her chamber, a captive to his authority, until she agrees to this plan. In the second and longer section of the story, set a century later, a young couple rent the old house and invite several friends for a visit. They consider the man-

"Charlotte Perkins Gilman's 'The Giant Wistaria': A Hieroglyph of the Female Frontier Gothic." From *Frontier Gothic: Terror and Wonder at the Frontier in American Literature*, David Mogen et al., eds. (Rutherford, NJ: Fairleigh Dickinson University Press, 1993), 156–74. Reprinted by permission.

sion "a *real* ghostly place" (482) nestled in a riot of savage nature. The grounds, "once beautiful with rare trees and shrubs," have now gone to seed and become "a gloomy wilderness of tangled shade."

> The old lilacs and laburnums, the spirea and syringa, nodded against the second-story windows. What garden plants survived were great ragged bushes or great shapeless beds. A huge wistaria vine covered the whole front of the house. The trunk, it was too large to call a stem, rose at the corner of the porch by the high steps, and had once climbed its pillars; but now the pillars were wrenched from their places and held rigid and helpless by the tightly wound and knotted arms. (482)

The visitors, particularly the women, soon begin "to see bloodstains and crouching figures" (482) in the sinister landscape, including the silhouette of a woman in the trunk of the ancient wistaria. That night, the ghost of the woman appears to two of the male visitors. The next morning, one of them reports that the "poor creature looked just like" all "those crouching, hunted figures" (483) they had discerned the night before in the dark landscape. The other reveals that he followed the ghost into the cellar, where it rattled the chains of the draw-bucket in the well. Each of them mentions a small red cross the she-ghost wore on a necklace of gold. The residents of the house quickly descend to the cellar, haul the mud-laden bucket to the surface of the well, and discover in it the tiny skeleton of a month-old child. The story ends as workmen find, beneath the rotting planks of the old porch and "in the strangling grasp of the roots of the giant wistaria," the bones of a woman with "a tiny scarlet cross on a thin chain of gold" (485) around her neck.

On first reading, the story seems a chilling if rather transparent indictment of sexual oppression. By piecing together a number of disparate clues, the reader may guess the ending to the tale of tyranny and woe recounted in part one: The young woman apparently escaped from her chamber, hid under the porch, drowned her baby rather than abandon it, and then starved to death rather than submit to her father's demand that she marry for the sake of propriety and return to England. As in other works of female gothicism, the protagonist is "simultaneously persecuted victim and courageous heroine."[5] Her literary forebear is not so much Hester Prynne of Hawthorne's *The Scarlet Letter*, however, as the maddened slave Cassy of Harriet Beecher Stowe's *Uncle Tom's Cabin*. Lest this point seem forced or contrived, note that Gilman considered Stowe, her great-aunt, "one of the world's greatest women" and her novel "a great book," the most popular and influential "work of fiction that was ever written."[6] Like Cassy, the heroine of "The Giant Wistaria" kills her child rather than allow it to suffer ostracism or persecution. In her early poem, "In Duty Bound," Gilman had alluded to childbearing as an "obligation preimposed, unsought. / Yet binding with the force of natural law."[7] In "An Old Proverb," written some months after the "Wistaria" story, Gilman would again illustrate this horror of maternity in a man-made world:

No escape under heaven! Can man treat you worse
After God has laid on you his infinite curse?
The heaviest burden of sorrow you win
Cannot weigh with the load of original sin;
No shame be too black for the cowering face
Of her who brought shame to the whole human race!
    No escape under heaven!

For you feel, being human. You shrink from the pain
That each child, born a woman, must suffer again.
From the strongest of bonds hearts can feel, man can shape,
You cannot rebel, or appeal, or escape.
You must bear and endure. If the heart cannot sleep,
And the pain groweth bitter,—too bitter,—then weep!
    For you feel, being human.[8]

Under the circumstances, the murder and suicide seem acts of heroic defiance which save child and mother from lives of shame. Much as Cassy haunts Simon Legree in *Uncle Tom's Cabin* until she has literally scared him to death, moreover, the ghostly presence in Gilman's story appears to exact her own measure of revenge upon her persecutors. Terrorized by men in the first part, she becomes the source of terror to men in the second.

"The Giant Wistaria" is not merely a tract in the gothic mode, however. Gilman also assimilated in it various elements of frontier mythology. Like many another American writer, she viewed the American West in paradoxical terms, as both promised land and howling wilderness. In her early allegorical poem "Nature's Answer," for example, she wrote of a man who homesteaded on the fairest spot on earth, with its "Soft hills, dark woods, smooth meadows richly green, / And cool tree-shaded lakes the hills between." But a pestilence in the night swept "his paradise so fair" and "killed him there."

"O lovely land!" he cried, "how could I know
'That death was lurking under this fair show'?"
And answered Nature, merciful and stern.
"I teach by killing: let the others learn."[9]

Gilman expressed similarly ambivalent views about the American wilderness in "The Giant Wistaria." On the one hand, the mother in the story has fled the oppressive Old World for a new start in the "luxuriant" New World garden. She yearns to walk in the "green fields" of the frontier or virgin land. Elsewhere in her writings, Gilman clearly associated the westering experience with freedom and opportunity, especially for women. "As American women are given higher place—have won higher place—than any women on earth," she wrote in 1897, "so the women of the west stand higher than any in America."[10] Or as she wrote in her poem "In Mother-Time,"

We come to California for the sunshine and the flowers:
Our motherhood has brought us here as one:
For the fruit of all the ages should share the shining hours.
With the blossoms ever-springing
And the golden globes low swinging,
In the sun.[11]

On the other hand, however, the mother in "The Giant Wistaria" fails to realize the freedom and independence promised in the west. Like the biblical Eve, she is banished from the garden for her sexual sin and cursed to suffer in childbirth. The cross on the chain around her neck represents the noose or halter of orthodoxy. The grotesque wistaria which takes root in her corpse, a mere seedling in the first part of the story, even figures as a tree of knowledge, botanical cousin to Beatrice's flowery shrub in Hawthorne's "Rappaccini's Daughter."

In her art no less than in her life, moreover, Gilman revised the traditional pattern of male flight to the geographical frontier. For the record, the story is moored autobiographically: Gilman wrote it after she left her husband in Rhode Island and moved to southern California, "the Garden of the Lord,"[12] with her infant daughter: that is, both the displaced author and protagonist flee (New) England for the West. Like conventional western male heroes, it seems, women might retreat westward from the sexual battlefield, albeit with one crucial difference: Whereas Natty Bumppo and Huck Finn "light out for the Territory ahead of the rest," preserving their bachelor freedoms, Gilman (like the woman she portrayed in the story) headed west with a cradle in tow. Obviously enough, mothers could not simply flee into the forest. For them, there was "no escape under heaven." They could not merely abandon off-spring, as the patriarch in Gilman's story proposes. At the very least, they had to arrange for alternative child care.

When she wrote the story in the winter of 1890,[13] Gilman was (like her character) at the center of a brewing scandal, caught in a double bind, both under fire as an irresponsibly single mother and under pressure to return east cloaked in marital respectability. "The Giant Wistaria" thus betrays the author's own predicament. As Juliann Fleenor explains, women writers have often used the gothic form "to convey fear of maternity and its consequent dependent mother/infant relationship."[14] Whereas Cassy and the heroine of "The Giant Wistaria" kill their children, Gilman in 1894 would dispatch her daughter to live with her former husband, the artist Charles Walter Stetson, and his second wife, the poet Grace Ellery Channing. As an adult, Katharine Stetson Chamberlin would complain that her mother had "seized the opportunity to get her freedom by shipping me East,"[15] but such a comment fails to account for Gilman's genuine regret that she had been forced to relinquish custody of her child. As she wrote later in her autobiography, "There were years, years, when I could never see a mother and child together without crying."[16] Gilman desperately wished to be free of the burdensome routine of motherhood, to be sure, but she purchased her freedom at a terrible price: a wrenching and permanent physical separation from her daughter, a premeditated and "guilt-producing form of death"[17] which she had anticipated and symbolically described in "The Giant Wistaria."

Unfortunately, this all-too-tidy biographical analysis of Gilman's tale may tend to obscure some of its startling formal characteristics as a literary text. As Leslie Fiedler reminds us, gothicism is an avant-garde literary movement, a protest or "rebellion of the imagination" against fiction of the commonplace.[18] An ambiguous, half-told tale disrupted by silences and ellipses, "The Giant Wistaria" is a type of open-ended riddle rather than a closed authorial monologue, an alternative fiction which reaches across the frontier of expression. The text responds to problems of authority by declaring its own indeterminacy. The story consists almost entirely of dialogue. Events are narrated by several distinct voices, none of them privileged, a cacophony of language akin to Bakhtin's notion of *heteroglossia*.[19] The decentralizing, centrifugal forces tearing at the discourse, Gilman's refusal to employ a single perspective or intelligence which can be trusted to observe and explain, compels the reader to sift through the fragments of debris and puzzle over the sequence of episodes. These parts, by any method of addition, yield no simple sum or symmetrical whole. Gilman's tale resolves no mysteries of historical causation, repairs no rifts in the mosaic of the past. Like the wistaria vine grown from an innocuous sprig, the past has become a Gordian knot or monstrous tangle of events which can never be straightened.

The narrative is, perhaps, all the more terrifying for the questions it leaves dangling. Who really kills the child? The heroine seems the most likely candidate, but her despotic father had earlier wished aloud that his pregnant daughter had been "cleanly drowned, than live to this end" (480). Does the heroine really hide under the porch and starve to death, or is she murdered (again, by her father?) and her body secreted beneath the loose boards? And who fathered her child? Might the heroine have been the victim of incest, given her father's insistence on abandoning the infant and returning immediately to England? None of these questions can be definitively answered on the basis of what we are told in the story, though we might reasonably expect some or all of them to be answered in a traditionally unified authorial monologue. Like other female gothicists such as Mary Shelley, Gilman amplifies the terror her story evokes by refusing to resolve it.

Nor are these the only gaps or "places of indeterminacy" (in Wolfgang Iser's phrase)[20] which appear in the text. For example, the heroine (the conventional designation never seemed less appropriate) is never directly described. Her presence is signified in the first part of the story by two brief comments: from the beginning, it seems, she is virtually a disembodied voice. Her father quickly silences her, significantly enough, by striking her across the mouth. As a ghost in the second part of the story, she does not speak at all. When addressed "rather fiercely" by one of the men, "she [doesn't] seem to notice" (484). Instead, her eerie presence is reported at second-hand by those visitors to the mansion who see her in the nightmare landscape. Gilman underscores the deceptions author(iz)ed by patriarchy when one of the weekend visitors, a reporter for a New York newspaper, declares upon his arrival that "if we don't find a real ghost, you may be very sure I shall make one. It's too good an opportunity to lose!" (482). After the ghost appears, he proposes to "put it in the Sunday edition!" (483). Without the dialogue available only to the reader in the first part of the story, however, the journalist in "The Giant Wistaria" can neither raise the salient issue of sexual oppression nor pose questions about the identities of murderer and victim. Blind to the intimations of sexual and maternal terror in the wilderness, he will trivialize the mystery by writing a spooky little story for the Sunday supplement about rattling chains and bumps in the night.

In retrospect, then, "The Giant Wistaria" is an experiment in the female frontier gothic worthy of the author of "The Yellow Wallpaper," a tale Gilman completed only five months later. Both stories oppose sexual stereotypes and extend the frontiers of female identity. The heroine of the first no less than the narrator of the second is confined in a prisonhouse of language, represented by a turret-room and an attic-nursery, respectively. Neither woman is permitted to describe her predicament as a victim of patriarchy; indeed, the first disappears from the story, at least in a corporeal sense, after speaking a total of three sentences while the second writes a clandestine epistolary tale, an absolutely forbidden discourse. Each of them, rather than submit to the demands of male authority, devises a set of signs which defy patriarchal control. As Paula Treichler observes, the narrator of "The Yellow Wallpaper" by the close of her story has changed "the terms in which women are represented in language" and extended "the conditions under which women will speak."[21] In "The Giant Wistaria," Gilman had written a tale with similar implications. The doltish men who visit the haunted mansion initially ridicule the women for seeing ghosts. One of the men imagines "a woman picking huckleberries," a benign form of domestic drudgery, where a woman had perceived "a crouching, hunted figure" (482). Another of the men cracks wise when his wife discerns in the trunk of the wistaria a "writhing body—cringing—beseeching!" (482). The narrative's young mother has become, it seems, a natural hieroglyph in the hallucinatory wilderness or liminal frontier. Much as the narrator of "The Yellow Wallpaper" reads in the pattern on the walls of her attic prison "sprawling outlines" of her predicament, the women visitors in "The Giant Wistaria" detect the intimations of sexual horror in the retrograde garden. Each of them respects the indeterminacy inscribed by the foreboding hieroglyphics of the landscape. "I'm convinced there is a story, if we could only find it" (482), one of them declares—a far cry from the male reporter's avowed intention to tell a story even if he cannot find one.

"The Giant Wistaria" is, of course, the story as one of the women characters might have written it, not the authoritative half-truth of the journalist. The implied author of the narrative understands that the land is cursed, not in this case by the blood of bondsmen or the victims of genocidal war—the dark figures in the landscape are neither supplicant slaves nor crouching Indians—but by the tears of anguished women on the most ancient of frontiers, the interstice defining the status and distinguishing the roles of men and women in patriarchal society. As Gilman wrote in "Nature's Answer," a young maid once

> found such work as brainless slaves might do.
> By day and night, long labor, never through;
> Such pain—no language can her pain reveal. . . .[22]

Like the young woman in this poem, like the narrator of "The Yellow Wallpaper," even like the author in her autobiography, the heroine of "The Giant Wistaria" devises a language to express ineffable pain—in her case, a hieroglyphic of natural symbol. Ironically, her tale has been lost and unread for nearly a century now—the same length of time that elapsed between the heroine's death and her revelation in the shadows and twisted vines. Eerily, the story seems to have anticipated its reception.

Notes

1. Carl Degler, "Introduction" to *Women and Economics* (New York: Harper & Row, 1966), xiii.

2. *Harper's Weekly*, 25 January 1896, 79; *North American Review*, 168 (May 1899): 589–590.

3. Ellen Moers, *Literary Women: The Great Writers* (Garden City, NY: Doubleday, 1977), 148.

4. C. P. Stetson, "The Giant Wistaria," *New England Magazine*, NS 4 (June 1891): 480–485. Gilman was married to Charles Stetson at the time of publication. All subsequent references are to this publication. "The Giant Wistaria" was recently reprinted in *Legacy*, 5 (Fall 1988) with an introductory essay by Gloria A. Biamonte.

5. Moers, 139.

6. *Forerunner*, 2 (July 1911), 196–197; "Social Darwinism," *American Journal of Sociology*, 12 (March 1907): 173.

7. *In This Our World* (Boston: Small, Maynard, & Co., 1898), 34.

8. *In This Our World*, 137–138.

9. *In This Our World*, 3.

10. "Woman Suffrage and the West," *Kansas Suffrage Reveille*, 2 (June 1897): 2.

11. *In This Our World*, 146.

12. *In This Our World*, 145.

13. Diary, 11 March 1890, vol. 29, Charlotte Perkins Gilman Papers, Schlesinger Library, Radcliffe College.

14. "The Gothic Prism: Charlotte Perkins Gilman's Gothic Stories and Her Autobiography," in *The Female Gothic*, ed. Juliann Fleenor (Montreal: Eden Press, 1983), 227.

15. Quoted in Mary A. Hill, *Charlotte Perkins Gilman: The Making of a Radical Feminist 1860–1896* (Philadelphia: Temple University Press, 1980), 234.

16. *The Living of Charlotte Perkins Gilman: An Autobiography* (New York and London: Appleton-Century, 1935), 163–164.

17. Hill, 232.

18. *Love and Death in the American Novel* (New York: Dell, 1966), 122.

19. *The Dialogic Imagination*, ed. Michael Holquist, trans. Caryl Emerson and Michael Holquist (Austin: University of Texas Press, 1981).

20. *The Act of Reading* (Baltimore: Johns Hopkins, 1978), 170–178.

21. "Escaping the Sentence: Diagnosis and Discourse in 'The Yellow Wallpaper,' " *Feminist Issues in Literary Scholarship*, ed. Shari Benstock (Bloomington and London: Indiana University Press, 1987), 75.

22. *In This Our World*, 4.

Kenneth Huntress Baldwin

In chapter 12 of her autobiography, Charlotte Perkins Gilman recalls one of the false starts that punctuated her life and career: "I left Oakland in debt and failure, and moved to San Francisco in the summer of 1894, beginning again, with a great new hope—the *Impress*."[1] The period immediately preceding her relocation to San Francisco featured dramatic events in both her private and public life—her mother, who had come to live with Gilman during a terminal illness, died in 1893; her estranged father remarried in 1894; *In This Our World*, her first collection of verse, was published in 1893; what was to become her single most famous literary work, "The Yellow Wall-Paper," appeared in 1892; and in 1893 she was elected president of the Pacific Coast Women's Press Association for a one-year term. The chief source of her "failure" was quite clearly and painfully the public reaction to her domestic situation. To compound the stigma of having recently divorced her first husband, Walter Stetson, while remaining on friendly terms with both him and Grace Ellery Channing, her closest friend and Walter's second wife, she had committed the unforgivable sin of sending her only child, Katharine, east to live with Walter and Grace in May. The accusations of being an unfit mother finally drove Gilman across the bay in an attempt to escape scorn and seek fulfillment in her new role as editor of the *Impress*.

The *Impress*, originally the *Bulletin* of the Pacific Coast Women's Press Association, was an eight-page monthly of interest mainly to members of the sponsoring organization. In anticipation of realizing the possibilities of the *Impress*, Gilman incorporated the Impress Company in September 1894, under the name Charlotte Perkins Stetson, with herself as president of the company and editor of the periodical.[2] With the help of an associate editor and a managing editor, Gilman turned a monthly publication into a weekly one, doubled its size to 16 pages per issue, and strove to achieve general interest and a national readership, as par-

Published here for the first time.

tially indicated by the prominently featured new subtitle—"A Journal for Men and Women." Gilman's regular contributions included "articles, verses, editorials, ethical problems—a department, and reviews" (*Living*, 173). In addition, she singled out for special mention an innovative series that she created especially for the *Impress:*

> I instituted a series of "Studies in Style," producing each week a short story, or a chapter from a long one, in avowed imitation of a well-known author. The readers were to guess the original, and the first correct guesser to receive a copy of one of that author's books. (*Living*, 173)

What is perhaps most surprising today is that neither Gilman's overall contributions to the *Impress*, so clearly a precursor of the well-known *Forerunner*, nor the "Studies in Style" series, a landmark in her work as a fiction writer, have been adequately studied. The lack of critical attention is a result of radical inaccessibility; the *Impress* remains the last major known writing by Charlotte Perkins Gilman yet to be issued in a format that would make it readily available to students and scholars. Since the series remains so overlooked, a variety of critical concerns have yet to be explored, including a statistical analysis of imitated style compared with representative original texts, an evaluation of Gilman's role as literary critic, and close readings of individual stories. The emphasis here is on a holistic approach in an attempt to stimulate interest in the neglected enterprise; at the same time I attempt to replace the common view of "Studies in Style" as a relatively uninteresting exercise in apprenticeship with recognition of Gilman's sophisticated performance as imitator, originator, and experimenter.[3]

The general format of the series was tripartite, consisting of an imitation, a critique of the prior week's imitation, and an announcement of the winning "guesser" for the imitation from two weeks previous. The imitations, always titled and ending with a question mark in place of the "author's" name, appeared on the fourth and fifth pages of each issue under the interrogative heading "Who Wrote It?"—followed by an asterisk to a repeated footnote:

> The above is the [number] of a series of studies in style; careful presentations of forms of literature; following various well known authors. The stories themselves are original, in no way copied or even parodied; the intention being to develop a wider knowledge and more delicate appreciation of distinctive literary method. The reader who first

names the writer represented will receive a copy of his choice of that author's works.

In the first 16 of the 20 issues of the *Impress* Gilman edited, 15 *identified* imitations appear, interrupted only by a holiday break in number 12 (22 December 1894) for an unsigned Christmas story presumably written by the editor herself. The 15 authors, in order of appearance and as actually named, are Rudyard Kipling, Mary E. Wilkins, Olive Schreiner, Nathaniel Hawthorne, Hamlin Garland, Maurice Maeterlinck, Edward Everett Hale, George Eliot, Louisa M. Alcott, Edgar Allan Poe, Charles Dickens, Henry James, Edward Bellamy, Mark Twain, and Washington Irving. Occasional references to a 17-part series are explained by the presence of "Who Wrote It?" stories appearing in the expected place in number 17 and number 19 and footnoted as the 16th and 17th entries; but the authors imitated are never identified, and no "Story Study" or "Story Study Prize" columns exist for them. In fact, Bellamy is the last person for whom both a study and an announced winner is published; he is also the last person for whom a correct guesser is identified (for whatever reason, no winner notification appeared for the earlier Hale entry or for the two authors who follow Bellamy: Twain and Irving).

With two exceptions, the imitations of Maeterlinck (a minidrama) and Eliot (an extract from a chapter from an imagined three-volume novel), the productions are limited in form to short stories composed in the manner of nineteenth-century British and American writers (excepting the Belgian Maeterlinck). The basis of selection, I suggest, corresponds closely and simply with Gilman's activities as a reviewer for the *Impress* itself. Beginning with the earliest issues of the journal in its *Bulletin* days, and continuing until the last issue, Gilman contributed literary reviews. In a regular feature entitled "Magazines of the Month," she discussed significant items from the latest issues of *Cosmopolitan, Century, New England Magazine, Overland Monthly, Dial, Atlantic Monthly, McClure's, Scribner's,* and others, periodicals likely to be read by *Impress* subscribers and surely outlets for the fiction of the authors imitated. In addition, she also critiqued specific works by Howells, Garland, Schreiner, Kipling, Maeterlinck, Twain, Wilkins, and Hale—fully half of the "Studies in Style" roster.

Existing critical references to the *Impress* stories give the impression that the stories were already published passages merely cut and pasted rather than original impersonations. As a consequence, Gilman's creative ability is slighted today although it was appreciated by nineteenth-century readers. In "The Prize Winner" column for issue 4, for instance, Gilman notes with obvious pleasure:

> The large number of letters received plainly show the widespread and vivid interest taken in these story studies. It is significant that no other than Miss Wilkins was named in connection with "A Day's Berryin'"—significant alike of the unmistakable individuality of Miss Wilkins' style, and of the faithfulness of Mrs. Stetson's presentation of it. (p. 5)

Supplemental evidence that Gilman upheld the "standard of excellence" she had established is provided by an occasional promotional feature of the *Impress*, appropriately titled "As Others See Us." The full-page column quoted prominent readers and reviewers, including educators, literary figures, ministers, and other public figures, all of whom enthusiastically endorsed the new journal. The laudatory comments single out "Studies in Style" for special mention with some regularity, thus providing testimony that Gilman's skill in producing literary impressions was readily acknowledged by informed contemporaries.

The "Studies in Style" are indeed a landmark in Gilman's career as a short-fiction writer. Besides being the only unified collection of short fiction ever written by Gilman, the *Impress* series equals in volume all of the short fiction she published, beginning with her 1886 debut; more strikingly, if we except the chapbook publication of *The Yellow Wall-Paper* in 1899, the stories are five times as long as all of the short fiction she produced from 1894 to 1909, the year the *Forerunner* began publication.

The "Studies in Style" should also be invaluable in augmenting Gilman's reputation as a literary artist. In considering the aesthetic quality of the imitations, it is important to distinguish between the story proper and the stylistic analysis that followed in the next issue. The title of the series specifically references the stylistic and thematic critiques that appeared under the title "Story Studies" rather than signifies the actual stories. The studies reveal Gilman's critical capabilities, while the stories evidence her creative abilities. Also, as we are reminded in each issue, the stories are "original"; this originality, generated weekly with remarkable stylistic variety, overshadows the commendable imitative skill, since the answer to the question "Who Wrote It?" is always the same—Charlotte Perkins Gilman.

If we reconsider key elements of Gilman's autobiographical recollection of the origin of her unique project, we find her reasoning problematical; for instance, imitations were necessitated by the fact that she "could not write a good story every week" (*Living*, 173). But she did, of course, just that, *adding* to the weekly task the demanding requirement of conforming each original story to the style of a different and influential author. A proper appreciation of Gilman's literary powers will challenge her own negative self-assessment, undercut subsequent critical judgment, and foreground the "Studies in Style" in the trajectory of her career as a fiction writer.

Gilman often disparaged her creative abilities, most clearly and bluntly in a frequently quoted passage in her autobiography—"I have never made any pretense of being literary" (p. 284)—a blanket disclaimer that is echoed two sentences later. More than a half-century later, Ann J. Lane, usually appreciative of Gilman as woman and writer, dismissed her fiction (excepting "The Yellow Wall-Paper") in harsher words: "Gilman gave little attention to her writing as literature, and neither will the reader, I am afraid."[4] And although the list of exceptions has steadily grown since Lane's 1980 pronouncement, it is still common to apologize for Gilman's literary deficiencies and to characterize her fiction as didactic.

In the very passage in which Gilman disavows any literary pretensions, though, she tentatively suggests that she " 'had a style of my own' " (*Living*, 285; author's punctuation), an interesting variation of Virginia Woolf's later and famous "room of one's own." Recognition of Gilman's individualized style points the way to a more accurate and positive summation of her literary expertise, as in Denise D. Knight's suggestion that Gilman resists "easy classification" precisely because she was unique and thus cannot be defined in terms of the major literary movements of her era—realism, naturalism, sentimentalism, regionalism.[5] Such a perspective resolves the apparent contradiction of Gilman's abdication of "any pretension to literature" with a coincidental claim to a specific, individualized style. Any contradiction evaporates if we translate "literary" as a reference to writers and writing identified with particular and popular schools or movements. As both stories and studies demonstrate, Gilman could create and analyze stylistic features—country dialect (Wilkins), parataxis (Schreiner), musical cadence (Dickens), absence of style (Bellamy)—as well as such thematic tendencies as Alcott's suggestion of buried lives, Maeterlinck's decadent pessimism, Hawthorne's unforgiven and unforgotten family secrets, and Garland's rebellion against the hopelessness of circumstance. Gilman actually effected a tour de force, showing her ability to echo masters of various schools, all the while speaking in her own idiomatic voice.

The "Studies in Style" should also be recognized as experiments in form since they constitute an important contribution to the development of the short story or, more precisely, the short-short story. Gilman's *Impress* texts are uniformly about two thousand words long, veritable miniatures of the original models. Gilman was well aware of the effect of length on total effect, as partially indicated by a pertinent 1893 diary entry in which she suggested that two thousand words amounted to "a little [sketch]".[6] On this basis alone, Gilman's creations could be considered translations as well as imitations, translations of one category of prose fiction into another.

One should also recognize that her *Impress* series anticipates sudden fiction, as the short-short story form is now commonly called. The key document for this new literary form is *Sudden Fiction: American Short-Short Stories* (1986), at once a representative anthology of creative efforts and a collection of critical definitions of the subgenre. While the critical positions taken in *Sudden Fiction* relate to contemporary texts, the origins of the form are traced to late-nineteenth-century American magazines and newspapers. Many features of sudden fiction—for example, concision, stress on a key moment in the relationship of two protagonists, surprise treatment of familiar material, emphasis on mood rather than on action—characterize Gilman's stories as well. Barry Targon, a contributor to the *Sudden Fiction* critical anthology, equates the form with the classic étude, a term that captures Gilman's "Studies in Style" both conceptually and etymologically.[7]

Even if we withhold final judgment on the literary merits of "Studies in Style," the project should be valued as a turning point in Gilman's search for an authentic authorial self. The *Impress* imitations exist as a vital developmental link in Gilman's progress toward a style of her own, mediating between the repressed, conflicted, relentless "I" of "The Yellow Wall-Paper" and the eventual independent and self-validating "I" of the *Forerunner*.

In *The Madwoman in the Attic*, a study of nineteenth-century women writers, Sandra Gilbert and Susan Gubar argue that the anxiety of influence necessarily experienced by male writers is experienced by women "as an even more primary 'anxiety of authorship'—a radical fear that she cannot create, that because she can never become a 'precursor' the act of writing will isolate or destroy her."[8] For Gilbert and Gubar, "The Yellow Wall-Paper" is paradigmatic of the struggle of nineteenth-century foremothers to overcome the symptomatology of this psychoriterary complex. By extension, Gilman stands as testimony to at least one nineteenth-century woman's ability to work through and move beyond the isolation and inertia she inherited. To read the stories and studies in the context of the anxieties of influence/authorship is to acknowledge a depth and complexity usually not granted them; to dismiss them as mere practice pieces is equivalent to seeing "The Yellow Wall-Paper" as nothing more than a gothic tale narrated by an insane woman for effect.

Given the interactive basis of the endeavor and the weekly announcement of a winner, one is surprised to learn, according to Gilman's own later recollection, that the *Impress* did not last long enough for any weekly prize to be awarded (*Living*, 173). One can only imagine the chagrin of the successful guessers, especially Mrs. K. P. S. Boyd of Berkeley, who, singled out for special mention in issue 16 for her "brilliant record of winning three prizes in succession," was left waiting for the volumes of Dickens, James, and Bellamy to which she was entitled. The admission raises a different question of intention, almost certainly a rhetorical one: were the imitations composed for the interests of subscribers or for Gilman's own ulterior, reflexive interests? Thus viewed in the light of anxiety/influence, the prizes exist as a pretense, a defense mechanism that deflects attention (and possible criticism) away from her creative abilities. Charlotte Perkins Gilman, the authorial self supposedly unable to create independently due to preemption by precursors, frees her fictive self by avowing only imitation, at once retreating to a belated position and deflecting charges of plagiarism. Because the author deferred to is well known, though, admiration of the original begets admiration of the imitator. Overall, Gilman's pretense of being nobody allows her the freedom to be anybody, a tactic permitting her to collapse recognized creative identities with her own and, in effect, to erase their signatures since they existed only by virtue of her mediation. The sole real author, Charlotte Perkins Gilman, is, like Poe's purloined letter, always hidden in plain sight.

The 20 installments maintain a near-consistent pattern of story/study/ winner until number 15, at which point the paradigm starts to disintegrate: studies appear without winners and two imitations without identification. Surprisingly, the terminal entry in the series consists of a story titled "An Unnatural Mother," composed by Gilman herself, in the place previously reserved for imitations. The abrupt appearance of such an explicitly autobiographical narrative at the conclusion raises the possibility of an autobiographical impulse underpinning the whole endeavor. As

Lane reports in her Gilman reader, "An Unnatural Mother" came "out of Gilman's private pain, for it was a phrase often used against her in the press" (*CPG*, xxi). The essence of the grim tale consists of a community's refusal to view a woman as anything but depraved, a woman, now dead, whose unforgivable sin was to bypass her own house, thereby endangering her own daughter, in order to save the population of three villages by warning them of an imminent dam collapse. But despite Lane's appreciation of "An Unnatural Mother" and choice of it for a selection of Gilman's best fiction, she documents it as a *Forerunner* item (Gilman in fact republished it twice there) with no reference to the original *Impress* appearance. As a result, the reader loses a sense of the coincidence of experienced pain and fictional representation. Gilman, we recall, had moved to San Francisco to escape gossip campaigns and newspaper columns labeling her "an unnatural mother" because of her decision to send her daughter Katharine east to live with Charles and Grace Stetson. While Gilman saw herself, like the protagonist of her story, as sacrificing personal desires for communal good, the decision was tantamount to child abandonment in the public mind. In his literary biography, Scharnhorst cites "An Unnatural Mother" as one of Gilman's "most popular stories,"[9] providing a detailed analysis that highlights autobiographical aspects focusing on Gilman's personal situation at the time of publication; Scharnhorst, though, isolates his treatment of the story from a consideration of its original appearance.

What we must finally consider is that the markedly antiautobiographical essence of the imitations is the very feature that gives integrity to the 20-part series. Gilman's autobiography and her diary alike attest both to her desire to escape public censure by moving to San Francisco and to her energetic involvement with the *Impress*. The "Studies in Style" experiment must have been a stimulating feature of her new literary life, enabling her to escape, as it did for several months, the felt pressures of her public and private selves. Gilman was able to sustain the imitations for only three months, however, at which point the story/study/winner framework collapsed, as we have seen, blurring the distinction between Gilman and the accepted writers ostensibly being mirrored in the studies. The imitative enterprise terminated, quite possibly with intention, in a dramatic reversion to the very autobiographical impulse that the series was intended to suppress. Having initiated the cycle with an emulation of Rudyard Kipling, she concluded with her own "Unnatural Mother," her most autobiographical fiction after "The Yellow Wall-Paper." The bibliographic history of "An Unnatural Mother" is revealing; written in June 1893, it may itself have been a version of a story called "An Unnatural Daughter" that Gilman reported working on as early as 1891 but never again mentioned in her diaries. She withheld this personal story until she found its appropriate purpose, as admission that attempts to elude herself—to be equated with and admired as Eliot or Alcott, Dickens or Twain—would ultimately fail. In the end she could write only as herself.

Nor could Gilman escape the viciousness of public opinion. Censure reached a new high during her brief *Impress* career, epitomized by Ambrose Bierce's persistent campaign against her lifestyle, her writing ability, and the journal itself in a widely read column, appropriately titled "Prattle," in the San Francisco *Examiner*. Gilman's notoriety was the direct cause of withdrawal of support for the journal by the Pacific Coast Women's Press Association, and the *Impress*'s failure occasioned Gilman's decision to leave California and head east. She would not produce any significant fiction for the next decade until, happily married and her reputation restored, she could express herself freely again in her own journal, the *Forerunner*. It remains an irony of literary history that, while Gilman is now safely ensconced in the canon, her other writings admired and her reputation assured, the "Studies in Style," her most ambitious project in short fiction, remains unstudied.

Notes

1. Charlotte Perkins Gilman, *The Living of Charlotte Perkins Gilman* (Madison: University of Wisconsin Press, 1990), 171. Hereafter, *Living*.

2. Beginning with the 6 October 1894 issue (volume II, number 1) and continuing to the last issue of the *Impress* on 16 February 1895 (volume II, number 20), the periodical, while still the official organ of the PCWPA, was published by the Impress Company.

3. One contextual aspect of the imitations demands notice here, the "Everyday Ethical Problems," a column found immediately preceding "Studies in Style" in every issue. Each week Gilman presented "a problem in the ethics of familiar life"; readers submitted solutions, the best of which were printed, and an occasional prize was awarded to the person "sending in the largest number of clever solutions." Both literally premised on reader response, the two series amount to companion pieces, different versions of story problems.

4. Ann J. Lane, ed., *Charlotte Perkins Gilman Reader* (New York: Pantheon, 1980), xvi. Hereafter, *CPG*.

5. Denise D. Knight, ed., *"The Yellow Wall-Paper" and Selected Stories of Charlotte Perkins Gilman* (Newark: University of Delaware Press, 1994), 24.

6. Denise D. Knight, ed., *The Diaries of Charlotte Perkins Gilman* (Charlottesville: University Press of Virginia, 1994), 537.

7. From the French "study," an étude is a musical exercise for a single instrument that, while designed to increase the technical quality of a performance, may sometimes be performed and appreciated as a completed composition.

8. Sandra M. Gilbert and Susan Guber, *The Madwoman in the Attic* (New Haven: Yale University Press, 1979), 48–49.

9. Gary Scharnhorst, *Charlotte Perkins Gilman* (Metuchen, NJ: Scarecrow Press, 1985), 34.

Works Cited

Gilbert, Sandra M., and Susan Gubar. *The Madwoman in the Attic.* New Haven: Yale University Press, 1979.

Gilman, Charlotte Perkins, ed. *The Impress.* San Francisco: The Impress Company. (6 October 1894–16 February 1895).

———. *The Living of Charlotte Perkins Gilman: An Autobiography.* Foreword by Zona Gale. New York: Appleton-Century, 1935; rpt. New York: Arno Press, 1972.

———. *The Diaries of Charlotte Perkins Gilman.* Vol. 2. Ed. Denise D. Knight. Charlottesville: University Press of Virginia, 1994.

Knight, Denise D., ed. *"The Yellow Wall-Paper" and Selected Stories of Charlotte Perkins Gilman.* Newark: University of Delaware Press, 1994.

Lane, Ann J., ed. *The Charlotte Perkins Gilman Reader.* New York: Pantheon, 1980.

———. *To "Herland" and Beyond: The Life and Work of Charlotte Perkins Gilman.* New York: Pantheon, 1980.

Scharnhorst, Gary. *Charlotte Perkins Gilman.* Scarecrow Author Bibliographies. 71. Metuchen, NJ: Scarecrow, 1985.

———. *Charlotte Perkins Gilman: A Bibliography.* Twayne's United States Author's Series. 482. Boston: Twayne, 1985.

Shapard, Robert, and James Thomas, eds. *Sudden Fiction: American Short-Short Stories.* Salt Lake City: Gibbs-Smith, 1986.

Monika M. Elbert

In her fiction as well as in her sociological works, such as *Women and Economics* and *The Home*, Charlotte Perkins Gilman seems to focus on the middle-class woman's lack of economic power and stability in society, but she is also aware of and sympathetic toward the middle-class man's plight in the business world. If Gilman perceives modern economics as threatening to woman's sense of self, as it makes her a nonproducing consumer and a captive of the domestic sphere, she also realizes that for man, the pressures of being the sole breadwinner for the family detract from his overall growth as a creative, fully realized individual. Certainly, one could point out that in some of her short fiction, many more women than men suffer dramatically, because of the philandering and neglectful males who disappoint their mothers and wives (e.g., "His Mother," "Being Reasonable," "Turned"). But in many other stories, men suffer silently: for each woman trapped in "The Yellow Wall-Paper," there is also a crawling man trying to escape.[1]

It is precisely the masculine tendency toward overdeveloped familial duty and allegiance to a mercenary business system that brutalize and desensitize men to the point where they are reduced to victims of inertia and lethargy, so that their situation is not much different from that of the nonproducing class of homebound women. Men are caught in the stultifying web of domesticity as surely as women:

> Social progress rests on the smooth development of personal character, the happy fulfillment of special function.... A man's best service to society lies in his conscientious performance of the work he is best fitted for. But the service of the home demands that he do the work he is best paid for. Man after man, under this benumbing, strangling pressure, is diverted from his true path in social service, and condemned to "imprisonment with hard labour for life."[2]

Published here for the first time.

Following this startling passage, Gilman points out that most men start
life rather idealistically, but when they "marry and start a home," they
must give up their dreams for a job that is economically profitable. Having such employment forces men to be industrious in a wrong, befud-
dled way, so that they abandon the work they love best for work that
"commands the greater wages" (p. 320). These skewed priorities result
from "the market," which "will pay best for what it wants," thus creating a "world . . . full of struggling men" (p. 320). In *Women and Economics,* Gilman shows the consequences of men's misplaced ambitions and
overriding passion for success in the work world: "cruelty . . . begotten
by irresponsible power," "pride and self-will," and selfishness.[3] If
Gilman is applauding women's efforts to escape the home and the
drudgery of housework and babysitting, she is also applauding men's
efforts to escape the business realm they are relegated to.

In her critique of the division of labor in *The Home,* Gilman shows how
the idea of public and private spheres creates categories that are arbitrary, misleading, and false.[4] In her description of the evolution of the
home, Gilman asserts, "With the steadily widening gulf between the
sexes which followed upon this arbitrary imprisonment of the woman in
the home, we have come to regard 'the world' as exclusively man's
province, and 'the home' as exclusively woman's (*The Home,* 22). Gilman
insists that by "maintaining this artificial diversity between the sexes,"
we "have preserved in our own characters the confusion and contradiction which is our greatest difficulty in life" (*WE,* 331). Many of Gilman's
female protagonists find redemption in crossing the threshold from the
private to the public realm, in moving away from home, in becoming a
public persona, through travel and/or work (e.g., "The Widow's Might,"
"Three Thanksgivings," "Old Mrs. Crosley," "An Honest Woman," "My
Poor Aunt," and "Mrs. Beazley's Deeds"; most of Gilman's heroic
women are liberated when they are widowed, abandoned, or divorced).

But how is it with the males in her fiction; what recourse do they
have when the public self of the work world weighs so heavily on them?
Is the movement a reversal of women's? Do they go home, and if so, do
they encounter a private self, or does the domestic house of horrors prevent them from ever finding another sense of self? In her nonfiction,
Gilman suggests that the feminizing effect of the home wreaks havoc on
the man's psyche: "if he has to stay in it too much, he knows it softens
and enfeebles him" (*The Home,* 284). The antidote to is go out, engage
in some male bonding, have " 'a real good time'—rest, recreation,
healthful amusement . . . with 'the boys.' The distant camp in the

woods, the mountain climb, the hunting trip,—real rest and pleasure are found with men away from home" (p. 284). She further asserts that the 99 percent of males who are gainfully employed in the business world are compelled to leave home for work, but even the fortunate "feminized" few, whose livelihood is not money oriented and outside-based, escape home: "The artist flees to a studio apart, if possible; the author builds him a 'den' in his garden, if he can afford it; the clergyman strives mightily to keep 'the study' to himself" (p. 40).

Lest I paint the bleak picture of a misogynistic world of men who escape the civilizing effects of women, I would like to suggest that in her short stories, Gilman really does offer a different portrait of men. Her vision of men's problems doesn't accord with the picture some historians have given us of the plight of turn-of-the-century men. One group of historians, from the 1970s onward, depicted turn-of-the-century middle-class men as becoming increasingly anxious about manliness and rebelling against the constraints of "an urban-industrial culture"; this new cult of masculinity advocated adventure and sports for men.[5] Recently, historian Margaret Marsh has painted another picture of turn-of-the-century suburban man as a "contented suburban father," who enjoyed the leisure a stable job afforded him (Marsh, 112). The term Marsh uses, "masculine domesticity," shows this other view of middle-class men as being true companions to their wives and ideal fathers, and happy in these roles; they had even started to share in the onerous household tasks (pp. 112–13).

Though Gilman's portrait of men is generally not as positive in terms of domestic bliss, she would agree with Marsh, or her fiction, at least, shows that "changing roles for women also meant changes in male roles. As women entered the masculine world, men began to enter the spheres assigned to women" (p. 113). Gilman was able to capture man's sense of liminality, as he is caught in a no-man's land, between the home and the workplace. There are three groups of men in the Gilman canon who are most successful in gaining an identity that encompasses both realms as they negotiate between public and private spaces: the artistic/creative types; the men who quit traditional business jobs to enter another realm (the countryside, Europe); and the men who become somewhat domesticized as they accept the changing roles of women and come to terms with their own feminine side. These men leave the public realm and dare to enter the more private sphere of masculine domesticity. For the home breakers who resist domestication and who dwell in the realm of the material world, Gilman offers moral censure in the shape of cautionary tales (e.g., "An Honest Woman," "Three Thanksgivings," "Mrs. Beazley's Deeds," "Mrs. Elder's Ideas," "His Mother," and "His Excuse"), in which men end up lonely and spiritually destitute if they are not willing to reform and accommodate woman's changing roles and newly acquired strength.

"Making a Living," which belongs to the category of male-artist story, is an idyllic, delightful tale that shows that men who follow their creative impulse won't go wrong and will find a home and a woman—as just rewards for not forfeiting their integrity—in the process. As Gilman succinctly puts it elsewhere, "[Woman] gets her living by getting a husband. [Man] gets his wife by getting a living" (*WE*, 110). In this particular story, though, the protagonist, Arnold, is able to achieve his dream in spite of finding a wife; precisely because he refuses to "get a living" in the normal fashion, he is able to attract good fortune and a utopian lifestyle in the country. Arnold's father tells him that he will never amount to much because he is a poet; he advises him to take over the family property in the country, to "rebuild that old-saw mill and make a living off it!"[6] He bequeaths him the old country place and admonishes him, "[Y]ou can sit in that handmade hut of yours and make poetry and crazy inventions the rest of your life" (*Herland*, 238). Upon his retirement, the father leaves his property and business to his favorite son, John. But John is a base materialist, the kind of man whom Gilman always attacks in her stories. She ironically states that John, "pattern and image of his father[,] came into possession of large assets and began to use them in the only correct way; to increase and multiply without end" (p. 239).

The moment of truth comes when both brothers, Arnold and John, vie for the attention of Miss Ella, who promptly turns down John's offer of marriage; to his offering of her great wealth in the future, she responds, "I'm not for sale . . . even on futures" (p. 239). When Arnold humbly but poetically offers his hand in marriage, he realizes that he will never be able to offer her the wealth necessary to make a good marriage. He hesitates, ". . . I've nothing to offer," to which she proclaims, "There's you" (p. 239). At that point, Arnold embarks on his adventure in the country; his playful and poetic spirit becomes the source of his income. Significantly, he goes back to the "small solid house" that he built as an adolescent and that so pleased his mother: it "was a growing joy as long as the dear mother lived" (p. 240). The maternal memory and the domestic legacy sustain him. When Arnold was "a great hulking brooding boy," "while his father stuck to the office and John went to Bar

Harbor with his chums" (p. 240), Arnold inhabited the house he made of stone quarried from his Hill with his mother; "he could work hard even if he was a poet" (p. 240). Now an adult, Arnold continues the dream his mother cherished—to study forestry and arboriculture, and to graft a certain kind of chestnut—pursuits his father shunned. But Arnold makes his fortune, despite his seemingly slothful activities of meditating on nature and scribbling "at any sudden moment when the fit seized him" (p. 243). A college friend, now in advertising, helps him achieve a livelihood: they market and sell the "Hill Mill Meal" cereal produced on his land. Though Arnold refuses to overexpand (he asserts that he does not want to be a millionaire), he makes enough money to afford a wife: "There's the house," he tells her, "furnished—there's a new room built on—for you, dear; I did it myself. There's the hill—and the little lake and one waterfall all for us!" (p. 246). The jingling advertisements and his cereal earn him a living, much to his father's consternation, and Arnold and Ella, like two pastoral creatures, "watch[ed] the sunset from their hammock, laughed softly together, and lived" (p. 248).

In contrast to "Making a Living," there are many other examples of thwarted artists/failed husbands, who succumb to the pressures of economics and so lose their integrity. In "Her Beauty," the male protagonist, Weldon Thomas, an aspiring poet, is seduced by the superficial beauty of Myra Hall. But when he marries her, he realizes too late that he has compromised his love of aesthetics for a boring job. She, a soulless beauty, too quickly grows old and ugly, and meanwhile he has lost touch with his poetic spirit. Amaryllis, Weldon's jilted lover, undergoes a more positive transformation; her love for Weldon, though ill-begotten, sends her on a lifelong quest for beauty. She imbibes the poetic spirit that he has lost when she becomes a first-rate dressmaker, and in pursuing her passion for beauty she attracts wealth and creates a lovely home. Weldon, who has moved from the countryside to New York and long since abandoned his poetry career for the eminently safe career of journalism, finds himself a failure at 42; his fellow journalists also consider him a failure, as he loses "his job on one big daily after another" (p. 299). Moreover, there are direct attacks on his manhood: "He hasn't snap enough," "[l]acks ginger," "[d]oes good work, but too slow," and "he's too old" (p. 299). Facing a desolate life as a widower in New York, he decides to return to the countryside to find solace and is startled by the beauty he now detects in Amaryllis, who has transformed herself and her surroundings into one harmonious landscape. His poetic spirit is revived, as he finds home in the feminine realm that she has created:

"His soul was stirred and comforted first by that broad stretch of garden ground, then by the gracious house, then by this satisfying restful room, with its windows into heaven, and now he felt in her something like all of them, and something better still" (p. 301).

This paradigm of the artist-man gone astray for the love of a woman is seen with more dire consequences in "His Excuse." Norman Parker, the protagonist, falls in love with Willie Carruthers, a proud southern woman. Because he is a mid-westerner (from New England stock) without a name and without wealth, Willie's surrogate father, her grandfather, the eminent Colonel Carruthers, forbids her to associate with Norman and threatens her with disinheritance if she should marry him. She falls in love with Norman despite his warnings, for Norman is sensitive, with an artist's soul; as she tells her father, "He's not like the other Northerners.... He is no mere business man. He doesn't care for money. He is going to be a writer, a poet. He is a gentleman even if his name is Parker" (*Yellow*, 89). It is true that Norman is interested in literature, and especially in poetry, but he is not very stable; as a student at Yale, he had "something of a breakdown, ascribed to overstudy" (p. 88). But when Willie falls in love with him, he gives up what he perceives as foolish dreams and resolves to return to ask for her hand in marriage when he has made it financially in the world. Giving up the realm of literature, he settles for journalism. He becomes a hack reporter "for the sake of that fair image still enshrined in his heart" (p. 92). Though his motives are noble, his job is not; with his gift for "vivid word-painting," he writes the most "lurid 'stories'" of "divorce, police, and criminal courts" (p. 92). He feeds off the misery and decline of others in writing these spectacular stories, and unwittingly finds himself, one day, writing the story of Willie herself, who has been left penniless at her grandfather's death, because of the many debts he incurred. When Willie discovers her maligner's identity, she casts him from her side forever, a bit infelicitously, since Norman was, after all, only trying to purchase a fine specimen of southern womanhood whom he otherwise could not afford, an atrocity to be expected in a system that confuses "the economic relation" with the "sex-relation" (*WE*, 5).

The second category of stories about men who escape the workplace involves those men on the verge of retirement who choose to go back to a cherished dream of the past (associated with the now-defunct creative spirit). Significantly, just as Gilman's widows are rejuvenated when their husbands die, at which time they can take on a new public role (often as organizers of clubs and boardinghouses), her male protagonists who are cut off from the work world through retirement enjoy the same kind of freedom and rebirth. It is as if the women, when denied access to the role they have always had, can now transcend the boundaries into the uncharted territory of men's public space; and men, when cut off from the workplace that has nearly strangled them, can cross the boundaries into women's feminine, private space. The roles are often reversed by the end of the story. For example, in "Mrs. Elder's Idea," Mrs. Elder is bored silly with her inattentive husband, who always repeats, "What's that?" after not listening to her long conversations. In fact, her problem is that she is "a woman naturally chatty, but skilled in silence" (*Yellow*, 139). Mrs. Elder has a passion for the urban scene—where she could shop as well as attend the theater. Mr. Elder, on the other hand, prefers the country; though he "had to work in the city to maintain his family . . . what he liked above everything else was the country; the real, wide, open country" (p. 140). For 22 years they have compromised by living in a town that is too urban for Mr. Elder's taste and too rural for Mrs. Elder's. When he has performed his paternal duty successfully, Mr. Elder decides that he can fulfill his "fondest hope—retirement" and sells the business he's always hated to buy a farm in the country, where he can retire "into the remote and lonely situation which his soul loved" (p. 141). Mrs. Elder, appalled at the thought of living in the country-side, rents a furnished floor with her children in Boston and decides to become a "professional shopper" (p. 144). Though this does not bode well in terms of Gilman's distaste for the consumer-woman, it does give Mrs. Elder access to the public arena. Ultimately, the couple compromises, each partner accepting the other's living arrangements for half the year.

In a variation of this story, "Mr. Peebles' Heart," Gilman portrays a man also nearing retirement and with that, the prospect of uselessness in a utilitarian and duty-bound society. At the age of 50, Arthur Peebles has become "the slave of duty"; for his whole life, his duty has been "carrying women," first his mother, then his wife, Emma, who is portrayed as one of the most unsavory female characters in the Gilman canon. Not only does she spend most of her time chattering away at the local ladies' club, but she is a "careless, clinging little person" who has sapped Peebles of his energy and strength (*Other*, 77). Parasitically inter-twining her life around his, she keeps him busy working at the store. The enlightened woman in the story, Emma's sister, Dr. Joan, can diagnose and alleviate Mr. Peebles's sense of malaise and despair. Like the type of good medical doctor in the Gilman canon (cf. Dr. Warren in

"Joan's Defender," so unlike the doctors in "The Yellow Wall-Paper"),
Dr. Joan understands the psychology of those around her. As an independent woman, she can certainly understand the limitations placed on
a duty-driven husband. Emma admits of her husband that "now and
then he's had a kind of a breakdown" (p. 81). After engaging in conversation with Arthur, Dr. Joan discovers that he hates his job at the store
and that he'd rather be traveling. And when she asks him about his preferred profession, had he been free to choose, he promptly responds,
"Music!" (p. 79) and tells the sad tale of how his father brought home a
guitar when he was just a boy, but his sisters (and not he) had been
expected to learn to play. Music, as a feminized activity, was denied the
growing boy. Dr. Joan prescribes the opposite of the rest cure—a kind of
activity cure, as she brings home records and maps to whet his dead-
ened appetite for life. After taunting him with the question "Why not
be your own man for once in your life—do what *you* want to—not what
other people want you to?," Arthur is jolted back into a sense of adven-
turous manhood (p. 83). He sells the store and takes an extended vaca-
tion to England, where he writes letters to his wife that manage to
broaden her limited horizons.

The third type of story can be considered an exemplum of the New
Man's behavior toward the New Woman. In *The Man-Made World*,
Gilman asks, "[W]hat will men lose" by women gaining equality?[7]
Some men will be fearful about "some new position of subservience
and disrespect," while "[o]thers laugh at the very idea of change in
their position, relying as always on the heavier fist" (p. 244). Gilman's
fictional accounts of enlightened men responding to changes in
women's roles provide some answers to the question of what the
changes will do to men.

In "Her Housekeeper," Gilman portrays a feminized, domesticated
man who falls in love with one of the boarders in his boardinghouse, the
actress Mrs. Leland. Though initially repulsed by the rather common
appearance of Arthur Olmstead, the owner of the boardinghouse, she
grows to appreciate the feminine touch with which he makes the boardinghouse a home. At first, she thinks he is some real estate agent, who
is simply a fellow boarder. It is not until the end of the story, when she
accepts his hand in marriage, that she realizes that she has him to thank
for all the amenities granted her, a temperamental actress and an unwed
mother. These luxuries include her choice of servants and cooks, and
the privacy of her own "skylight room": "I have the privacy, the detachment, the carelessness of a boarding-house, and 'all the comforts of a

home' " (*Herland*, 196). Though Olmstead's final confession moves her to accept his marriage proposal, she is aware throughout the story that he is nurturing and sensitive, qualities in a man that at first repel her. Olmstead shows a "most improper domesticity of taste by inviting friends to tea," about which Mrs. Leland taunts him, "[j]ust like a woman!" (p. 197). Olmstead's calm response is "[W]hy not? Women have so many attractive ways—why not imitate them?" (p. 197). The whole story offers a role reversal of the traditional male-female roles. Mrs. Leland wants her freedom, her profession, her lovers, and she hates her housekeeping. The nurturing Olmstead says he will continue to take care of her housekeeping needs when they are married, and that he prizes her more as a working woman than if she were a sedentary housewife or servant housekeeper. In fact, he has been the perfect househusband; as he tells her, "I have kept this house—for you—for three years," to which the incredulous Mrs. Leland responds, "It seems such a funny business—for a man" (p. 206). Moreover, Olmstead turns out to be a better mother to her child than she could ever be; he is more patient and understanding than "either mother or governess" (p. 198).

Gilman condemns the type of man who will make "a housekeeper of his wife" (*The Home*, 226). Since he has such low expectations of her, he does not really get much in return.

> A man . . . has his position in the world and in the home, and finds happiness in both. He loves his wife, she meets his requirements as a husband, and he expects nothing more of her. His other requirements he meets in other ways. That she cannot give him this, that, and the other form of companionship . . . is no ground of blame; the world outside does that. (pp. 226–27)

In "The Cottagette," Gilman portrays a man who tries to encourage the creativity of woman. When the male protagonist, Ford Mathews, meets the vacationing Malda, he is enchanted by the home she has made of the cottagette and impressed by her embroidery work. A thwarted artist, he can appreciate her eye for beauty; he himself is in a transitional mode from popular writer (of newspaper and magazine articles) to author of books. When Lois advises her girlfriend Malda to cook for Ford Mathews if she wants to win him over as a husband, the rationale is, "What [men] care for most, after all, is domesticity" (*Other*, 45). But Malda becomes exhausted and less charming when she tries to nurture Mathews all day with her cooking; finally, she even irritates Mathews, so that he explodes when he perceives that her diminishing artistic powers are a result of the frenzied housework. He proposes to her, on the condition that she must not cook.[8] The feminized Ford, with his eyes as clear as a girl's (p. 45), turns out to be a better cook than she could have dreamed: the lunch and tea he prepares on their outing "tasted better" to Malda "than her own cooking" (p. 49). In fact, in telling her his own history as a cook, Mathews shows that he does not need a wife to be his cook, and more important, he shows that he has successfully crossed the gender boundaries.

One might ponder the final question that the narrator of "The Cottagette" poses, "Was there ever a man like this?" It might have been a utopian wish on Gilman's part, but it also reflects the changing times, with the pressure on men to share in the nurturing and housekeeping functions associated with the mother/wife. What Gilman consistently shows is the need to subvert and redefine gender roles, so that both sexes are finally empowered. In *The Home*, Gilman critiques the false definitions of manhood and womanhood: "The home, its labours, cares, and limitations we have called womanly; and everything else in life manly; wherefore if a woman manifested any power, ambition, interest, outside the home, that was unwomanly and must cost her position as such" (p. 280). One could finish this thought for her and speculate that for men, any interests outside the business world were considered unmanly and cost him his position as such.

Notes

1. Gilman herself was aware that the businessman's fate was comparable to that of the homebound woman. She points out that Dr. S. Weir Mitchell also treated "the businessman exhausted from too much work." See Gilman, *The Living of Charlotte Perkins Gilman* (Madison: University of Wisconsin Press, 1990), 95. Hereafter, *Living*.

2. Charlotte Perkins Gilman, *The Home: Its Work and Influence* (New York: McClure, Phillips, and Co., 1903), 319. Hereafter, *The Home*.

3. Gilman, *Women and Economics* (Boston: Small, Maynard, and Co., 1898), 338. Hereafter, *WE*.

4. To their credit, some recent literary critics and historians have tried to show how the public and private spheres overlapped, thus bridging the gaps between the sexes. See Nina Baym, *American Women Writers and the Work of History, 1790–1860* (New Brunswick, NJ: Rutgers University Press, 1995), 1–10; Paul Lauter, "Teaching Nineteenth-Century Women Writers," in *The (Other) American Traditions: Nineteenth-Century Women Writers*, ed. Joyce W. Warren (New

Brunswick, NJ: Rutgers University Press, 1993), 73–91; and Margaret Marsh, "Suburban Men and Masculine Domesticity, 1870–1915," in *Meanings for Manhood: Constructions of Masculinity in Victorian America*, ed. Mark C. Carnes and Clyde Griffen, (Chicago: University of Chicago Press, 1990), 111–28. Marsh asserts that "the doctrine of the separate spheres began to break down after the Civil War" (p. 113). For an account of how the idea of separate spheres affected Gilman personally, see Carol Ruth Berkin's essay "Private Woman, Public Woman: The Contradiction of Charlotte Perkins Gilman," in *Critical Essays on Charlotte Perkins Gilman*, ed. Joanne B. Karpinski (New York: G. K. Hall, 1992), 17–42.

5. Cf. note 4. Marsh refers to the seminal essay by John Higham in 1970, "The Reorientation of American Culture in the 1890s," and shows how his essay generated many similar interpretations regarding the anxieties of manhood: "We owe the association of the corporation drone with the flamboyant Rough Rider to an influential essay by John Higham, who argued that one of the most significant American cultural constructs at the turn of the century was a growing cult of masculinity" (p. 111).

6. Citations to the stories "Making a Living" (pp. 238–48), "Her Beauty" (pp. 294–301), and "Her Housekeeper" (pp. 195–207) are from Barbara H. Solomon, *Herland and Selected Stories by Charlotte Perkins Gilman* (New York: Signet, 1992); hereafter, *Herland*. References to "His Excuse" (pp. 88–95) and "Mrs. Elder's Idea" (pp. 138–45) are to Denise D. Knight, *The Yellow Wall-Paper and Selected Stories of Charlotte Perkins Gilman* (Newark: University of Delaware Press, 1994); hereafter, *Yellow*. References to "The Cottagette" (pp. 41–51) and "Mr. Peebles' Heart" (pp. 76–85) are to Lynne Sharon Schwartz, *The Yellow Wallpaper and Other Writings by Charlotte Perkins Gilman* (New York: Bantam Books, 1989); hereafter, *Other*.

7. Gilman, *The Man-Made World; Or, Our Androcentric Culture, Forerunner* 1 (1909–10); rpt., (New York: Charlton Co., 1991), p. 244.

8. One might recall Gilman's outspoken statement that men are not attracted to the domestic woman; the powerful women, "[t]he breakers of hearts, the queens of romance, the goddesses of a thousand devotees, have not been cooks" (*The Home*, 280–81).

Works Cited

Baym, Nina. *American Women Writers and the Work of History, 1790–1860*. New Brunswick, NJ: Rutgers University Press, 1995.

Berkin, Carol Ruth. "Private Woman, Public Woman: The Contradiction of Charlotte Perkins Gilman." In *Critical Essays on Charlotte Perkins Gilman*, ed. Joanne B. Karpinski. New York: G. K. Hall, 1992. 17–42.

Gilman, Charlotte Perkins. *Women and Economics*. Ed. Carl N. Degler. 1898. Rpt., New York: Harper and Row, 1966.

————. *The Home: Its Work and Influence.* Intro. William L. O'Neill. 1903. Rpt., Urbana, IL: University of Illinois Press, 1972.

————. *The Man-Made World; Or, Our Androcentric Culture.* 1911. Rpt., New York: Johnson Reprint Corp., 1971.

————. *The Living of Charlotte Perkins Gilman: An Autobiography.* 1935. Rpt., intro. by Ann J. Lane. Madison: University of Wisconsin Press, 1991.

————. *"The Yellow Wallpaper" and Other Writings by Charlotte Perkins Gilman.* Intro. by Lynne Sharon Schwartz. New York: Bantam, 1989.

————. *Herland and Selected Short Stories by Charlotte Perkins Gilman.* Ed. and intro. Barbara H. Solomon. New York: Signet, 1992.

————. *"The Yellow Wall-Paper" and Selected Short Stories by Charlotte Perkins Gilman.* Ed. and intro. Denise D. Knight. Newark, DE: University of Delaware Press, 1994.

Lauter, Paul. "Teaching Nineteenth-Century Women Writers." In *The (Other) American Traditions: Nineteenth-Century Women Writers.* Ed. Joyce W. Warren. New Brunswick, NJ: Rutgers University Press, 1993. 73–91.

Marsh, Margaret. "Suburban Men and Masculine Domesticity, 1870–1915." In *Meanings for Manhood: Constructions of Masculinity in Victorian America.* Ed. Mark C. Carnes and Clyde Griffen. Chicago, IL: University of Chicago Press, 1990. 111–28.

Barbara A. White

A major issue in lesbian feminist criticism has been the definition of "lesbian," or how we decide, as Bonnie Zimmerman puts it, "when a specific writer is a Lesbian writer or a text a Lesbian text."[1] The issue is complicated when the writer lived before our time and the act of recovering her for lesbian history may mean projecting current understandings onto a very different past. Zimmerman wonders, "Should we limit this appellation to those women for whom sexual experience with other women can be proven?" ("What," 37). But in the case of Charlotte Perkins Gilman (1860–1935) we already have the evidence. Although "proof" is lacking for such nineteenth-century writers as Emily Dickinson and Sarah Orne Jewett, who are often claimed to have been lesbians, Gilman herself admitted sexual experience with women. One wonders why, then, Gilman is almost universally presented as a heterosexual writer and her works analyzed accordingly. This essay will suggest some reasons and examine Gilman stories that are unmistakably "lesbian texts."

In observing that Gilman is presented as heterosexual, I do not mean to imply that her biographers completely ignore her close relationships with women. Everyone notes Gilman's youthful passion, well documented in her diaries and letters, for Martha Luther, the "pussie" and "little chick" with whom she planned to spend her life.[2] But Ann J. Lane concludes (correctly) that "it is impossible to read widely in the correspondence of most nineteenth-century women without stumbling across language similar to that used by Charlotte to Martha" and (less persuasively) that "deep as these loving relationships were, there were far fewer that sought sexual expression than would be imagined today."[3] Whether or not the latter statement is true, Gilman herself in her autobiography described her romance with Martha as "love, but not sex,"[4] and we might be willing to read it as an "episode" in an otherwise unblemished heterosexual life were it not for Gilman's subsequent rela-

Published here for the first time.

tionships with women. Here she is at age 30 writing to her friend Grace Channing, who was about to marry Gilman's ex-husband:

> Do you know I think I suffer more in giving you up than in Walter—for you were all joy to me.
> It is awful to be a man inside and not be able to marry the woman you love!
> When Martha married it cracked my heart a good deal—your loss will finish it.
> I think of you with a great howling selfish heartache. *I* want you—*I* love you—*I* need you myself![5]

The next year Gilman began a two-year relationship with journalist Adeline Knapp that apparently did include sex. Before she married Houghton Gilman she confessed that "I loved her that way" and worried that Knapp might produce her love letters—"Fancy the San Francisco Papers with a Profound Sensation in Literary Circles! Revelations of a Peculiar Past! Mrs. Stetson's Love Affair with a Woman. Is this 'Friendship'! and so on" (*Journey*, 246).

Unfortunately, Gilman's statements have been minimized by her biographers and critics. One reads as late as 1993 that the early relationship with Martha Luther was "ambiguously affectionate, suggesting the possibility of repressed homosexuality; but close friendships, often expressed in romantic if not erotic language, were not unusual between artistic intellectual women of the day"; the later relationship with Adeline Knapp is not mentioned.[6] Lane argues that Gilman and Knapp may not have been lovers; perhaps they slept together because Gilman "needed physical demonstrations, not necessarily sexual, of the affection she craved" (*To Herland*, 166). She concludes that Gilman "is reported to have said to E. A. Ross, 'I am altogether heterosexual and cannot do my best work unless in love and loved,' a statement which is confirmed by her life's work" (p. 349). This comment to Ross, a sociologist with whom Gilman was friendly, has deflected critics who seemed headed toward a lesbian analysis of Gilman.[7] Gilman did not make the statement, however—Ross says it of *himself* in his autobiography.[8]

But Gilman's status as a heterosexual writer is not completely an invention of her biographers, for lesbian critics have not been anxious to claim her.[9] In our current classification of sexualities, Gilman was bisexual, and bisexuals have tended to slip through the cracks, ignored by both lesbians and heterosexual women.[10] Furthermore, Gilman's most famous work, "The Yellow Wall-Paper," is a heterosexual text about a wife and mother in which relations between women are presented as bleak.[11] In the utopian *Herland,* today the second-best-known Gilman text, women reside in perfect harmony separate from men, but without sex—"they hadn't the faintest idea of love—sex-love, that is";[12] the women reproduce by parthenogenesis and live in a state of compulsory celibacy. Gilman herself, then, would seem to be rejecting lesbian identity as a viable option.

Of course she had her reasons. We might wish that Gilman, the leading feminist philosopher at the turn of the century, had openly discussed lesbianism; yet as Mary A. Hill points out, "to promote the positive value of lesbian relationships in articles and lectures was not, realistically, a nineteenth-century option. The resulting scandal almost certainly would have discredited her life and work" (*Journey,* 233). Gilman's fantasy of being exposed in the San Francisco newspapers was by no means paranoid—she had already been attacked as antifamily when she divorced Walter Stetson and sent her daughter to live with him. Even so, Gilman might have braved further ostracism were it not for the fact that emphasizing lesbian possibilities would have contradicted her major reason for writing. The bedroom lay in the home, and Gilman wanted to portray women moving out of the home, acting competently and efficiently in the world. She deplored literature wherein "love, good love and bad love, natural and unnatural, legitimate and illegitimate" is "continually vocalized and overestimated . . . with the unavoidable inference that there is nothing else going on."[13] She noted that "We have long since seen that there were other interests than those of sex, for men. We must learn that these exist for women as well."[14]

Yet if Gilman banished sex from *Herland,* she did not keep it out of her short stories. In many tales women are sexually attracted to women, and once one woman has saved another from patriarchy, there is little else going on. The central situation in most of Gilman's stories is rescue.[15] Often a woman succeeds in rescuing another woman from an oppressive man or constricting gender role—Gilman even invented for a series of stories a character whose sole function is to carry out this pattern. In seven stories from 1909 to 1912, Benigna MacAvelly (a benign Machiavelli) quietly pulls strings in the background to give older women a much-needed profession or to protect younger women from unwanted sexual advances by men.[16] Perhaps Gilman conceived similarly of her own role as writer.

Gilman inaugurated the woman-rescues-woman pattern in one of her earliest stories, published even before "The Yellow Wall-Paper." In "My

Poor Aunt" (1891), the 21-year-old narrator, Kate Bennett, is trapped in a scenario from Gilman's youth: living at home with her economically struggling mother, she feels alone and useless; her mother and aunt want to marry her off to a man she "hated to have . . . touch me."[17] To the rescue rides Kate's other aunt, for whom she was named, an aunt labeled "poor" because unmarried. But Aunt Kate proves to be "young, handsome, well-dressed—the picture of health, happiness, and success" (*Herland*, 164); she owns a newspaper in Nebraska and offers young Kate the position of assistant editor. The plot is remarkably similar in Gilman's last published story, "A Growing Heart," which appeared a quarter of a century later. Here the 21-year-old Agnes (Gilman was 21 when she lost Martha to marriage) consults a minister because she has no marriage prospects and feels trapped by her mother, "the anchor which held the girl, or the chain which bound her" (p. 309). The female minister breaks the chain, explaining that marriage and motherhood are not the whole of life; having "exhibited the world" to Agnes (p. 310), she helps her found a town in the West.[18]

But, we must inquire, are these rescue stories really lesbian? It is one thing to deliver a woman from compulsory heterosexuality and another to allow her the "sex-love" between women that is denied in *Herland*. One could argue that Aunt Kate and the minister save the heroine from the wrong man only to supply her with the right one. In "My Poor Aunt" the good man follows the two Kates west, and in "A Growing Heart" he is even more of an afterthought—at the end of the story we are told that Agnes married after age 40 and had two children.[19] The relationships between the women are so much more intense and central in the stories that if one wanted to minimize the lesbian content it would work better to read the relationships as mother-daughter in nature. A critic's comment about Gilman's autobiography—that she "searches for mother figures, women she hoped would give her the approval and love she needed" and would act "to save and to guide her"[20]—also applies to the fiction. There is certainly an element of wish fulfillment in "My Poor Aunt" and "A Growing Heart": a miserable 21-year-old Charlotte Perkins is provided with the feminist writer's dream—a better mother, a wise older woman who not only wants Charlotte to be free and feminist but also will publish her work![21]

The protagonists of the two stories do not feel "daughterly" toward their mentors, however. A strong erotic current pulses throughout, and this is why the stories need to be read as lesbian texts. In "My Poor Aunt" the first-person narrator seems obsessed with watching her aunt

Kate, framing and reframing her as "the picture of health, happiness, and success." "With what infinite satisfaction did I look upon a woman who was sufficient to herself and a little over! . . . I feasted my eyes upon . . . this hale, bright, blooming creature." Finally Kate "fell into her arms literally and metaphorically" (*Herland*, 164). The same thing happens to Agnes in "A Growing Heart" as the minister "took her in her arms and kissed her."[22] Agnes compares the minister's smile to a sunrise; when she talks, "Agnes was facing her, leaning forward, breathing quickly, her eyes aflame" (p. 311).

In other woman-rescues-woman stories the protagonists are old school friends who once had a relationship like Charlotte Perkins and Martha Luther had. "Lost Women" (1912) has a first-person narrator whose aunt tells her a story about two young women who "worshipped each other": "Those girls were just wrapped up in each other, the way girls are, only there seemed to be more to it. To hear either of them tell, it was one of those very special friendships that mean more than anything else on earth—except love. Sometimes I think they are about as good as love—but I don't know."[23] Nellie and Mary get "lost" when they marry Smith and Brown and change their names; only as widows do they accidentally find each other—"Nellie just swept her off. . . . I guess there weren't any happier women in Texas those days" (p. 284). The frame of this story enacts a familiar mentoring relationship as the aunt informs the narrator about "special friendships" that can be "as good as love" and warns her not to change her name (Gilman wished she herself had remained "Perkins" instead of adding men's names [*Living*, 284]).

"Mrs. Power's Duty" (1913) depicts the rescue of the title character by her old school friend Georgy Hammond. Georgy travels west to find Julia "indifferent to everything in life," dazed by the heat of her husband's beloved Sinkville, Arizona.[24] Georgy, who is her friend's minister, convinces her to resume teaching in the East, arguing that she commits a "sin" when she wastes her life serving a man. But Georgy's means of persuasion are hardly religious: much of the story is given over to sensuous description of the friends' hand-holding, hugging, and "cuddling" (p. 255) and of the tasty lunch Georgy has brought. Julia drops her head on Georgy's shoulder and cries from hunger—"and it's the first time I've been hungry for—*years*, it seems" (p. 255). As in other Gilman tales of "special friendships," food is central and scenes of eating seem to stand in for sex.[25] Both "Mrs. Power's Duty" and "Lost Women" shy away in the end, though, from a full endorsement of love between women. Julia's husband follows her east, and Nellie and Mary contact an old suitor (though the point here may be that men, by keeping their names, are easier to locate). It could still be argued that Gilman was unconscious of the implications of her portrayals of women's relationships, just as Lane reads her "awful to be a man inside" outcry to Grace Channing as an expression of "unrecognized sexual feelings" (p. 151).

But Gilman does not always bow to convention and provide a man in the background. Sometimes the women involved in "special friendships" end up happy together, as in "Encouraging Miss Miller" (1915), in which a secretary, "little Miss Sayles," rescues Miss Miller from being exploited by relatives and becomes her "lover."[26] Occasionally the relationship is explicitly marriagelike. "The Boarder Bit" even includes a proposal, for when Lucy Magway inherits money she convinces the friend of her girlhood, Georgiana, to divorce her husband, who "has ruined your health, and broken your heart, and spoiled your life—just leave him, my dear, for good and all!"[27] Lucy suggests that she and Georgiana travel abroad and on their return board out. "'Oh, Georgiana, wilt thou be mine!' cried Mrs. Magway, with juvenile abandon." Georgiana accepts, and "the two women were as happy as schoolgirls in their renewed intimacy" (p. 173). The fact that Gilman buries Lucy and Georgiana's romance in a story ostensibly about boarding suggests that her depiction of the relationship made her nervous, as does the mock-heroic wording "wilt thou be mine." Indeed, the latter is reminiscent of the self-conscious language Gilman used in her diary entries about Martha Luther, as in "Verily I love the damsel" (*Diaries*, 43).

A more straightforward story, and the best of her women's marriage tales, is "Turned" (1911). Here two women are "turned" from heterosexuality by the behavior of a man. While her husband travels abroad on a business trip, Marion Marroner discovers that he has impregnated their 18-year-old Swedish maid. Marion's first impulse, to dismiss young Gerta in a jealous rage, gives way to pity and understanding: "Mrs. Marroner stood and watched her, and as she watched she considered the helpless sweetness of the face; the defenseless, unformed character; the docility and habit of obedience which made her so attractive—and so easily a victim" (*Herland*, 263). Perhaps Gerta should have "resisted temptation," Marion thinks, but how could she have recognized it disguised as friendship from her employer? And so Mr. Marroner returns to an empty house and has to hire detectives to locate his wife, who has started teaching in another town. When he rings her bell, he is greeted by "two women. One like a tall Madonna, bearing a baby in her arms. Marion, calm, steady, definitely impersonal, nothing but a clear pallor to hint of inner stress. Gerta, holding the child as a bulwark, with a new intelligence in her face, and her blue, adoring eyes fixed on her friend—not upon him" (p. 267).

Marion and Gerta are thus framed as a couple in what must have seemed to Gilman's contemporaries a surprise ending. Of course, Gilman prepared for it by noting early in the story that even though Gerta seemed a child, there were "but fifteen" years between them (p. 260), and Marion's occupation as a teacher means that she can develop that new intelligence of Gerta's all the more quickly. The "blue, adoring eyes" have also been mentioned earlier. "Turned" resembles, and even surpasses, "My Poor Aunt" in its heavy emphasis on looks. Gerta's "splendid, clean young beauty" (p. 264) is lauded on nearly every page: she is a "young goddess" who exhibits "rich womanhood," and "her braided wealth of dead-gold hair, her grave blue eyes, her mighty shoulders and long, firmly moulded limbs seemed those of a primal earth spirit" (p. 259). In a phrase that has somewhat different connotations for today's readers, she was "grandly built" (p. 258). There is no mistaking that Marion has gained an attractive partner.

Gilman wrote other stories that resemble "Turned." "Mrs. Beazley's Deeds" (1911) concludes in exactly the same way, with the callous husband returning from a trip to find that his wife has left him for a woman. Mr. Beazley has been coercing his wife to sign away property deeded her by her late father. She is rescued when a boarder from the city, who Mr. Beazley assumes is a vacationing schoolteacher, turns out to be "the best woman lawyer in New York" (*Herland*, 348). Miss Lawrence, who is also "fairly young, undeniably good looking" (p. 340), helps Mrs. Beazley keep her last deed and escape her overbearing husband. As Miss Lawrence and Mr. Beazley face off at the end of the story, he gives a double meaning to the word "property": " '[Y]ou seem to have found a good deal more in that property than I did,' said he with a sneer. 'That's not improbable,' she replied sweetly" (p. 349).

In "Being Reasonable" (1915) two women again turn the tables on a man. Mary Cunningham and Betty Henderson discover that they are married to the same traveling salesman and decide to divorce him and live together with their young children. The characterizations are similar to those in "Turned"—Mary practical and reasonable but Betty soft and "foolish,"[28] and the tableau at the end, in which the women confront Mr. Cunningham/Henderson, is exactly the same. Mary has hidden Betty in her closet(!) and at the proper moment she emerges: "Then Mary raised her eyes to the closet behind her husband; and there came forth from it a cold, stern woman, looking older, looking taller, looking even more beautiful" (p. 191). Then "Mary rose and went to her friend's side, standing, her arm about her," and the couple announces they are divorcing him—"we have each other" (p. 192). Although the resemblance to "Turned" is close, this story is weaker because it depends on absurd coincidences. Mary discovers her husband's bigamy only when she goes to a movie and happens to find him there with Betty (in New York City); Betty just happens to be Mary's long-lost school friend. Gilman was never scrupulous with her plots, caring most that her message get across, but "Being Reasonable" sinks to an unusual low, perhaps signaling how much she needed to tell this particular story. As Lucy Magway urges her friend Georgiana in "The Boarder Bit": "Just leave him, my dear."

It does seem that in order to be left the man has to be demonstrably evil—a tyrant, a thief, a bigamist, capable of seducing a young dependent in his home. This defensiveness implies some apprehension on Gilman's part that she was breaking the rules in her women's marriage stories. However confused she may have been about her sexual identity (as evident in the "man inside" comment), she was most likely conscious of her erotic attraction to women and the stigma placed on it—hence her fear of the California newspapers and insistence in the autobiography that her relationship with Martha excluded sex. In the stories it may have been acceptable to plot women rescuing women from patriarchy or to linger over descriptions of women's bodies, their golden hair or "bare white back" or "smooth brown arms."[29] Or perhaps women could be shown leaving their husbands at the end of a story and living together happily ever after. But for a turn-of-the-century writer to combine all these elements, as Gilman did in what I have been calling the women's marriage stories, bordered on subversion.

To some modern readers, Gilman's stories might not be considered "radical transgressors of heterosexual codes," as Marilyn Farwell puts it. Farwell argues that many lesbian works cannot be so described because "the dualities of the male active and female passive spaces are reconfirmed."[30] In other words, female characters can temporarily occupy "male narrative space" and lesbians "heterosexual space" without challenging the dualism of the basic structure. *The Well of Loneliness,* for example, "depends structurally on the maintenance of gender difference. Stephen is identified with male desire, she moves through female space and almost wins the female as her reward" (p. 97). Such is the case also in Gilman's marriage stories, with difference always being stressed. The women have unequal status, and the aggressor in the relationship is the one who plans, thinks, and earns the money—the teacher, the lawyer, the inheritor, the scientist. The characters in the "female passive spaces"—wife, maid, and secretary—are recipients of the "male" gaze and exhibit stereotypically female qualities. Gilman describes Betty, for instance, as weak and childish, a "credulous, too-affectionate little thing" (*Yellow*, 187). The adjective "little" is applied also to Mrs. Beazley, Miss Sayles, and Gerta, even though Gerta, like Betty, is taller than her partner. One recalls the youthful Charlotte Perkins's favorite name for Martha Luther—"little girl" (*Diaries*, 88). Clearly in the story in which Charlotte lived she intended to occupy the hero space with Martha as "damsel" and "little girl." But Martha's marriage showed her that however strongly a woman is identified with male desire, she cannot, in Farwell's words, "ultimately possess male space" (p. 97).

Farwell calls for a "space of sameness" (p. 97) in lesbian fiction that would "confuse the boundaries" between subject and object and lover and beloved, undercutting "the heterosexuality which is based on this dualism" (p. 98). Gilman would have been uncomfortable blurring the boundaries: even as she struggled to make Gerta and Betty wiser and thus more appropriately equal mates for Marion and Mary, she preserved the basic distinctions she had established between them; even in the all-female country of Herland, the presence of the male narrator and his friends works to enshrine dualism. Interestingly, in stories of female utopias that lack a male narrator, at least one recognizable lesbian character usually appears; in "Bee Wise" (1913) she is called "Manager" and is plain, strong, and sturdy, described by her uncle as "a man after his own heart!"[31]

But the utopias are another story, and Farwell's theory is only one among many that might be used in interpreting Gilman's work; for instance, Bonnie Zimmerman, who is quoted at the beginning of this essay, questions Farwell's conclusions and claims "it may be that lesbian space is defined as much by difference as by sameness. It is the differences within our difference that carry such exciting potential" (*Lesbians*, 12). Difference or sameness, the important point here is that Gilman's writing shows enough lesbian sensibility to deserve the benefit of a variety of lesbian feminist readings. Gilman criticism would certainly be enriched by a less exclusively heterosexual approach, one that instead of viewing her attraction to women in terms of discrete biographical episodes to be explained away, acknowledges it as a central force in her life and work. When such a body of criticism comes into being, Gilman can be claimed more firmly for lesbian history and tradition.

Notes

1. Bonnie Zimmerman, "What Has Never Been: An Overview of Lesbian Feminist Criticism for the Nineties," in *New Lesbian Criticism: Literary and Cultural Readings,* ed. Sally Hunt (New York: Columbia University Press, 1992), 34. Hereafter, "What."

2. See *The Diaries of Charlotte Perkins Gilman,* ed. Denise D. Knight (Charlottesville: University Press of Virginia, 1994) 16, 22; hereafter *Diaries.* See also Juliet A. Langley, " 'Audacious Fancies': A Collection of Letters from Charlotte Perkins Gilman to Martha Luther," *Trivia* (Winter 1985): 52–69. Gilman's biographers fit her in the framework of Carroll Smith-Rosenberg's theories on the prevalence and acceptability of romantic friendships between women in the nineteenth century; see "The Female World of Love and Ritual: Relations Between Women in Nineteenth-Century America," *Signs* 1.1 (1975): 1–29.

3. Ann J. Lane, *To Herland and Beyond: The Life and Times of Charlotte Perkins Gilman* (New York: Pantheon, 1990), 78. Hereafter, *To Herland.*

4. Charlotte Perkins Gilman, *The Living of Charlotte Perkins Gilman* (Madison: University of Wisconsin Press, 1990), 78. Hereafter, *Living.*

5. Mary A. Hill, ed., *A Journey from Within: The Love Letters of Charlotte Perkins Gilman, 1897–1900* (Lewisburg, PA: Bucknell University Press, 1995), 404. Hereafter, *Journey.*

6. Thomas L. Erskine and Connie L. Richards, introduction to *The Yellow Wallpaper: Charlotte Perkins Gilman,* Thomas L. Erskine and Connie L. Richards, eds. (New Brunswick, NJ: Rutgers University Press, 1993), 4.

7. See Joanne Karpinski, ed., *Critical Essays on Charlotte Perkins Gilman* (Boston: G. K. Hall, 1992), 4.

8. See Edward Alworth Ross, *Seventy Years of It: An Autobiography* (New York: D. Appleton-Century, 1936), 20.

9. For instance, Gilman does not appear, as do Dickinson and Jewett, in the syllabi and bibliographies of the groundbreaking *Lesbian Studies: Present and Future,* ed. Margaret Cruikshank (Old Westbury, NY: Feminist Press, 1982). Nor is she mentioned 10 years later, as are Dickinson and Jewett, in the articles and extensive bibliographies of *Sexual Practice, Textual Theory: Lesbian Cultural Criticism* (see Zimmerman, "What"). Nor does Gilman appear in anthologies of lesbian writing or in reference books, such as *Gay and Lesbian Literature* (Detroit: St. James Press, 1994).

10. See, for example, Loraine Hutchins and Lani Kaahumanu, eds., *Bi Any Other Name: Bisexual People Speak Out* (Boston: Alyson, 1991). See also Elizabeth Reba, ed., *Closer to Home: Bisexuality and Feminism* (Seattle: Seal Press, 1992).

11. All the living women in the story collaborate with the patriarchs who seek to control the heroine. One might, however, view "The Yellow Wall-Paper" as a heterosexual text only on the surface. Carla Kaplan has recently pointed out that the story can be read as a critique of compulsory heterosexuality—see "Reading Feminist Readings: Recuperative Reading and the Silent Heroine of Feminist Criticism," *Listening to Silences: New Essays in Feminist Criticism*, ed. Elaine Hedges and Shelley Fisher Fishkin (New York: Oxford University Press, 1994): 168–94.

12. Barbara H. Solomon, ed., *Herland and Selected Stories by Charlotte Perkins Gilman* (New York: Signet, 1992), 89. Hereafter, *Herland*.

13. See Charlotte Perkins Gilman, *The Man-Made World; Or, Our Androcentric Culture, Forerunner* 1 (1909–10); reprint (New York: Charlton Co., 1991), 101.

14. See Gilman, "Coming Changes in Literature," *Forerunner* 6 (September 1915): 234.

15. Characters are rescued from a variety of threats, often those that once plagued Gilman herself: a conventional mother ("A Growing Heart"), a teasing brother ("Joan's Defender"), a sexist fiancé ("Three Women"), postpartum depression ("Making a Change"), patriarchal doctors ("Dr. Clair's Place"), and even nosy reporters ("An Unwilling Interview"). Sometimes the rescuer is male ("Old Mrs. Crosley"), and sometimes a man is rescued ("Mr. Peebles' Heart"). Occasionally an attempted rescue is refused by the character in need ("Through This").

16. The seven stories are the following: "According to Solomon" (1909); "Martha's Mother" (1910); "A Coincidence" (1910); "Mrs. Potter and the Clay Club" (1911); "Mrs. Elder's Idea" (1912); "An Innocent Girl" (1912); and "Maidstone Comfort" (1912). The Benigna MacAvelly of the stories is a middle-aged matron, older than the protagonist of Gilman's novella *Benigna Machiavelli* (1914), which follows the young woman to age 21, when she marries a man named MacAvelly.

17. *Herland*, 161. Gilman gives him the ironic name "Boon"; "Kate Bennett" recalls the marriageable Bennets of Jane Austen's *Pride and Prejudice*. The story is also similar to Mary Wilkins Freeman's "Louisa" (1891), in which a young woman resists her poverty-stricken family's pressure to marry. A Gilman story with the same plot is "Mr. Robert Grey, Sr." (*Forerunner* 1 [September 1910]: 1–4). Just as the heroine decides to concede, Robert Grey Sr. kisses her: "I jerked away from him—he almost fell over. 'No. O NO!' I cried. 'I can't do it Mr. Grey. I simply *can't!* . . . I can't bear to have you touch me—never could' " (p. 4).

18. A female minister similarly saves an oppressed daughter in "What Occupation?" (1911).

19. The strength of the heterosexual plot was such that Gilman sometimes contrasts successful, happy "old maids" with broken-down wives, only to "reward" the old maid in the end with a superfluous husband. See, for instance, "Five Girls" (1894), "Fulfillment" (1914), "Mrs. Mann's Clothes" (1914), and "A Gift for Needle Work" (1915).

20. See Juliann E. Fleenor, "The Gothic Prism: Charlotte Perkins Gilman's Gothic Stories and Her Autobiography," in Erskine and Richards (cf. note 6), 154–55.

21. Another possible reading of these stories is to interpret Kate and Kate (conveniently named) and Agnes and the minister as different aspects of the self; as Bonnie Zimmerman points out, however, this type of reading "serves to mask a relationship that a lesbian reader might interpret as bonding or love between women" ("What," 36).

22. Gilman, "A Growing Heart," *Forerunner* 7 (December 1916): 311.

23. Gilman, "Lost Women," *Forerunner* 3 (November 1912): 281.

24. Gilman, "Mrs. Power's Duty," *Forerunner* 4 (October 1913): 153.

25. See, for instance, the Benigna MacAvelly story "A Coincidence" (1910).

26. Gilman, "Encouraging Miss Miller," *Forerunner* 6 (December 1915): 311.

27. Gilman, "The Boarder Bit," *Forerunner* 6 (July 1915): 173.

28. See Denise D. Knight, *"The Yellow Wall-Paper" and Selected Stories of Charlotte Perkins Gilman* (Newark: University of Delaware Press, 1994), 187. Hereafter, *Yellow*.

29. "An Innocent Girl," *Forerunner* 3 (March 1912): 57; "Old Water," in *"The Yellow Wall-Paper" and Selected Stories*, ed. Denise D. Knight (Newark: University of Delaware Press, 1994), 122. Both of these stories contain further sensuous descriptions of women's bodies. In "Old Water" the "smooth brown arms" of the heroine are favorably compared to the arms of the "disgusting" man who unsuccessfully pursues her (p. 128)—she "felt a real dislike for the heavy fell of black hair on his arms and hands" (p. 126).

30. See Marilyn R. Farwell, "Heterosexual Plots and Lesbian Subtexts: Toward a Theory of Lesbian Narrative Space," in *Lesbian Texts and Contexts: Radical Revisions*, ed. Karla Jay and Joanne Glasgow (New York: New York University Press, 1990), 96.

31. Gilman, "Bee Wise," *Forerunner* 4 (July 1913): 171. It is probably not accidental that Gilman often chose a male name for one partner in a dyad—Georgy, Georgiana, Marion (the male spelling with "o" rather than the female spelling with "a"), and Miss Lawrence (no first name given).

Works Cited

Erskine, Thomas L., and Connie L. Richards. Introduction to *"The Yellow Wall-paper": Charlotte Perkins Gilman*, Thomas L. Erskine and Connie L. Richards, eds. New Brunswick, NJ: Rutgers University Press, 1993.

———. *Herland and Selected Stories by Charlotte Perkins Gilman*. Ed. Barbara H. Solomon. New York: Penguin, 1992.

Farwell, Marilyn R. "Heterosexual Plots and Lesbian Subtexts: Toward a Theory of Lesbian Narrative Space." In *Lesbian Texts and Contexts: Radical Revisions*. Ed. Karla Jay and Joanne Glasgow. New York: New York University Press, 1990. 91–103.

Fleenor, Juliann E. "The Gothic Prism: Charlotte Perkins Gilman's Gothic Stories and Her Autobiography." In Thomas L. Erskine and Connie L. Richards, eds., *"The Yellow Wallpaper"*: *Charlotte Perkins Gilman.* New Brunswick, NJ: Rutgers University Press, 1993. 139–158.

Gilman, Charlotte Perkins. *The Man-Made World; Or, Our Androcentric Culture.* New York: Charlton, 1911.

———. "Lost Women." *Forerunner* 3 (November 1912): 281–84.

———. "Bee Wise." *Forerunner* 4 (July 1913): 169–73.

———. "Being Reasonable." In *"The Yellow Wallpaper" and Selected Stories.* Ed. Denise D. Knight. Newark: University of Delaware Press, 1994. 185–92.

———. "The Boarder Bit." *Forerunner* 6 (July 1915): 169–73.

———. "Mrs. Power's Duty." *Forerunner* 4 (October 1913): 253–57.

———. "Coming Changes in Literature." *Forerunner* 6 (September 1915): 230–36.

———. "Encouraging Miss Miller." *Forerunner* 6 (December 1915): 309–13.

———. "A Growing Heart." *Forerunner* 7 (December 1916): 309–13.

———. *The Living of Charlotte Perkins Gilman: An Autobiography.* 1935. Rpt., Madison: University of Wisconsin Press, 1990.

———. *The Diaries.* Ed. Denise D. Knight. 2 vols. Charlottesville: University Press of Virginia, 1994.

———. *A Journey from Within: The Love Letters of Charlotte Perkins Gilman, 1897–1900.* Ed. Mary A. Hill. Lewisburg: Bucknell University Press, 1995.

Hutchins, Loraine, and Lani Kaahumanu, eds. *Bi Any Other Name: Bisexual People Speak Out.* Boston: Alyson, 1991.

Karpinski, Joanne, ed. *Critical Essays on Charlotte Perkins Gilman.* Boston: G. K. Hall, 1992.

Lane, Ann J. *To Herland and Beyond: The Life and Work of Charlotte Perkins Gilman.* New York: Pantheon, 1990.

Reba, Elizabeth, ed. *Closer to Home: Bisexuality and Feminism.* Seattle: Seal Press, 1992.

Ross, Edward Alsworth. *Seventy Years of It: An Autobiography.* New York: D. Appleton-Century, 1936.

Zimmerman, Bonnie. "Lesbians Like This and That: Some Notes on Lesbian Criticism for the Nineties." In *New Lesbian Criticism: Literary and Cultural Readings.* Ed. Sally Munt. New York: Columbia University Press, 1992. 1–15. Hereafter, *Lesbians.*

———. "What Has Never Been: An Overview of Lesbian Feminist Criticism" (1981). In *Sexual Practice/Textual Theory: Lesbian Cultural Criticism.* Ed. Susan J. Wolfe and Julia Penelope. Cambridge: Blackwell, 1993. 33–54.

Carol Farley Kessler

The utopian fiction of Charlotte Perkins Gilman takes on as its "cultural work" the demonstration that women are not confined to one traditional mode of being—wife/motherhood—but can fill as varied social roles as can male counterparts.[1] Jane Tompkins in her introduction to *Sensational Designs* (1985) suggests that we can speak of the "cultural work" of texts as an "attempt to redefine the social order" (xi). Further, Tompkins argues that we should study novels and stories "because they offer powerful examples of the way a culture thinks about itself, articulating and proposing solutions for the problems that shape a particular historical moment" (xi). Like her great-aunt Harriet Beecher Stowe, included in Tompkins's study, Gilman wrote "to win the belief and influence the behavior of the widest possible audience": she had "designs upon her audiences, in the sense of wanting to make people think and act in a particular way" (xi).

In her 1910 study called *The Man-Made World; or, Our Androcentric Culture*, Gilman devoted one chapter to discussing what she labelled "Masculine Literature." Here Gilman explains her understanding that readers would more readily accept heretical views if presented as stories with morals for future action. In her stories, Gilman "re-presented" her ideas clothed as characters. She explains this view of the social function of literature:

> The thought of the world is made and handed out to us in the main. The makers of books are the makers of thoughts and feelings for people in general. Fiction is the most popular form in which this world-food is taken. If it were true, it would teach us life easily, swiftly, truly; teach not by preaching but by truly *re-presenting* [emphasis added]; and we should grow up becoming acquainted with a far wider range of life

"Consider Her Ways: The Cultural Work of Charlotte Perkins Gilman's Pragmatopian Stories, 1908–1913." From *Utopian and Science Fiction by Women*, Jane A. Donawerth and Carol A. Kolmerten, eds. (Syracuse: Syracuse University Press, 1994). 126–36. Reprinted by permission.

in books than could even be ours in person. Then meeting life in reality we should be wise ["Bee Wise" or be utopian, which is a pun on one of her titles]—and not be disappointed. (21)

She thus subscribes to a literature that can be called "cultural work," can enact social changes, can function as social action, can convey alternative versions/visions of human action—a position of clear self-consciousness regarding literary didacticism.

To this end of advocating particular changes, Gilman has situated her utopian fiction on the cultural boundary between genders. In "Response to a Question from *Novy Mir*," the Russian cultural critic Mikhail Mihailovitch Bakhtin (1895–1975) reminds us that

In our enthusiasm for specification we have ignored questions of interconnection and interdependence of various areas of culture; we have frequently forgotten that the boundaries of these areas are not absolute, that in various epochs they have been drawn in various ways; and we have not taken into account that *the most intense and productive life of culture takes place on the boundaries of its individual areas* and not in places where these areas have become enclosed in their own specificity (p. 2).[2]

This productivity of culture then occurs exactly along such boundaries as gender, and utopia becomes a primary locus for culture-creation, or "cultural work." By refusing to accept definitions of traditional "male" and "female" roles and instead offering clear alternatives to such mainstream notions, Gilman forces readers to question boundaries defining behavior assumed acceptable on the basis of gender—her views being still in the 1990s ahead of widespread social practice. This discussion recovers from oblivion nine lesser known short stories, seven from Gilman's magazine *The Forerunner.*[3] These stories taken as a group offer as great a challenge for social transformation as do Gilman's utopian novels: three stories suggest transformations specifically for men, complementing those suggested for women.

In contrast to Gilman's utopian fantasies, her utopian short stories could be labelled "pragmatopias," a term which Riane Eisler coined in *The Chalice and the Blade: Our History, Our Future* (1988) and defines as a "realizable scenario for a partnership future."[4] The "partnership" society that Eisler defines seems already to have been present in the "pragmatopian" imagination of Charlotte Perkins Gilman as revealed in her turn-of-the-century fiction, especially the short stories: the alternative or partner-oriented gender roles she depicts *could be* realized or attained then or in the present-day society that we know. To convey her view Gilman relies not so much upon fantasy in these *Forerunner* short stories—as one might anticipate in utopian writing, but in fact upon realism. But she uses realism subversively, her "design" for effecting the "cultural work" of her utopian fiction. Most often, as Anne Cranny-Francis reminds us in her recent study, *Feminist Fiction: Feminist Uses of Generic Fiction* (1990), realism is the narrative mode employed to naturalize ideology into the lives of readers (137).[5] These are, of course, her words for naming the "cultural work" of texts, which may (1) encourage the maintenance of a status quo—that is, may make what is ideology appear as if derived from natural order—as well as (2) encourage the social transformation that is the goal of utopian writers. Thus Gilman in a realistic mode[6] seeks to dislodge traditional gender ideology by presenting alternative, "realizable" possibilities for more egalitarian gender roles: critics typically decry "alternative" possibilities by alleging how "unrealistic" they are. It is this quality of "realizability" that I wish to examine in these nine utopian short stories.

Traditionally these stories might not have been included in bibliographies of utopian fiction: their mode is realistic. They are "thought experiments" which extrapolate possibilities from present-day society. They make explicit how Gilman's readers might go about realizing her utopian visions. They locate us in the here and now: the setting is her contemporary United States. The nine stories present re/locations (or is it dis/locations?) of the individual with respect to gender in the structuring of families, neighborhoods, occupations, and societies as a whole. I discuss these stories in an order of increasing social complexity—an ordering that in Eisler's terminology could be conceptualized as an "actualization," instead of as a "domination," hierarchy. Social structure need not encase us in oppression: democratic and socialist structures can be envisioned as liberating or actualizing. In these stories, Gilman focuses not upon the macro-structure of a capitalistic economy (which she ignores here as a social problem), but upon the micro-structure of everyday living that Erving Goffman first problematized in *The Presentation of Self in Everyday Life* (1959) and Bettina Aptheker in *Tapestries of Life* (1989). As her strategy for effecting "cultural work," Gilman creates subversively realistic fictions that offer us in "pragmatopias," or realizable utopias, erasure and redrawing of gender boundary lines.

At the lowest level of social organization is the family, the usual location in Western and European cultures for the process of child care, examined in two early stories, both of which adjust the male gender role to provide greater autonomy and support to women. The earlier story, "A Garden of Babies," particularizes the role of the female child-nurturer, while at the same time showing that not all women have either the desire or the ability to be good at nurturing. Both men and women work together to establish a baby garden for the health and welfare of mothers and children. Women provide the actual care; men provide medical expertise. Together they make possible mothers' recovery from the physical exhaustion of caring for small children, a necessity Gilman learned from personal experience and fictionalized in "The Yellow Wallpaper."[7] "A Garden of Babies" demonstrates men participating in the changed behavior necessary for women's lives to expand. It also presents child care as a societywide responsibility by including specialized training in the proper nurturing of small infants and children, and thereby contradicts the then-prevailing assumption that every mother naturally knew how to care for her baby. On the other hand, Gilman's fiction demonstrates her agreement, for the most part, with the assumption that primarily women should perform child care. The insight of Nancy Chodorow—that we need to experience as children nurturance from adults of both sexes—was not then current.[8]

Published a half year later, "Her Housekeeper," however, does anticipate Chodorow. A male realtor and manager of boardinghouses provides the environment in which the woman he loves, also mother of a son not his own, can pursue her career: he finds for her live-in help—a governess to provide child care and a maid to keep house; a cook to her taste; and friends as co-tenants. He provides tea and conversation by a fireside, but no "undesired affection" (150), and for her boy his own listening ears, real artifacts for play, large books for perusal spread out upon a floor. She finds him a "real comfort" because he can "leave off being a man" and "just be a human creature" (151). The "plot" consists of his refutation of her list of six reasons why she won't "remarry." (We eventually learn that she has never married, however, and had born a son out of wedlock.) Gilman has placed the institution of marriage at the center of this story—an institution requiring radical reform for a woman to flourish. Reform, it receives: she may retain her freedom, keep her profession, take lovers—so long as she doesn't love them, and need never keep house (155–57)! Her son would figure as "an added attraction" to this successful suitor (155): if she wanted to take a foreign tour, he would care for her son (156). What appears is a model feminist partner, as caring of a woman as of her child. Dare we call him, by analogy to

Joanna Russ's *Female Man* (1975), a "male woman"? The transformative redrawing of male gender boundaries enacted in both these family stories is "realizable," pragamatopian.

At the second level of social organization—the neighborhood—three stories pertain: "Her Memories," "Maidstone Comfort," and "Mrs. Hines' Money." Over two and a half years after "Her Housekeeper," Gilman published "Her Memories," another story with a central male presence, this time as an unnamed narrator, who recounts his female companion's memories of life at Home Court. This utopian community, situated in four highrise buildings, provided child care and baby culture in covered, connected rooftop playgrounds; its adult amenities included a quiet, central courtyard with fountains, surrounded by cool arcades. Individual families resided in kitchenless apartments, their meals coming up from a common basement kitchen on a service elevator. Gilman regularly privileges the nuclear family unit in her realistic stories. Again she stresses the varied capacities that different women have for mothering—some suited to the very young, some to the school-aged, some utterly out-of-tune with any children, including their own. And Gilman forces us to rethink commonplace daily activities and recognize their relatedness to larger social goals. Although not limited to gender adjustments, "Her Memories" restructures the domestic environment to permit more equitable relations between the sexes.

The next month after "Her Memories," Gilman published "Maidstone Comfort"; here, utopia is a summer resort community of the same name, featuring kitchenless cottages. The female narrator is a friend of the manager-owner Sarah Maidstone Pellett, and Mrs. Benigna McAvelly,[9] who in connecting the inheritance of Molly Bellow with the ideas of Sarah Pellett at Maidstone Comfort located the funding for this enterprise. The capitalistic basis of this tale may seem at odds with Gilman's professed socialist beliefs: rather than her earlier more radical innovations, after her 1900 marriage, she appears more willing to depict bourgeois, middle-class solutions, but she makes women the primary actors on her stage. The next spring in "Mrs. Hines' Money," Gilman again depended upon capital, rather than behavioral and structural change—the basis she credits for social improvements in the first three stories discussed.

In "Mrs. Hines' Money," Eva Hines independently creates social innovations that improve the quality of life in her town. Widowed as the result of an accident, she retains her own legal counsel (rather than depending upon that of her brother) and obtains additional information from the social service-oriented magazine *The Survey*,[10] as well as from her own travels. Then with careful planning according to the new ideas she has gained, she uses money inherited from her husband Jason to build in his memory The Hines Building—a utopian scheme to raise the consciousness and knowledge of the town by housing within this building a library, an auditorium or theatre, men's and women's lounges, a swimming pool and a gymnasium, a roof tea-garden, and meeting rooms for clubs with memberships of all ages. Capital to support social services could, of course, accumulate from taxes rather than private inheritance, but the 1990s egocentricity of voters makes taxes now appear an unrealizable mode for financing social change. Although these last two tales may be less convincing to us today as social change than the first three stories discussed, we must recall that in Gilman's time, family summer "resorts" were commonplace and a women's club movement was strong and influential. What remains nonetheless transformative about them is the broad social agency attributed to individual, capable neighborhood women.

Occupational structure, especially of gender, is the third locus for utopian concern in an actualization hierarchy of social organization. In addition to the already-discussed "Her Housekeeper" are two more stories: "Aunt Mary's Pie Plant" and "Forsythe & Forsythe." An editorial headnote to "Aunt Mary's Pie Plant" proclaims that "Mrs. Gilman's characters show in a convincing way how her beliefs and remedies would work out in practice. [In this story] will be found a realistic miniature 'Looking Backward'" (117–18). The traveler to utopia here is a reporter, Aunt Mary's niece, who has come to describe the sleepy town she expects to find. Instead, encouraged by the town's minister, women of rural New Newton have established businesses offering various household services. A cooked-food service, run by the best cooks, delivers hot fare "better and cheaper" than individual homes earlier provided.[11] Aunt Mary now runs a factory, M. Gardiner, Pies, and has organized a Woman's Farm and Garden Club, whose members bolster each other's business projects: their cooperative networking has changed their town. Traditional women's work is more efficiently, profitably, and competently accomplished as businesses run by skilled practitioners. Overall town prosperity has led to the construction in a parklike setting of a New Central School, equipped both to serve luncheon to students and to offer a crèche and kindergarten facilities. This story demonstrates how evolution toward cooperation and community might occur through club activity. It also suggests—through both Aunt Mary, and her niece, the reporter who will marry, reside in New Newton, and mail her articles to journals wherever they may be located—that women can pursue the world's work in a domestic setting, an early version of flex-time.

Treating primarily the mesh between domestic relationships and occupations, "Forsythe & Forsythe" stars husband-wife law partners, George Forsythe, and his cousin and wife Georgiana Forsythe, whose firm is located in Seattle, Washington. They resolve the problem of housekeeping by living in a residence hotel. A former best friend from college days, businessman James R. "Jimmy-Jack" Jackson, renews his friendship with George. He finds that his wife Susie, a self-centered pleasure seeker, pales in contrast to his first love, George's sister, Clare Forsythe, now a sanitary engineer who lives in the same residence hotel. With the arrival of Susie's divorce decree, he proposes marriage to Clare, whose independent competence he admires. Gilman undermines popular wisdom by showing a nondomestic career woman to be more attractive to a suitor than a woman for whom marriage is the "crowning event of her life" (196). She also suggests that men might find female competence not a threat, but a boon. In both these tales, gender adjustments erase the separation of private and public in the occupational structure, and thereby permit the equal participation of both sexes.

Finally during the summer of 1913, Gilman published two visions of a whole society, the last and most complex level of a social actualization hierarchy included in this discussion—"Bee Wise" and "A Council of War." In "Bee Wise," as in "Mrs. Hines' Money," an inheritance again makes possible the establishment of a utopian experiment: a ten-million-dollar gift permits a group of friends at a women's college to form a "combination" to create "a little Eden" in California (215). Their college Morning Club of some twelve to twenty members—including Mother, Teacher, Nurse, Minister, Doctor, Statesman [*sic*], Manager, Artist, Architect, Engineer—becomes the nucleus for this experimental community. A utopian visitor, again in the guise of a reporter as in "Aunt Mary's Pie Plant," arrives to discover that the Mayor of Herways is a former college classmate. Reporter Jean finds "a perfectly natural little town, planned, built, and managed—. . . by women—for women—and *children*" (215). She learns that the founders aimed "to show what a bunch of women can do successfully": they were willing that men help, but they expected to manage (217). The reporter remains, working in the beach town of Herways (the location of businesses and industries) and living in Beewise (the Residence Club), according to the community's plan. Herways and Beewise take their names from a Biblical verse found in Proverbs 6.6: "Go to the ant, thou sluggard; consider her ways and be wise" (219).[12] As the fictional social structure becomes more complex, Gilman correspondingly expands women's social roles: what a woman has done, women can do, she demonstrates.[13]

The next month Gilman published another woman-centered story focused upon the larger society, "A Council of War." Here, in the only story I discuss not set in the United States, London women plan "to remove this devastating error in relation [namely, male rule, the "war" of the title] and to establish a free and conscious womanhood for the right service of the world" (223). They plan "a government within a government; an organization of women," or "an Extension Committee," "a Co-operative Society" (224). They would employ "women only," or the "right kind" of man (225). At the prospect of a "woman's world, clean and kind and safe and serviceable, . . . the women looked at one another with the light of a new hope in their eyes" (228). This conclusion, however, verges on an essentialism that many feminists today find problematic, nor is this consistent with Gilman's own recognition in "A Garden of Babies" that nurturing skills must be learned, even by mothers. These last two stories strongly prefigure 1915 and 1916 utopias to come, namely, the all-female society of *Herland* and the critique of modern society found in *With Her in Ourland*.

In the utopian stories published between 1909 and 1913, Gilman seems to have moved first, from imagining changes for men that would permit women to achieve the emancipation that she suggests in *Women and Economics* to second, deciding that a better persuasive strategy would be to suggest to (especially male) readers that women have abilities important to society as a whole. Perhaps she thought that persuasion including an appeal to male self-interest might be more effective than an appeal based solely upon altruism: needed transformations improve women's lives, and such improvement could make women more substantially contributing members of society—a benefit to men as well. Demonstrating in *Herland* how benefits to women could be benefits to the whole of society is part of Gilman's two-pronged strategy for improving women's lot: change minds to change behavior. Gilman's utopian stories exemplify the didactic literary purpose to which she unashamedly subscribed. As her strategy for effecting "cultural work," Gilman created subversively realistic fictions that offer us in "pragmatopias," or realizable utopias, erasure and redrawing of gender boundaries. Gilman's demonstration of various grassroots innovations and reforms suggests the utopian potential of the realistic mode. What we might be tempted to dismiss as UNrealistic—when located in realizable, gylanic pragmatopia—may subvert our tendency to dismiss and instead transform our vision of the possible. Such is the "cultural work" of Charlotte Perkins Gilman.

Notes

1. I owe to Lee Cullen Khanna the insight to apply Jane Tompkins' concept of "cultural work" to feminist utopian fiction. Jane Donawerth and Carol Kolmerten provided invaluable encouragement and sound advice regarding revision, as did my Penn State colleagues Shirley Marchalonis and Ian Marshall.

2. Bakhtin, however, missed recognizing the applicability of his insight to boundaries marking gender, a locale of social change that was engaging ever more interest as he began his career. He lived from 1895–1975, overlapping with the last forty years of Gilman's life. During the 1920s he worked on a treatise about the nature of moral responsibility and aesthetics, a relationship that had concerned Gilman during the previous two decades.

3. All of the stories discussed in this essay are reprinted in Carol Farley Kessler, *Charlotte Perkins Gilman: Her Progress Toward Utopia with Selected Writings* (1995). Pages cited refer to this reprint.

4. Eisler's study suggests an updated version of Gilman's 1898 *Women and Economics*, now including recent archeological discoveries and evolutionary theory. For further information on this recent research, see works cited by Elinor W. Gadon, Marija Gimbutas, and Lucy R. Lippard for archeology, and Stephen Jay Gould for evolution.

5. Cranny-Francis, discussing Marge Piercy's *Woman on the Edge of Time* (1976), writes, "three intersecting narratives—realist, utopian, dystopian—construct a complex text in which Piercy deconstructs dominant ideological discourses [and] examines the interpellation of the individual in ideology and[,] one of the principal means by which ideology is naturalized into the lives of individuals, the realist narrative (137)." See her chap. 4, "Feminist Utopias," 107–142.

6. That "literary realism"—which I would define here as a rationally constructed vision of what could be possible in a currently existing society, hence "realistic"—was in fashion during Gilman's time offered her a serendipitous coincidence, even though she wrote at the very end of that era. Perhaps one reason why all of her work was out of print by 1930 was that she had held to this literary fashion beyond its passing. The fact of a Great War did not dampen her expectation of human progress, nor did the furor over Freud temper her belief in the human capacity to choose rationally.

7. "Dr. Clair's Place" reverses "The Yellow Wall-Paper" by demonstrating what *should be done* for exhausted women.

8. *The Reproduction of Mothering: Psychoanalysis and the Sociology of Gender*

(1978); for a critical discussion of the theory, see also *Signs* 6, no. 3 (1981): 482–514, for critiques.

9. Benigna McAvelly (with its pun on Machiavelli) also appears in the novel serialization *Benigna Machiavelli* (1914; rpt. 1994).

10. Gilman's good friend, Martha S. Bensley Bruère, wrote for *The Survey* and in 1919 published in *Ladies Home Journal* a serialization of a utopian novel, *Mildred Carver, U.S.A.*—an updated, gender-revised version of the universal service to one's country imagined by Edward Bellamy in *Looking Backward*.

11. Hayden, in *The Grand Domestic Revolution* (1981, p. 197), argues that Gilman, though a self-proclaimed socialist, in fact supported highly individualistic social solutions based upon a "benevolent" capitalistic economy. As Hayden notes, however, Gilman did not disturb the hierarchy of class structure.

12. From King James's Bible, Proverbs 6.6–11:

6 Go to the ant, thou sluggard; consider her ways, and be wise:

7 Which having no guide, overseer, or ruler,

8 Provideth her meat in the summer, *and* gathereth her food in the harvest.

9 How long wilt thou sleep, O sluggard? when wilt thou arise out of thy sleep?

10 *Yet* a little sleep, a little slumber, a little folding of the hands to sleep:

11 So shall thy poverty come as one that travelleth, and thy want as an armed man.

13. Gilman may have read the juvenile serialization, "A Brave Girl" by Elizabeth Stuart Phelps the daughter, in *Wide Awake* (1883–84), in which a former college woman becomes a business success.

Bibliography

Aptheker, Bettina. *Tapestries of Life: Women's Work, Women's Consciousness, and the Meaning of Daily Experience.* Amherst: U Massachusetts P, 1989.

Bakhtin, M[ikhail] M[ihailovitch]. "Response to a Question from *Novy Mir*" (1970) in *Speech Genres and Other Late Essays.* Trans. Vern W. McGee. Ed. Caryl Emerson and Michael Holquist. Austin: U Texas P, 1986.

Bellamy, Edward. *Looking Backward, 2000–1887.* 1888; rpt. edited by John L. Thomas. Cambridge, MA: Harvard Univ. Press, 1967.

Bruère, Martha S. Bensley. *Mildred Carver, U.S.A. Ladies Home Journal* 35–36 (June 1918–February 1919); rpt. New York: Macmillan, 1919.

Chodorow, Nancy. *The Reproduction of Mothering: Psychoanalysis and the Sociology of Gender.* Berkeley: U California P, 1978. See also *Signs* 6.3 (1981): 482–514 for critiques.

————. "Being and Doing: A Cross-Cultural Examination of the Socialization of Males and Females." In *Woman in Sexist Society: Studies in Power and Powerlessness.* Eds. Vivian Gornick and Barbara K. Moran. New York: Basic Books, 1978, pp. 173–197.

Cranny-Francis, Anne. *Feminist Fiction: Feminist Uses of Generic Fiction.* New York: St. Martin's, 1990.

Eisler, Riane. *The Chalice and the Blade: Our History, Our Future.* San Francisco: Harper & Row, 1988.

Gadon, Elinor W. *The Once and Future Goddess: A Symbol for Our Time.* San Francisco: Harper & Row, 1989.

Gilman, Charlotte [Anna] Perkins [Stetson]. "Aunt Mary's Pie Plant." *Woman's Home Companion* 6 (June 1908): 14, 57, 58.

————. "Bee Wise." *The Forerunner* 4.7 (July 1913): 169–73.

————. *Benigna Machiavelli. The Forerunner* 5.1–12 (1914); rpt. Santa Barbara, CA: Bandanna, 1994.

————. "A Council of War." *The Forerunner* 4.8 (August 1913): 197–201.

————. "Dr. Clair's Place." *The Forerunner* 6.6 (June 1915): 141–45.

————. *The Forerunner* 1–7. New York: Charlton Company, 1909–1916. Reprinted with an Introduction by Madeleine B. Stern. "Radical Periodicals in the United States, 1890–1960" series. New York: Greenwood Reprint Corporation, 1968.

————. "Forsythe & Forsythe." *The Forerunner* 4.1 (January 1913): 1–5.

————. "A Garden of Babies." *Success* 12 (June 1909): 370–71, 410–11.

————. "Her Housekeeper." *The Forerunner* 1.4 (January 1910): 2–8.

————. "Her Memories." *The Forerunner* 3.8 (August 1912): 197–201.

————. *Herland. The Forerunner* 6 (1915). Reprint *Herland: A Lost Feminist Utopian Novel,* introduced by Ann J. Lane, New York: Pantheon Books, 1979.

————. "Maidstone Comfort." *The Forerunner* 3.9 (September 1912): 225–29.

————. "Masculine Literature," Ch. 5 of *The Man-Made World; or, Our Androcentric World. The Forerunner* 1.5: 18–22.

————. "Mrs. Hines' Money." *The Forerunner* 4.4 (April 1913): 85–89.

————. *With Her in Ourland. The Forerunner* 7 (1916); rpt. "Radical Periodicals in the United States, 1890–1960," Westport, CT: Greenwood Press, 1968; excerpt *The Charlotte Perkins Gilman Reader,* Ann J. Lane, ed., NY: Pantheon, 1980.

————. *Women and Economics: A Study of the Economic Relation Between Men and Women as a Factor in Social Evolution.* Boston: Small, Maynard & Company, 1898. Reprinted, edited and introduced by Carl N. Degler, New York: Harper Torchbooks, 1966.

————. "The Yellow Wallpaper." *New England Magazine* NS 5 (January 1892): 647–56. Rpt., Afterword by Elaine R. Hedges, New York: Feminist Press, 1973; rpt. Knight, Denise D., ed. *"The Yellow Wallpaper" and Selected Stories of Charlotte Perkins Gilman.* Newark, DE: University of Delaware Press,

1994; rpt. Golden, Catherine, ed. *The Captive Imagination: A Casebook on The Yellow Paper.* New York: The Feminist Press, 1992; rpt. Erskine, Thomas L. and Connie L. Richard, eds. *"The Yellow Wallpaper"/Charlotte Perkins Gilman.* New Brunswick: Rutgers University Press, 1993.

Gimbutas, Marija. *The Gods and Goddesses of Old Europe: Myths and Cult Images.* Berkeley: U California P, 1982.

Goffman, Erving. *The Presentation of Self in Everyday Life.* Garden City, NY: Doubleday, 1959.

Gould, Stephen Jay. *The Mismeasure of Man.* New York: Norton, 1981.

Hayden, Dolores. *The Grand Domestic Revolution: A History of Feminist Designs for American Homes, Neighborhoods, and Cities.* Cambridge: MIT Press, 1981.

Kessler, Carol Farley. *Charlotte Perkins Gilman: Her Progress Toward Utopia with Selected Writings.* Utopianism and Communitarianism series. Syracuse: Syracuse University Press, 1995.

———. "Consider Her Ways: The Cultural Work of Charlotte Perkins Gilman's Pragmatopian Stories, 1908–1913." In *Utopian and Science Fiction by Women: Worlds of Difference,* edited by Jane Donawerth and Carol A. Kolmerten. Utopianism and Communitarianism series. Syracuse: Syracuse University Press, 1994, pp. 126–36.

Lippard, Lucy R. *Overlay: Contemporary Art and the Art of Prehistory.* New York: Pantheon, 1983.

Phelps, Elizabeth Stuart. "A Brave Girl." *Wide Awake* 18–19 (December 1883–August 1884).

Piercy, Marge. *Woman on the Edge of Time.* New York: Knopf, 1976.

Russ, Joanna. *The Female Man.* New York: Bantam, 1975; rpt. Boston: Gregg/G. K. Hall, 1977.

Tompkins, Jane. *Sensational Designs: The Cultural Work of American Fiction 1790–1860.* New York: Oxford UP, 1985.

Chronology

1860   Charlotte Anna Perkins is born on 3 July in Hartford, Connecticut, to Mary Fitch Westcott and Frederick Beecher Perkins.

1869   Parents separate; mother retains custody of Charlotte and her brother, Thomas (b. 1858).

1873   Mother moves family to Providence, Rhode Island.

1878–1879   Gilman enrolls in the Rhode Island School of Design.

1880   Publishes first poem, "To D. G.," in May 20 issue of *New England Journal of Education.*

1881   MARCH. Establishes "Perkins & Co. Designers" with cousin Robert Brown. Designs advertising cards for Soapine, a household cleaning agent produced by Kendall Manufacturing Co.

           NOVEMBER. Is devastated when her closest friend, Martha Luther, becomes engaged and subsequently marries and moves away.

1882   JANUARY. Meets Providence artist Charles Walter Stetson (1858–1911), who proposes marriage 17 days later. She declines.

1883   Agrees to marry Stetson after he suffers "a keen personal disappointment."

1884   Marries Stetson on 2 May.

           AUGUST. Discovers she is pregnant; episodes of depression increase.

1885   Gives birth to her only child, Katharine Beecher Stetson, on 23 March.

1885–1886   Suffers severe postpartum depression.

1887   APRIL. Travels to Philadelphia to undergo the rest cure for nervous prostration under the direction of noted nerve specialist Dr. S. Weir Mitchell. Her health rapidly declines; she suffers nervous breakdown.

1888   Separates from Stetson; spends several weeks with Providence friend Grace Ellery Channing in Bristol, Rhode Island. Gradually recovers from illness.

OCTOBER. Moves with Grace and daughter Katharine to Pasadena, California.

DECEMBER. Joined by Stetson, who attempts a reconciliation.

1890   JANUARY. Walter Stetson is called back to Providence to be with his dying mother; the couple permanently separates. Becomes active in the Nationalist movement; begins lecturing career.

APRIL. Her poem "Similar Cases" appears in *Nationalist*.

JUNE. William Dean Howells writes to praise the poem.

AUGUST. Writes her most famous short story, "The Yellow Wall-Paper."

1891   Moves to Oakland, California; joins the Pacific Coast Women's Press Association.

1892   Publishes "The Yellow Wall-Paper" in *New England Magazine*.

1893   Publishes *In This Our World*, a book of verse.

1894   Divorce from Walter Stetson is finalized; Stetson marries Grace Ellery Channing; Katharine moves East to live with her father and stepmother. Charlotte moves to San Francisco and assumes the editorship of the *Impress*.

1895   *Impress* folds. Publishes second edition of *In This Our World*. Visits Jane Addams at Hull House in Chicago. Begins lecturing extensively throughout the United States.

1896   JANUARY. Attends Women's Suffrage Convention in Washington, D.C.

JULY. Attends International Socialist and Labor Congress in London.

1897   Becomes reacquainted with first cousin George Houghton Gilman; courtship ensues.

1898   Publishes *Women and Economics* and third edition of *In This Our World*.

1899   Attends Congress of the International Council of Women in London.

1900   Marries Houghton Gilman in Detroit on 11 June. Publishes *Concerning Children*. Moves to New York with Houghton; Katharine comes to live with them.

1903   Publishes *The Home: Its Work and Influence*.

1904   Publishes *Human Work*. Attends the International Congress of Women in Berlin, Germany.

1905   Embarks on international lecture tour of England, Holland, Germany, Austria, and Hungary.

1907   Publishes *Women and Social Service*.

1909–1916   Writes, edits, and publishes the *Forerunner*, a monthly magazine.

1910   Publishes her first novel, *What Diantha Did*.

1911   Publishes *The Man-Made World; Or, Our Androcentric Culture* and two novels: *The Crux* and *Moving the Mountain*.

1913   Attends the International Women's Suffrage Congress in Budapest, Hungary.

1915   *Herland*, a utopian novel, is published serially in the *Forerunner*.

1922   Moves to Norwich Town, Connecticut.

1923   Publishes *His Religion and Hers*.

1925   Begins to write her autobiography, *The Living of Charlotte Perkins Gilman*.

1932   Diagnosed with inoperable breast cancer.

1934   Houghton Gilman dies suddenly after suffering a cerebral hemorrhage. Moves to Pasadena, California, to be near daughter Katharine.

1935   Grace Channing Stetson joins her in California. On 17 August, Gilman ends her life by inhaling chloroform.

        OCTOBER. *The Living of Charlotte Perkins Gilman* is published posthumously.

1994   Gilman is inducted into the National Women's Hall of Fame in Seneca Falls, New York.

Selected Bibliography

PRIMARY SOURCES

Short Story Collections

Charlotte Perkins Gilman Reader. Edited and with an introduction by Ann J. Lane. New York: Pantheon, 1980.

Herland and Selected Stories by Charlotte Perkins Gilman. Edited and with an introduction by Barbara H. Solomon. New York: Signet, 1992.

The Yellow Wallpaper. Boston: Small, Maynard & Co., 1899. Reprint, with an afterword by Elaine Hedges. Old Westbury: Feminist Press, 1973.

The Yellow Wallpaper and Other Writings by Charlotte Perkins Gilman. Introduction by Lynne Sharon Schwartz. New York: Bantam Books, 1989.

"The Yellow Wall-Paper" and Selected Stories of Charlotte Perkins Gilman. Edited and with an introduction by Denise D. Knight. Newark, Del.: University of Delaware Press, 1994.

Other Works by Charlotte Perkins Gilman

Benigna Machiavelli. Serialized in *Forerunner* 5 (1914). Reprint. Santa Barbara: Bandanna Books, 1993.

Concerning Children. Boston: Small, Maynard & Co., 1900.

The Crux. Serialized in *Forerunner* 2 (1911). Reprint. New York: Charlton Co., 1911.

The Diaries of Charlotte Perkins Gilman. Edited by Denise D. Knight. Charlottesville: University Press of Virginia, 1994.

Forerunner. Vols. 1–7 (1909–1916). Reprint, with an introduction by Madeleine B. Stern. New York: Greenwood, 1968.

Herland. *Forerunner* 6 (1915). Reprint, with an introduction by Ann J. Lane. New York: Pantheon, 1979.

His Religion and Hers: A Study of the Faith of Our Fathers and the Work of Our Mothers. New York: Century Company, 1923.

The Home: Its Work and Influence. New York: McClure, Phillips & Co., 1903.

Human Work. New York: McClure, Phillips & Co., 1904.

In This Our World. Oakland: McCombs & Vaughn, 1893. 3rd ed. Boston: Small, Maynard & Co., 1898. Reprint. New York: Arno, 1974.

The Living of Charlotte Perkins Gilman: An Autobiography. Foreword by Zona Gale. New York: Appleton-Century, 1935. Reprint, Madison: University of Wisconsin Press, 1990.

Mag-Marjorie. Serialized in *Forerunner* 3 (1912).

The Man-Made World; Or, Our Androcentric Culture. Forerunner 1 (1909–10). Reprint, New York: Charlton Co., 1911.

Moving the Mountain. Forerunner 2 (1911). Reprint. New York: Charlton Co., 1911.

Our Brains and What Ails Them. Serialized in *Forerunner* 3 (1911).

Social Ethics. Serialized in *Forerunner* 4 (1914).

What Diantha Did. Forerunner 1 (1909–10). Reprint. New York: Charlton Co, 1910.

With Her in Our Land. Serialized in *Forerunner* 3 (1911).

Women and Economics: A Study of the Economic Relation Between Men and Women as a Factor in Social Evolution. Boston: Small, Maynard & Co., 1898. Reprint, with an introduction by Carl Degler. New York: Harper & Row, 1966.

Won Over. Serialized in *Forerunner* 4 (1913).

SECONDARY SOURCES

Books

Allen, Polly Wynn. *Building Domestic Liberty: Charlotte Perkins Gilman's Architectural Feminism.* Amherst: University of Massachusetts Press, 1988.

Bellamy, Edward. *Looking Backward, 2000–1887.* Boston: Ticknor, 1888.

Ceplair, Larry, ed. *Charlotte Perkins Gilman: A Nonfiction Reader.* New York: Columbia Press, 1992.

Clapperton, Jane Hume. *A Vision of the Future, Based on the Application of Ethical Principles.* London: Swan Sonnenschein, 1904.

Golden, Catherine. *The Captive Imagination: A Casebook on "The Yellow Wallpaper."* New York: The Feminist Press, 1992.

Hill, Mary A. *Charlotte Perkins Gilman: The Making of a Radical Feminist 1860–1896.* Philadelphia: Temple University Press, 1980.

———. *Endure: The Diaries of Charles Walter Stetson.* Philadelphia: Temple University Press, 1980.

Karpinski, Joanne B. *Critical Essays on Charlotte Perkins Gilman.* Boston: G. K. Hall, 1991.

Kessler, Carol Farley. *Charlotte Perkins Gilman: Her Progress Toward Utopia with Selected Writings.* Syracuse: Syracuse University Press, 1995.

Lane, Ann J. *To Herland and Beyond: The Life and Work of Charlotte Perkins Gilman.* New York: Pantheon, 1990.

Meyering, Sheryl L., ed. *Charlotte Perkins Gilman: The Woman and Her Work.* Foreword by Cathy N. Davidson. Ann Arbor: UMI Research Press, 1989.

Scharnhorst, Gary. *Charlotte Perkins Gilman.* Boston: Twayne, 1985.

Schreiner, Olive. *Dreams.* London: T. Fisher Unwin, 1890.

Veblen, Thorstein. *The Theory of the Leisure Class.* New York: Macmillan, 1899.

Ward, Lester. *Dynamic Sociology.* New York. D. Appleton, 1883.

Bibliographies

Scharnhorst, Gary. *Charlotte Perkins Gilman: A Bibliography.* Metuchen: Scarecrow, 1985.

Critical Articles and Essays

Bader, Julia. "The Dissolving Vision: Realism in Jewett, Freeman, and Gilman." In *American Realism: New Essays*, ed. Eric J. Sundquist. Baltimore: Johns Hopkins University Press, 1982, 176–98.

Bassuk, Ellen L. "The Rest Cure: Repetition or Resolution of Victorian Women's Conflicts?" In *The Female Body in Western Culture: Contemporary Perspectives*, ed. by Susan Rubin Suleiman. Cambridge: Harvard University Press, 1986, 139–51.

Biamonte, Gloria. " 'There is a story, if we could only find it': Charlotte Perkins Gilman's 'The Giant Wistaria.' " *Legacy* 5:2 (Fall 1988): 33–43.

Degler, Carl N. "Charlotte Perkins Gilman on the Theory and Practice of Feminism." *American Quarterly* 8 (Spring 1956): 21–39.

DeLamotte, Eugenia C. "Male and Female Mysteries in 'The Yellow Wallpaper.' " *Legacy* 5:1 (Spring 1988): 3–14.

Fishkin, Shelley Fisher. "Making a Change: Strategies of Subversion in Gilman's Journalism and Short Fiction." In *Critical Essays on Charlotte Perkins Gilman*, ed. Joanne Karpinski. New York: G. K. Hall, 1992, 234–48.

Fleenor, Juliann E. "The Gothic Prism: Charlotte Perkins Gilman's Gothic Stories and Her Autobiography." In *The Female Gothic*, ed. Juliann E. Fleenor. Montreal: Eden, 1983, 227–41.

Howe, Harriet. "Charlotte Perkins Gilman—As I Knew Her." *Equal Rights: Independent Feminist Weekly* 5 (September 1936): 211–16.

Hume, Beverly A. "Gilman's Interminable Grotesque: The Narrator of 'The Yellow Wallpaper.' " *Studies in Short Fiction* 28:4 (Fall 1991): 477–84.

Johnson, Greg. "Gilman's Gothic Allegory: Rage and Redemption in 'The Yellow Wallpaper.' " *Studies in Short Fiction* 26:4 (Fall 1989): 521–30.

Kasmer, Lisa. " 'The Yellow Wallpaper': A Symptomatic Reading." *Literature and Psychology* 36:3 (1990): 1–15.

Kessler, Carol Farley. "Charlotte Perkins Gilman, 1860–1935." In *Modern American Women Writers*, ed. Elaine Showalter. New York: Charles Scribner's Sons, 1991.

Knight, Denise D. "The Reincarnation of Jane: 'Through This'—Gilman's Companion to 'The Yellow Wall-Paper.' " *Women's Studies* no. 20, 3–4 (1992): 289–302.

———. " 'Such a hopeless task before her': Some Observations on Hawthorne and Gilman." In *Scribbling Women: Engendering and Expanding the Hawthorne Tradition*, ed. John Idol and Melinda M. Ponder. Amherst: University of Massachusetts Press, 1997.

Lanser, Susan A. "Feminist Criticism, 'The Yellow Wallpaper,' and the Politics of Color in America." In *Feminist Studies* 15 no. 3 (Fall 1989): 415–41.

Shumaker, Conrad. " 'Too Terribly Good to Be Printed': Charlotte Perkins Gilman's 'The Yellow Wallpaper.' *American Literature* 57 no. 4 (1985): 588–99.

Veeder, William. "Who Is Jane? The Intricate Feminism of Charlotte Perkins Gilman." *Arizona Quarterly* 44 no. 3 (1988): 40–79.

Index

The Author

Denise D. Knight is associate professor of English at the State University of New York College at Cortland, where she specializes in nineteenth-century American literature. She is editor of *The Later Poetry of Charlotte Perkins Gilman* (University of Delaware Press, 1996), *The Diaries of Charlotte Perkins Gilman* (University Press of Virginia, 1994), *The Yellow Wall-Paper and Selected Stories of Charlotte Perkins Gilman* (University of Delaware Press, 1994), and *Nineteenth-Century American Women Writers: A Bio-Bibliographical Critical Sourcebook* (Greenwood Press, forthcoming, 1997). Her work has appeared in *Women's Studies, Walt Whitman Quarterly Review, American Journalism, ANQ: A Quarterly Journal of Short Articles, Notes, and Reviews,* and various essay collections on issues in American literature.

The Editors

Gary Scharnhorst is professor of English at the University of New Mexico, co-editor of *American Literary Realism,* and editor in alternating years of *American Literary Scholarship: An Annual.* He is the author or editor of books about Horatio Alger, Jr., Charlotte Perkins Gilman, Bret Harte, Nathaniel Hawthorne, Henry David Thoreau, and Mark Twain; and he has taught in Germany on Fulbright fellowships three times (1978–79, 1985–86, 1993). He is also the current president of the Western Literature Association and the Pacific Northwest American Studies Association.

Eric Haralson is assistant professor of English at the State University of New York at Stony Brook. He has published articles on American and English literature—with special emphasis on the topic of masculinity—in *American Literature, Nineteenth-Century Literature,* the *Arizona Quarterly, American Literary Realism,* and the *Henry James Review,* as well as in several essay collections. He is also the editor of *The Garland Encyclopedia of American Nineteenth-Century Poetry.*